Stage Whispers

DOUGLAS WILMER

Stage Whispers

The Memoirs

Porter Press International

First published in March 2009

ISBN 978-0-9556564-9-1

Published by
Porter Press International Ltd.

PO Box 2, Tenbury Wells,
WR15 8XX, UK.
Tel: +44 (0)1584 781588
Fax: +44 (0)1584 781630
sales@porterpress.co.uk
www.porterpress.co.uk

Designed by Grafx Resource
Printed by the MPG Books Group in the UK

COPYRIGHT

We have made every effort to trace and acknowledge copyright holders
and we apologise in advance for any unintentional omission. We would
be pleased to insert the appropriate acknowledgement in any subsequent
edition. We wish to thank the following Editors and publishers of the named
publications, which we have managed to trace, for their kind permission to
reproduce the cuttings and/or images – BBC Information & Archives, ITV,
Solo Syndications.

Contents

Acknowledgements

I would like to thank Philip Porter for his 15 years of friendship, for editing this book, and unfailing support and encouragement, without which this book would not have been even envisaged. Further thanks are due to Guy Marriott for his wise and kindly counsel, and to Julie Porter, Anne Harding and Celia Porter for reading the draft manuscript and valuable advice, based on their wide knowledge of the British theatre. I am grateful to the *Porter Press* staff for their most patient and helpful assistance, and especially Mary Fulford-Talbot, Claire Bryan and Abigail Humphries, who designed the jacket. Book design has been in the capable hands of Andy Garman. And, lastly, my long-suffering dear wife, Anne, without whose support and laughter these *Memoirs* would not have reached their conclusion.

Douglas Wilmer
Woodbridge
December, 2008

Introduction

Douglas Wilmer, as the reader will discover, has worked with all the thespian *greats*. The cast list of his life is a veritable *Who's Who* of the theatre from the '40s through to the '70s, as a glance at the Index will forcibly underline.

From the early part of his career, he acted alongside many of the pre-war grandees of the theatre. The roll-call is extraordinary. In almost every case, he earned their sincere respect as a very fine actor of immense sensitivity and intelligence, and in many cases he made great and enduring friendships with some of the mightiest names in the business: Guinness, Heston, Burton and Olivier, to name but four.

Wilmer was not famous for his patience and tolerance. With a sharp, incisive brain, he was impatient and especially of some directors, irrespective of their supposed eminence. This did not endear him to all and must have tempered his rise in his chosen profession. He was his own man: a trait that is either embraced or shunned, depending on the self-assurance of the other party.

In the '60s he found fame for a while as Sherlock Holmes on BBC television. I was 14 when I watched them and, like so many throughout the world for more than a century, became hooked on the mercurial Holmes and his faithful Boswell, Dr. John Watson. In the early '70s, I joined the *Sherlock Holmes Society of London*, which had been founded by London barrister, Tony Howlett, and others in 1951.

Such senior members had been brought up on Arthur Wontner and Basil Rathbone and, many decades later, Jeremy Brett achieved great notoriety for his curiously eccentric, and increasingly maniacal, portrayal of Holmes. As I became more established within the Society, a state of affairs assisted by Tony and Freda Howlett and other leading members staying annually for a weekend at my ancient home in Worcestershire, I ventured the opinion that the finest Sherlock Holmes of all time had actually been a chap called ... Douglas Wilmer.

To my astonishment, relief and pleasure, the cognoscenti did not demolish my assertion. Quite the reverse: they wholeheartedly agreed. Fortified by such views, I determined to *find* Mr. Wilmer and perhaps start a correspondence. Through another member with theatrical connections, I discovered that, though effectively retired, he still retained an agent and via this medium wrote. Almost immediately, I received a most charming letter from him, expressing pleasure at my compliments and stating, modestly and inexplicably, that he thought he had been written off long ago.

As Douglas explains in later pages, we met appropriately where Holmes and Watson were wont to dine, at *Simpson's in the Strand*. From this, a wonderful friendship has grown, which included my persuading him back to his old profession. The *talking books* that we subsequently produced for Penguin were described by Sir Christopher Frayling as "the finest of their genre". Richard Lancelyn Green, whom I had asked to co-produce with me, and I played a very minor role. Douglas, who read every part in character, was absolutely brilliant.

It was indeed an honour to work, in some small way, with him, just as it is an honour to be able to call him a close friend, and to have edited and published this volume.

For years I, and others, have been telling Douglas he should write a book about his extraordinary life. After gentle, but unremitting, bullying, here we are at last. Douglas does not pull any punches, irrespective of the stature of his one-time colleagues. The result, I think you will agree, is fascinating, amusing, controversial, thought-provoking, informative and compelling.

Philip Porter

Prologue

I have reached a time of life when I am frequently told by those who have endured, from time to time, my random and possibly incoherent reminiscences that I should really write it all down. Whether this is from a genuine desire that such memoirs should be recorded in some recognisable form before, with my eventual demise, they disappear altogether or simply in order to silence my anecdotage once and for all is entirely open to question.

It is, of course, possibly both.

Without question, I have encountered many people who certainly interested me. Whether or not I can similarly engage the attention of readers is, of course, another matter but I can think of no better method of going about such a task than the one I have chosen, which is by preparing a litany of names and dealing with them, one by one, or as they naturally occur in the narrative. These range from Joe Orton to Tyrone Guthrie, from Sofia Loren to Marilyn Monroe, from Celia Johnson to Dame Edith Evans, from Richard Harris to Christopher Plummer, from Dame Sybil Thorndike to Elizabeth Taylor, from Kenneth Williams to Sir Donald Wolfit, Burton, Olivier, Gielgud, Guinness, Heston... I am told I mention over 100 actors of note, plus a fair sprinkling of directors and producers. I am myself amazed when I look back and realise the number of famous names, with whom I have worked and/or had rewarding friendships.

I believe my recollections will bring a fresh view of some. They will certainly paint a picture of what it was like to work with many of them and, I fear, may ruffle a few feathers or explode the odd myth.

I have tried, as far as possible, to avoid hearsay and to stick to my personal experiences and, in the case of conversations, to record, as faithfully as possible, things said, either in my immediate hearing or directly addressed to me. In many of the cases I have reported, what passed was said to me and to me alone and was privy to no-one else. Whether it is of general interest or not is up to the reader to judge.

It is in the nature of memoirs that one topic leads to another. Anyway, it is certainly so with me. Undisciplined perhaps but I fear I know no other way, except in this somewhat conversational style. I find it difficult to marshal my thoughts in strict chronological order. Even when giving interviews, not one of my favourite pastimes, I have to rely on the skilfulness of the interviewer to keep me on course.

Without any doubt, I will inevitably leave myself open to the charge of the dropping of names; but one cannot have it both ways and, as I am not engaged in recording the doings of nonentities of no interest to anyone, I make no apology for this. Some will no doubt see it as a mere exercise in name-dropping. In extenuation, I can only quote David Niven, in reply to the same accusation: "If you have dinner with Mao Tse Tung, you don't write about the butler".

It has been my lot to have encountered many people in my long lifetime who still, it appears, arouse enough interest to warrant inclusion in my memoirs.

I have tried to present them truthfully, as I knew them, without undue emphasis on their failings, but by simply saying what actually happened or what I was told by them, face to face. I have also, wherever possible, told of their virtues. If my narrative sometimes appears to enter the sphere of detraction, then, short of producing a bland and limply untruthful history of events, so be it.

In Pilate's memorable phrase, "*Scripsi scripsi*". What I have written, I have written.

1

Early Days

"Begin at the beginning, go on 'til you come to the end and then stop," as the King said to the White Rabbit in *Alice*.

So to begin: I was born on January 8th 1920, sometimes described as the unluckiest day of the year, and not, as has been given out, in the fair city of Shanghai, but in a rather more prosaic situation in the less exotic purlieus of Middlesex.

I have been repeatedly told that a certain Nurse King, announcing my arrival to my mother, declared, "It's a boy, and he's as yellow as a guinea".

I cannot but feel that this remark has played its part in colouring the somewhat jaundiced attitude, which was to dog me, until more recently, for most of my life. It was certainly repeated to me, as a child, more times than I care to remember, either in anecdotal form or as a reproof for naughtiness. Indeed for some years in my infancy, and even later, I was haunted by the sneaking belief that I was, somehow, a Chinese changeling and nursed a deep shame at the thought.

I was, however, able to enjoy my first birthday, albeit at the time unconsciously, surrounded by the luxuries provided by the P&O Shipping Line (or to give it its more grandiose title: *The Peninsular and Oriental Steam Navigation Co.*), en voyage to Shanghai with my mother to join my expectant father. Those were the palmy days of *grande luxe,* as I was later to discover when I twice repeated the voyage to and from the Far East, when First Class P&O travel implied considerably more than a cattle-boat Channel crossing.

My father did something mysteriously to do with mathematics in the so-called *Princely House* of Jardine Matheson. I never quite discovered what but it must have been reasonably remunerative as we lived in a certain style in a large-ish house in the French Concession, with half a dozen living-in servants and a chauffeur-driven car.

I spent as much of my time as I could with the servants, whose company I enjoyed enormously. I can remember my doting mother, tucking me up in bed and kissing me goodnight, before going out to dinner.

I would feign sleepiness, wait until I heard the family car out of earshot, and then leap from my bed and run down to the kitchen where the servants were having their evening meal, which I would dip into with gusto, chattering away with them in Chinese with the greatest enjoyment. My natural affinity with them was perhaps due to my infantile fancies of being one of them. I loved being with them and they appeared to be fond of me. They certainly spoiled me.

As a result of all this, by the age of six I could chatter away in Chinese with some fluency, in the Shanghai dialect, of course, which was quite a different language from the more aristocratic Mandarin of official use, spoken in Peking. My parents, in common with most of the Europeans living in Shanghai, never got around to speaking Chinese in any dialect whatsoever, except for the odd word such as "hurry up" or "come here". However, my own proficiency in the language was, alas, not to last.

A friend of my father's, who could speak the language, came to lunch one Sunday and, the service hatch in the dining room being open, I could be heard chattering away in the kitchen. Apparently, as he listened, his eyes widened and his jaw dropped.

"Have either of you any idea what that child is saying? He's using the most filthy language and I would strongly advise you to keep him well away from the servants."

So, my secret life below stairs was, from then on, severely curtailed and when I came to school in England I gradually lost my Chinese.

I sometimes wonder if my early essays into Chinese and French have not given me a certain facility in picking up languages on the spot, so to speak. I have in my time, been reasonably fluent in a number of them: French, Spanish, German, Italian and even Haussa, the *lingua franca* of West Africa. However, they never seemed to stay with me once I was away from their native environment. A week or so, spent on my own, in their respective countries and I would slip back into them.

The only one that really seems to stay with me with any degree of permanency is French, and this is probably due to the Hell-Fire nuns of the Sacred Heart.

At the age of four, I had been put into a nursery-cum-kindergarten, run by French nuns of that Order, where I was taught the first rudiments of French. Indeed, nothing else was ever spoken, which has probably helped me to feel at home in that language ever since. I do not recall very much, except that it was strict and one called the nuns *ma mere* and had to ask their permission to *faire pee-pee*. But, above all, I recollect the horrifying lantern lectures with holy pictures in lurid detail, portraying the torments of Hell, which I was led to believe, as a non-Catholic, would be my ultimate destination.

This gloomy prediction filled me with terror and, upon my return home, I demanded of my mother that I should be allowed to become a Catholic forthwith. This brought about my removal from the nuns pretty *tout de suite*. However, I did learn quite a good deal of French and it is quite possible that their early indoctrination contributed to my later conversion to *The One True Faith*.

My next school was memorable to me chiefly because of my mathematics teacher, a Miss Hepburn, who was red-faced with red hair tied back in a bun and a wart on the end of her not-unnoticeable nose. She was severe, bordering on sadistic, taught mathematics - never my favourite subject - and rewarded all non-comprehension with hefty wallops on the hands with a stout ruler. This, almost certainly, was the root and cause of my total imbecility over all matters mathematical, which has dogged me all my life.

Among other recollections of my boyhood in the Orient, I can recall a strangely precocious distaste for the life-style of the Europeans out there. I was also aware of a strongly compulsive nostalgia for an England that I had never knowingly seen. This was probably brought about by my mother, who spent much of her life out there pining for an England she hardly ever had an opportunity to see. I am certain that much of this rubbed off on me.

She always spoke of it with longing. For her it was *Home* and she would talk to me very often about her "green and pleasant land" and, to my father's intense irritation, taught me racy music-hall songs, of which she seemed to have an inexhaustible fund, many of which I can remember to this day.

I can well recall my mounting excitement, in 1928, when the time came for *Home Leave* and I was to have my first sighting of my native land and the thrilling voyage by P&O through the South China Sea to such glamorous places, as they then most certainly were, as Penang and sailing up through the

Straits of Malacca, with its shoals of flying fish scudding over the waves before the bow of our ship, then on to Singapore and Colombo and the delights of curry at the Mount Lavinia Hotel, overlooking the palm-fringed beach with its fine silver sand and the sound of the sea. Surely the most sumptuous and varied curry in the world.

It was a tradition, whenever my parents landed in Colombo, to take a car to that delightful spot for lunch. We would always have curry, for which it was famous, at a table in the shade of the palm trees, served by gentle, smiling waiters in white sarongs, with semi-circular combs holding their long, oiled hair up in place, as was the custom then for Sinhalese men.

I thought it Paradise then. Now they probably all have crew-cuts, wear natty suits and carry guns.

I remember our ship, battling through a monsoon in the Indian Ocean on our way to Aden, and the intense heat, even at sea. Neither I, nor my parents, were ever seasick, unlike practically everyone else on board. To cool off, when it was calmer, I swam in the ship's pool, a kind of gigantic canvas bucket rigged up on deck.

I recall, with rather less pleasure, sharing the pool with a Russian, called Prince Mdvani, who looked like my young idea of a gigolo. He was engaged to Barbara Hutton, the Woolworth heiress, who was also one of the passengers. She was a haughty-looking peroxided lady, with heavy black eyebrows, naturally of tremendous wealth. Mdvani and I were alone in the pool one afternoon when, for some extraordinary reason, he swam over to me and held me under water for rather longer than was comfortable. I remember kicking him in the balls and making a spluttering and frightened escape.

My father had been appointed treasurer to the ship's sports fund and one of his unenviable duties was to collect subs for the prizes. The only flat refusal he met with was from the Woolworth lady, who said she was not taking part in the sports.

On that voyage we took on board, probably at Singapore, the Ranee of Sarawak and her two beautiful daughters, Princess Pearl, who later married Harry Roy, the band-leader, and her equally attractive sister. At the Fancy Dress Ball, the Ranee wore her national costume, but I principally remember Princess Pearl in a dashing Andalusian hat and shawl, dancing with a carnation between her teeth.

They were delightful.

To please my mother, and much to my youthful embarrassment, I was hotly-encased in red crêpe paper as a Christmas cracker, which actually won a prize, most probably of the booby variety.

I had read somewhere that in Aden there was an hotel that was reputed to have on show mummified mermaids and, when we went ashore there, I believe I pestered the life out of my parents to be taken to see them. Once ashore, finding themselves sorely in need of cooling refreshment, my ma and pa took me there and sat on the verandah, probably with a long ice-cold beer apiece, while I sat and chafed until taken to see these embalmed wonders. They were in a long wooden box with a lid which, when lifted, revealed what appeared to be two stuffed manatees, which I felt, even at my tender age, was a bit of a let-down. Otherwise Aden seemed remarkable only for its extreme heat and aridity.

We then had the wonders of the Suez canal, with Port Said and Suez at either end, and the excitement of watching strings of camels, plodding along its banks: scenes, which, to my boyish eyes, seemed to be straight out of the Bible.

As travellers' tales, unless crammed with remarkable incident, tend towards tedium, I will take a flying leap to Marseilles, where, to save time, we left the ship and travelled overland to Calais and sailed to Dover.

To this day I can see quite distinctly, in my mind's eye, my first glimpse of England and recall my great delight and breathless excitement.

After spotting the almost unbelievably white cliffs, as we came nearer and nearer the shore, I could see a green puffer train on the dockside, just like the Hornby toy model I had in Shanghai and there was a bobby, standing on the quay, looking just as I knew he would look. It was very early on a Summer's morning and everywhere looked very quiet and almost deserted.

I had a strange feeling, almost of relief, and recall thinking, "This is my home. This is where I belong and where I want to be."

I came home for the last time when my parents brought me back to school in England, aged 13. I never saw Shanghai again.

2

King's School, Canterbury

When prospective schools were being discussed by my parents, I always put in a special plea for King's School, Canterbury, which was reputed to be the oldest school in England, or possibly even Europe.

Having had, from an early age, a strongly developed sense of history such a claim made a great appeal to my sense of the romantic. It was, after all, the Alma Mater of Christopher Marlowe, Walter Pater, Somerset Maugham, Hugh Walpole, William Harvey and many other distinguished alumni. It was also the recipient of a royal charter from that lovable monarch, King Henry the Eighth. The original foundation, however, was by St. Augustine, no less, making it almost as old as the actual Christian religion in this country.

The factor which really influenced my father was, I believe, a rather more prosaic one. As I was to spend all my school holidays with my grandmother, who lived by the sea in Cliftonville where my parents also intended to reside until such time as they went back to China, it was a conveniently short train journey to Canterbury, should they desire to visit me for any reason. When we went to see the school, I was enchanted with the old buildings. Some of them were, in fact, Norman but all of them were almost as ancient and situated in the Precincts of the great Cathedral. I was duly entered and that was that.

I was disappointed in only one respect. It had been deemed a healthier option for me to live outside the city so I was entered into one of the two *Out Houses* a mile or so from the city. A late Victorian building of not much character, it was called Langley House and presided over, as it turned out, by a dreary clergyman and his wife.

The first day of term arrived and I was brought to the school by my parents, who left me there, on my poor mother's part, somewhat tearfully. Conditions were Spartan and I very soon discovered that the romantic illusions I had entertained were illusions indeed. It was tough and Langley House enjoyed the reputation of being tougher than most. Bullying was taken as a matter of course as the clerical housemaster left all disciplinary measures in the hands of the monitors, house prefects and the hierarchy of the older boys, without any apparent supervision whatsoever. His sole duty, seemingly, was to teach so-called Divinity in the main school, a subject that he managed to make both dull and depressing. Never having had any previous experience of prep-school boarding, I found it all very strange indeed and encountered rather more difficulty in coming to terms with my new condition of life than most of the other new boys who had enjoyed such earlier conditioning.

I made many mistakes, which did not pass unnoticed. Punishment was frequent and severe.

Not to put too fine a point on it, I found my new life miserable and frightening, and I had many occasions to be reminded of the unhappy experiences endured and described in the book of my illustrious predecessor, Somerset Maugham, in his barely disguised description of King's School in *Of Human Bondage*.

Unsurprisingly, the school numbers were not overly healthy; nor was its bank balance. The headmaster, a not particularly able man, was, suddenly and surprisingly, offered the headmastership of Merchant Taylors, a position he thankfully accepted, abandoning his sinking ship as soon as he decently could. The Governors had decided to close our ancient academy and actually caused circular letters to that effect to be printed. These were to be sent to all the parents, notifying them of this eventuality. At an emergency governors' meeting, however, someone spoke up and said he had heard of an extraordinarily gifted headmaster, who had taken command of a similarly *sinking ship* and, within a very short space of time, had restored it, not only to total buoyancy, but indeed to some considerable degree of affluence. Would it not, he asked, be worth a try, to lure him away, in an attempt to exercise a similar miracle at King's, which was, after all, a school of much higher repute than his present incumbency?

The approach was made and the Reverend Doctor John Shirley DD agreed to take on the task in hand, but subject to the most stringent conditions. He was to be made a Canon of the Cathedral Chapter, which would entitle him to a handsome house in the Precincts, rent free, and provide him with a stipend, which would enable him to forego any salary due to him as Headmaster until such time as he had achieved a solution to the financial difficulties of the school. It would also automatically ensure him a place on the governing body, where he would be in a position to exercise a veto on any matter relating to the school and to keep a watchful eye on any proposals likely to arise. He was also to have total power over which existing members of the teaching staff he chose to dismiss and which to retain. There were also many other draconian measures he proposed to adopt, all of which were agreed to by an understandably cowering board of Governors. In return, he undertook to have the School on its feet again, both financially and in reputation, within five years.

This was in 1935, by which time I had already spent two unenjoyable and largely unprofitable years in the school, so that when Shirley arrived, or *Fred* as he came to be called, it felt like a wild and cleansing wind and certainly made a strong impact on my life, then and thereafter.

To say that he transformed the school is something of an understatement. After a very short time, he fired a third of the staff, including my erstwhile housemaster, replacing them with younger men of much superior teaching ability and scholarship. My new English master, for instance, was the winner of the Oxford Newdigate poetry prize, an award previously made to such men as Ruskin, Matthew Arnold, Oscar Wilde and Julian Huxley. He was a man who could make the giants of English literature, such as Shakespeare and Chaucer, come alive for the dullest of boys.

Meantime, Shirley embarked on an ambitious refurbishing programme. He scrapped the two largely autonomous *Out Houses*, incorporating them into the Precincts, which brought me into a far more convenient situation with regard to attending classes. He had a new block of classrooms built and revised the entire layout of the school, modernising and extending out-of-date science laboratories and sanitation.

There was the famous occasion, the Governors demurring on the latter expenditure, when he personally went round with a hammer, smashing antediluvian urinals and loos. He then summoned the Sanitary Inspector, who promptly condemned them.

Where he got the money for all this Heaven alone knows, but among other accomplishments he was a financial wizard and seemed capable of coaxing cash out of thin air. He even got round Somerset Maugham, formerly an avowed detester of the school, and persuaded not only a considerable sum out of him, but also the gift of a valuable collection of rare books, manuscripts, letters from Nelson, Thackeray and many others, which went into showcases in the school museum.

Shirley also brought with him a fair number of boys from his former school to increase the numbers and thereby the fees, which, at the time seemed hardly ethical, but *Fred* was not a man to be troubled by such minor scruples. He was, however, suspended from the Headmasters' Conference because of it, a fact which appeared to trouble him not at all.

Without doubt, he must rank with the greatest of headmasters in the history of public schools, from Arnold onwards: eccentric, dynamic, a tyrannical and unpredictable despot, charged with an almost mesmeric charisma. He knew every one of the boys in his care by their names, retaining a keen interest in their welfare with an almost uncanny insight into their characters.

I loved and feared him. He had a strong influence on the course of my life, being, almost unwittingly, responsible for me taking to the theatre as a profession.

Visiting one of the later rehearsals of the school play, *Richard of Bordeaux*, he summarily evicted, for incompetence, a boy (ironically in later life an actual bishop) from the role of the Archbishop of Canterbury. He looked around him, spotted me, who had never acted in my life, and said, "You'll do, with your scoundrelly looks. Learn the part in two days. And don't go into any classes until you know it." This was a mere two days before the actual performance.

Quaking with fright, I did as commanded.

Dame Sybil Thorndike, who was then one of the country's greatest actresses, had a nephew, Dan Thorndike, playing one of the parts and she came to see the first performance. Despite my imperfect mastery of the lines, she made complimentary remarks to *Fred*, saying, "If that boy, playing the Archbishop, were to take to the stage, I think he could well make a go of it".

So, despite the most strenuous paternal opposition - Pa thought I was mad - I made that my determined aim. Both he and *Fred* opposed the idea, and *Fred* arranged for me to be taken on as a sort of articled pupil to the school architects in their City of London offices, as I describe at some length in the next chapter.

3

Seeley & Paget of Cloth Fair

So, towards the end of my schooldays at King's, Canterbury, it was decided by my father, since he had refused to support any notion I might have of a career in the theatre, that the nearest to any form of artistic future that could be hoped for was, perhaps, in architecture.

The grisly alternative to this was his suggestion that I should return to Shanghai where I could start a career devoted to the inner workings of the Hong Kong and Shanghai Bank, starting on the ground floor - in short, as a bank clerk.

Both options, of course, required some fairly considerable skills in mathematics, a facility much enjoyed by my father, but most certainly not inherited by me. I knew that, once I had been shipped off back to China, any possibility of later attempts to enter a stage career would be virtually nil. So, accordingly, I plumped for the less odious option and chose architecture.

It so happened that my headmaster, *Fred*, had recently employed a firm of architects to design some new school buildings and, as there were several further projects in the pipeline, he was able to exert some considerable leverage on my behalf. Thus a meeting was arranged with Messrs. Seeley and Paget, architects, to give me the once-over. This was to take place on their next visit to the school, which was fairly imminent. I believe that the outcome of this was pretty much of a foregone conclusion, due to *Fred* being in the habit of getting his own way, as he had doubtless made abundantly clear when the arrangement was made.

The practice was a *smart* one, both men occupying a *certain position* in the scheme of things; Seeley was heir to a peerage and Paget the son of the Bishop of Chichester. As this was in the days when such things mattered rather more than they do now, they had the House of Lords, the Commons and The Church Council pretty well sewn-up between them; and that was only for starters.

The practice was consequently a busy one. I was later to discover they also led a highly active social life, doubtless involving much networking and entertaining of the *right people*.

They were also both unmarried and quite plainly *an item*, so to speak, residing together in a charming and very substantial Jacobean house in Cloth Fair, overlooking the churchyard of St. Bartholomew the Great. Two floors were occupied by the practice.

However, perhaps *I run before my horse to market*. It was arranged that when my last term at school was concluded, I would have a few weeks' holiday before going to London to take up my new career. This would allow time to find a suitable place for me to live and any other necessary arrangements to be made. By this juncture, my mother had arrived in England, much to her delight, and was living with her mother in Cliftonville, the more polite part of rumbustious Margate. Here I joined her until the later arrival of my father when we moved to a comfortably-furnished flat in Hampstead where they were to spend their six months *home leave*. This plan was soon abandoned as the flat turned out to be seriously and quite definitely haunted, which made our continued existence there eventually impossible.

To those of you who are impatient of accounts of haunting and things that go bump in the night, and I must confess that I am of their number, I can only recommend that you skip the next page or so. I have boldly said it was haunted but I would like to add that I am not prone to such flights of fancy, nor am I any more superstitious than the next man. In fact, this is the sole occasion in my life when I can recall such an experience. But recall it I do, and with total certainty.

My father had announced with much pride that he had found the perfect place for us to reside until their departure back to the Far East. My mother and I visited it, and heartily agreed with him that he had indeed found somewhere that would more than fit the bill.

It was situated high up in Hampstead, in a quiet street called Lancaster Grove. Pleasantly furnished, it was light and airy in a cheerful chintzy sort of way, and on the top floor of a large converted house. The flat below was unoccupied, so there were no neighbours to bother about. It seemed ideal.

An appointment had been made through the agent to meet the owner, a widow whom we understood was in residence, but who could show us round strictly by appointment and with two day's warning. At the time we thought this a bit odd if the owner was, apparently, in residence but soon forgot about it.

We were, however, to be reminded of it before very long.

We met the good lady who showed us round her very pleasant apartment. She was amiable and Scottish. Over coffee, she related the sad circumstances of her husband's demise, which had occurred a year earlier. He had returned home one evening and she had found him lying dead at the front door. She seemed overcome by her recollections and indeed shed a tear.

The place seemed quite suitable; we sympathised with the lady and arranged to move in, which we did a short time after. We were still under the impression, which she did nothing to dispel, that she had been living there up to the time of our tenancy. We very much later discovered that she had, in fact, been resident in a hotel for some considerable time on the other side of London, which explained the slight difficulties in the initial viewing. The place was unlived in and required some preparation to give an otherwise impression.

At all events, we moved in and almost at once my mother, much to my father's irritation, expressed a sense of unease in the atmosphere. He put this down to an unwillingness to accept a change of scene and there it was left.

On the first night, I went to bed early and being a very sound sleeper was surprised to be suddenly wide awake, hear a door open and close, and heavy footsteps in the passage outside my bedroom. I looked at my watch. It was 1.30am. Dismissing this as the likely nocturnal visit to the loo by my father, I fell asleep at once. I thought no more of it until next morning when my mother asked me if my tummy was all right as she had heard me moving about in the passage to the bathroom in the early hours of the night. I told her not only had I not stirred from my bed all night, but I had been awakened by the same sound of doors and footsteps. Well, we shrugged that one off until my mother went to her wardrobe for her overcoat and the hat she was wearing the day before. She called me and told me that the veil which had adorned the hat had been removed and was nowhere to be seen. She knew she had put the hat away on the top shelf and there it was, where she had left it, but undoubtedly minus the veil.

A series of similar little oddities occurred for the first three weeks of our tenure of the place, over which my mother and I compared notes, and which then abruptly ceased. We had kept it between the two of us as we knew my father had no patience with *that kind of nonsense* and would only be intensely irritated.

I have not gone into the details of these happenings here as they were as nothing compared with what was later to follow. Such instances as hearing the sound of objects, like my mother's scent bottles and silver-backed hair brushes apparently performing a jig on the glass top of her dressing-table in a room which we knew to be empty, would be almost totally eclipsed by the violence of later events. How my father managed to ignore them or rationalise them as he did, one will never know.

However, after the initial three weeks, all was peace and tranquillity. And one really had almost come to believe that it had all been, perhaps, after all, a figment of one's imagination. The intermittent oppressive atmosphere had entirely vanished. It was not the same place at all.

Nevertheless, my parents decided that domestic chores on their home-leave were perhaps not quite the ticket. They had been accustomed, after all, to being waited on, hand and foot, so they found a set-up, where in a large house with a secluded garden, we would be catered for by a genteel Edwardian lady, who would cook and look after our creature comforts. The domestic daily help in our first situation had abruptly left after a couple of weeks and was never seen again and it had been difficult to replace her. So the owner of the apartment was given a month's notice, via the agent and almost at once, all hell, as the saying is, broke loose.

There would be loud knockings on the drawing room door which upon investigation would reveal nothing and no-one. My mother said she had seen the figure of a man one evening, standing at the end of the landing, watching her for several seconds before disappearing.

One evening soon after, we had decided to go to see a film at the Swiss Cottage Odeon, prior to which my father and I had been sitting in armchairs on either side of the fireplace, Pa reading the paper, while we waited for my mother who was titivating herself in her bedroom. After a few moments, he put the newspaper down and, removing his spectacles and placing them on the arm of the chair, got up and went out of the room to see how my mother was getting on.

I reached across and picked up the paper, holding it open in front of me, idly noticing as I did so my father's specs where he had placed them. Almost at once, he came back into the room with his coat on to retrieve his glasses and to get me moving. To our astonishment, they were no longer there. We made a quick search, without success and left for the film without them.

On our return we sat down to a cold supper, which we had on a card table in front of the fire. We never made use of the dining room as it was always very cold, particularly in the evening. Towards the end of our meal, we became aware of a strong smell of burning and saw that there were wisps of white smoke curling up on all sides of the table. Pa and I quickly lifted the table to see what on earth it could be, whereupon both the smell and the smoke quickly faded away. There was no sign of scorch marks or burning that we could see, so we replaced the table and finished our meal.

Almost at once there came a quite unmistakable and very loud knock on the door, heard by all three of us.

We looked at each other and my father got up, walked to the door and opened it. There was nobody there.

Later on I was deputed to return the knives and forks to the sideboard in the dining room, which, as I have said, was always very cold and which consequently we rarely used, except to get at the aforesaid knives and forks, etc. After I had put them away in their drawer, I turned my back to the window and, as I approached the door, there was a loud noise of splintering wood. Turning to see the cause, I became aware that the very substantial wooden curtain pole over the window appeared to have been wrenched away from the wall and was hanging at an acute angle, with its bracket dangling at one end and the wooden curtain rings, slithering down its length.

I lost no time in getting out of there and acquainting my parents with this; they came back into the room with me to survey the damage.

As may be imagined, the atmosphere was distinctly uneasy and quite justified the stiff Scotches my father poured.

Whatever my father made of this incident, I have no idea. I suppose he found some perfectly rational explanation. He had appeared momentarily disconcerted, but quite quickly recovered his cool. So far as I can remember, he made little comment on the matter. The subject of spooks was still most definitely off the agenda, as far as he was concerned.

To me, it seems almost inconceivable that he and my mother would not have spoken of such a train of events, but I suppose times and mores between married couples were very different then.

One Sunday morning I went into the kitchen to lend a hand with clearing away the breakfast things and my mother reached for the packet of washing-up powder which, to her astonishment, was completely empty. She told me that she had only a moment earlier opened the full new packet. It had been one of my weekend chores, since the sudden departure of our domestic, to take the rubbish down to the dustbin, which I had done on the Saturday morning, happening to notice, as I did so, the empty packet in the bin. It had a very noticeable blue and white check pattern. I took the packet from my mother and noticed that one side of it was smeared with wet tea leaves. It was almost certainly the one I had put into the rubbish-bin the day before.

We looked about us for any sign of the new packet and eventually espied it on a high shelf, jammed in between a line of old saucepans, which we never used and which could be reached only by standing on a chair. There and then, I decided that it was time to face up to my father and tell him exactly what had occurred.

He was in the drawing room, dealing with a back-log of correspondence. I went in and saw that he was standing behind his bureau, wearing a somewhat dazed expression. I started to relate what had happened when he cut me short, saying that something pretty damned odd had just happened to him. He went on to say that he had been sitting behind the desk and that he had a sudden feeling that he was being watched and upon looking up from his papers saw, quite distinctly, a man in a dark suit standing in front of him. It was just for a moment, he said, and then there was no-one there. This was a matter of seconds before I had entered the room and in broad daylight, with the sun streaming in through the window.

He looked pretty shaken and it was the first time that I had heard him admit to anything supernormal about the place.

He then started fulminating about, "giving that woman with her damned spooks a piece of my mind when I see her". My mother said he should do nothing of the sort. After all, the poor woman might have to live alone there herself one day. I could not quite follow her reasoning, but it seemed to pacify Pa in some way.

Instead, he decided on a good stiff whisky all round, which I thought a far more sensible notion.

After a few more words, he downed his drink and went back to his desk and

I followed my mother back into the kitchen, carrying her almost un-broached glass of whisky in my hand. This I set down on the kitchen dresser just inside the door. After a short time, I reminded her of her neglected drink and went to hand it to her. I was astounded to see that a very grubby rag, which I was able to identify as the one normally situated on the U bend under the sink, was stuffed tightly into her glass.

There were other events too numerous to merit any special mention in these pages, but there was one piece of unfinished business, which I feel bound to touch on.

It was on the last night we were to spend in Lancaster Grove and we were all packed up and ready for our departure on the morrow.

I have neglected to mention that in spite of the most rigorous search for my father's spectacles on the morning after their extraordinary disappearance a fortnight earlier, we had still not found them. About 10 o'clock in the evening, my mother went to her bedroom and called out to us. She was standing in the bedroom doorway, her hand still at the light switch. On the floor, just inside the door, in a most obvious place, were the missing spectacles.

When we returned the keys to the agent the next day, my father asked him if he had heard any complaints about the flat. The man appeared evasive. He did say that a German-Jewish family of refugees had taken it before us but had left abruptly after less than a week. They apparently gave no reason for their departure and it seems were content to forfeit three weeks' rental, which had been paid in advance. My father was true to his word and let the matter drop.

My mother's veil, along with other more trivial items, had never come to light.

In spite of experiencing all the foregoing events, as we all undoubtedly did, I still, perhaps unreasonably, find it sometimes hard to believe the evidence of my own senses.

Hamlet is a favourite play of mine and whenever I come to the line, "There are more things in heaven and earth than are dreamt of in our philosophy," my mind returns to the happenings at the seemingly prosaic number 21 Lancaster Grove.

To return to Seeley and Paget, the time soon came when I was to be unofficially articled to the firm from whom I was to receive what amounted to pocket-money, supplemented by a small amount from Pa, to enable me to live on my own once my parents had gone back to the Far East after their leave had come to an end. In return for this, I was put under the tutelage of one of the firm's senior draughtsmen and told to make myself useful in any way required of me, and that I should also attend evening classes in architecture.

My tutor in the firm was a pleasant man called Soper, who appeared to be afflicted with a mild form of religious mania, being a member of a sect known as *The Plymouth Brethren*. Among other things, he told me that Christmas trees were idolatrous and that every step taken in a dance was a step towards Hell. He also initiated me into the arts and use of architectural instruments and of mixing washes for watercolours, which I found rather more interesting. He was, it turned out, a very fine painter in that medium, and it was one of his duties to prepare drawings from Seeley's plans for proposed buildings, set in attractive, but entirely fictitious, surroundings for the information and possible entrapment of putative clients.

There were two other draughtsmen of talent, headed by the real lynchpin of the firm, an unsmilingly gaunt individual who was a veritable genius on building construction. It was he, I later discovered, who translated many of Seeley's less plausible plans into sound architectural possibilities. As to Paul Paget, in spite of some letters after his name, I do not think he knew one end of a pencil from the other. His chief duties appeared to be the liberal dispensation of charm and in concerning himself with such matters as consulting the cook as to a suitable lunch for the Bishop of London, who, it seems, had problems with his teeth.

In all fairness, I am sure his opinion was often sought in more professional matters by the Hon. John, as I feel sure he also had impeccable taste.

I was once sent upstairs to their bathroom for something and was quite surprised to see, in the middle of the room and side-by-side, two identical old-fashioned bath tubs. I remember thinking at the time, that it was really rather sweet.

As may be surmised from the foregoing, it was becoming clear that I could not look to the Partners for my transformation into Christopher Wren. This was left entirely, in whatever time was to spare, to *Holy Joe*, as he was affectionately known, plus whatever I could pick up on my own, by the exercise of my wits.

I have so far omitted to mention another member of the staff of this remarkable outfit. She comes last, but by no means least, in my recollections.

This was one, Mabel Ingram, personal secretary to the Hon. John, a dazzlingly blonde lady, lissom, leggy and, to my already discerning eye, of rather more than passing nubility. She obviously felt sorry for me in my predicament and began to drift into the Upper Plan-room, inhabited by *Holy Joe* and myself, fairly frequently, presumably to see how I was getting on.

I was greatly flattered by her motherly interest and remained so, until one day, she took advantage of Joe's temporary absence in the lavatory, by asking me how I spent my evenings and would I perhaps like to do a film with her.

In my innocence, I told her that I was obliged to attend evening classes on three days of the week, and that otherwise I went home to my mother and father, at which she laughed and said she was sure I could manage one evening some time or other; that is, of course, if I wanted to.

Well, to be perfectly truthful, the idea did rather appeal to me. Also, I was beginning to lose faith in my architectural potential and the position into which I had been so rudely thrust.

My mathematical problems had been a most decided obstacle to my advancement in that direction and I was being given such tasks as mapping out the lettering for the Earl of Beauchamp's tombstone or preparing a water-colour drawing of the proposed font in the new chapel at a home for unmarried mothers in Wantage or, more menially, sent on an errand to the bank to pick up Lord Mottistone's medals. I was also finding attendance at my evening classes increasingly irksome and had had enough of the study of stresses and strains in RSJs and the problems of drainage. So, perhaps it is more readily understandable that I was tempted to play truant for perhaps just one evening and to take advantage of Mrs. Ingram's kind invitation to accompany her to the cinema.

As I somehow had the feeling that she would prefer the matter to be kept *sub-rosa*, I was obliged to wait until her visit to our plan-room coincided once more with Joe's natural requirements before I was diffidently able to broach the subject with her.

She seemed pleased and suggested that, should we happen, quite by chance at the end of the day, to leave the building at the same time, we could also happen to be walking to St. Paul's tube station together and, perhaps, even stop on the way for refreshment of some kind.

She appeared to be a mistress of subterfuge and I admired her for that and was only too happy to fall in with her plan.

I was later to discover that she was married but, having left her husband whom she described, in an unflattering light, as a rugger-mad bore, she was living on her own in a small, but attractive apartment in St. John's Wood. This was a discreet area, formerly much-favoured by well-to-do gentlemen for keeping their mistresses in the reign of Edward the Seventh.

I also discovered that she was 32 years of age and had no particular intention to lead the life of a nun.

It will probably come as no great surprise then that my original intention to play truant for one evening from my classes in building construction soon became somewhat extended. It was on one such delightful occasion that our idyll was disturbed by a resounding ring at the door. She whispered to me to be silent and the ring was repeated, this time for very much longer and again and again.

Judging from its insistence, she was able to form the opinion that this was her husband, who had taken not too kindly to her leaving the marital nest and had come to persuade her return. As his vigil seemed destined to go on for ever and as the hour for my departure was upon us, this presented something of a difficulty.

I had been unable to let my parents know of my activities as they would certainly not have received the news with over-much pleasure. However, to confront an irate and cuckolded rugby footballer on the other side of the door seemed an unsuitable option.

I began, therefore, to cast about for some means of exit, other than the front door.

I was led to the kitchen with a window overlooking what appeared to be an unlit and uninviting abyss. The apartment was on the first floor and the window, as I was assured by my ladylove, gave on to an alley, not much frequented at night. So, having re-attired myself and snatched a last hasty embrace, I hoisted myself through it and, clutching the window ledge, with my heart in my mouth, allowed myself to drop into the night, whereupon, there was a most hideous clatter and I found myself on my back in a pile of evil smelling rubbish.

I had fallen on to a battery of dustbins and was lying on a bed of their contents.

Undeservedly unhurt, and having hastily removed whatever visible fragments of refuse were still adhering to my person, I ran as fast as my legs would carry me to the Underground station and home, hoping that any possible dishevelment in my appearance would escape parental notice.

My fears were unfounded as it was only remarked that I was rather later than usual.

I can no longer remember how Mabel dealt with her husband, which I suppose is unchivalrous of me, but I am sure she managed it somehow. She certainly did not allow it to disturb our existing arrangement, which was briefly interrupted only by a parental decision that, when my leave became due, we were to spend it *en famille*, somewhere by the sea.

Going abroad at that time was considered, in their circles at least, as rather outré, so a compromise was reached and they plumped for Jersey.

When I told Mabel of this, she said that we could continue to be in touch, by means of the system of *poste-restante* and that she would write to me c/o my local Post Office in Jersey, as indeed she did.

Unfortunately, on our return to London, my mother, wishing to send our holiday garments to the cleaner's, came upon one these missives, which I had, with classic carelessness, left in one of my pockets. In the permissive society of today, it may seem preposterous as to what degree *the proverbial hit the fan* but hit it, it most certainly did.

On my return from the office, my mother, who had been reduced apparently to instant hysterics, was nowhere to be seen, having shut herself in her bedroom, and I was met with a stony-faced paterfamilias who greeted me, as he held out the offending missive, saying, "How long has this *low intrigue* been going on?"

Such was the depth of my passion that I fear I responded with total fury. And I demanded of him how he dared to speak of my love in such terms, adding, perhaps somewhat unreasonably, that they had had no right to have read my private letters.

Be that as it may, he told me how deeply my mother had been hurt by this appalling behaviour and loftily demanded an undertaking from me that the affair would be terminated forthwith, a demand with which I told him I had no intention of complying.

He seemed somewhat taken aback at this and said that before notifying the Hon. John of his secretary's shameless conduct, he wished to interview the young woman and tell her that she must stop seeing me or he would immediately inform her employer of her perfidious betrayal of trust within the firm. I said I would convey this pompous message to her and leave it to her to decide on her own course of action. He then slightly surprised me by saying that perhaps they could meet for a quiet lunch somewhere, which sounded rather better, I thought.

I now had to face my sorrowing mother, who emerged from her *purdah* and had very little to say to me.

It is curious that in France such situations are, I believe, usually met with complete parental approval, when the further education of their sons into the spheres of Venus is often undertaken by an older and suitably-experienced woman. But unfortunately, such was hardly the case in this country, except possibly among the aristocracy, in the period of which I write.

Nowadays, of course, parents can consider themselves fortunate if their offspring can steer clear of booze, drugs or uncalled-for pregnancy. Once again *mores mutantur*.

To return to my father and, at that time, the *Light of my Life*, it was arranged for them to meet somewhere or other, when, over an extremely good lunch, he more politely, I believe, requested rather than demanded, that she would leave his only-begotten son alone. This in her turn, and I am sure with great charm, she refused, telling him that, should he be inclined to report the matter to the Hon. John, then, as in the aristocratic sphere in which he lived such an occurrence was pretty much of a commonplace, he would almost certainly wonder what all the fuss was about and it would get my father no further.

This clever and courageous reply seemed to baffle my Pa, who is reported at last to have said, "Well, if you won't, I suppose you won't. But at least will you tell him to get his hair cut?"

She then reported to me that he had been most charming, greatly complimentary, not to say flattering, adding moreover that he could quite understand his son's attachment to her.

I, of course, was extremely relieved.

Later on that same evening, over dinner, my mother was still in a state of considerable shock, ate little and spoke less. My father, possibly in deference to this, had resumed his former boot-faced countenance and at one point spoke of the meeting, with a slighting reference to Mabel in the terms more recently employed by President Clinton, regarding Miss Lewinsky, as "That woman".

I took exception to this and blew the whistle on him, saying, "That's rather a change of front, isn't it? She told me this afternoon you had taken her to a slap-up lunch and told her how attractive she was and how you could quite understand your son's attachment to her. But now she's gone back to being *That woman*, has she?"

At this, my mother broke her silence and, in icy tones, demanded to know if he had indeed said any such thing, whereupon, squirming somewhat, he admitted to words of that effect, adding that he had deemed it wiser to "butter her up a bit" if he was going to make any progress with her, whereupon my mother, after a long cold stare at him, returned to her former silence.

Not long after this unfortunate happening, my parents' time in England came to an end and they returned to the Far East, this time to Hong Kong. I went down to Southampton with them and saw them on board the Queen Mary, as, for some reason, which now escapes me, they were going via New York. As I saw them disappear into the canvas tunnel, covering the gangway to the ship, I did so with some regret, which, I must own, was not entirely free from relief.

It is more than likely that I may now be considered an unfeeling and thankless child but the six months I had just spent with my parents had not been easy.

To begin with, prior to their arrival from Shanghai, I had not seen them for a full five years, which, to a boy of between 13 and 18, is a long and formative period of time. It was a very different matter for a middle-aged couple, such as my parents, who arrived furnished, I feel sure, with the idea of carrying on from where they left off with a child of 13, only to find in his place a young man with ideas of his own and who had also had to make a life of his own. The first thing that struck my Pa was that my voice had broken, which was hardly surprising. I had been singing as bass in the school choir for the last two years. With their arrival back into my life, I felt confronted with what amounted to a couple of strangers and this took considerable getting used to.

This was, I fear, particularly hard for my mother, who still seemed to regard me as her *one ewe-lamb*. She made endless demands for affection and made scenes if ever I made a move to see one of my friends.

Perhaps I should not labour the point any further as I am unable, even to this day, to rid my mind of a certain sense of guilt in the matter. For what it is worth, I speak of it here to make clear, to some small degree, some of the reasons why I should have viewed their departure with a certain sense of relief. Such feelings were of course compounded into remorse when I heard, very much later, of the death of my mother in a Japanese internment camp during the war.

But I digress.

Left once more to my own devices, I took up residence *en famille*, so to speak, with two ladies who had answered an advertisement in *The Times*, inserted by my father some time before. They were two retired school-mistresses, who had formerly run their own school in Lymington, which had apparently gone bust for some reason. They had taken a large-ish Victorian terrace house in London at Highgate Village, and offered digs with half-board (full board at weekends if required), to suitable young gents like myself.

I found it suited me splendidly. I had a large room at the top of the house, with fine views over London. I could see the Dome of St. Paul's. They were two cultivated ladies, who cooked and looked after me, and were able to provide me with interesting conversation. They had both resided at one time in Italy and were well informed in the Arts of that splendid country. They found in me an interested listener. In short, I was perfectly happy and counted myself as indeed fortunate to be there.

Furthermore, I was now totally free to continue my *low intrigue* as I chose.

This agreeable state of affairs was to continue for a few more months, marred only by rumours of war and then, finally, by war itself. I remember only too well sitting in the comfortably shabby sitting room in Highgate and listening to the voice of Chamberlain, pronouncing our present state of being at war. This was to have repercussions almost at once. Seeley and Paget decided to close down the practice and, in a fit of patriotic fervour, offered themselves and were accepted for the Barrage Balloon Department of the RAF.

Mabel took a secretarial job at the BBC and was promptly evacuated to the wilds of Evesham and I had a mysterious medical for the army, which referred me, for what reason I was never able to discover, to some sort of consultant in Harley Street. He, after a perfunctory examination of liver and lights and a general chat, I forget what about, beamed at me and told me I was A1, but that he was recommending me as not suitable for front line service.

I was somewhat disconcerted by this and asked him why not. He just smiled, saying that that was his opinion, there was nothing to worry about and, further than that, he flatly refused to be drawn. He went on to say that I would receive my calling-up papers eventually. However, it was unlikely I would receive them for another year, by which time the war would probably be over. He recommended me to get on with my life in the meantime and do whatever I felt inclined.

Feeling somewhat flat, I went home to my two ladies and gave them an account of all this. They told me not to worry and suggested I made the best of the situation. As I had told them the true direction in which my ambitions lay, they asked why I did not have a shot at RADA. Why not try for a scholarship?

Accordingly I wrote to the secretary of the Royal Academy for Dramatic Art (to give its full title) to enquire about such a possibility. I learned of various scholarships, but of only one which not only paid the fees but also provided a small amount for the student to live on. This was the much competed for *Leverhulme*, which was awarded only once a year.

As I knew it was unlikely that Pa would cough up for such a *harebrained* idea, I decided to apply for that as the only one which would be of any use to me. It consisted of a series of competitive eliminating auditions in which one performed set exam pieces, together with selections of one's own choice. To cut a long story, I reached the final round and was eventually summoned to the Principal's office to be interviewed by the august panel of judges, including the Principal himself, Sir Kenneth Barnes, his sister, Dame Irene Vanbrugh, and a couple of others.

Sir Kenneth told me that they had decided to make me an award under the terms of the *Leverhulme Scholarship*. I thanked them and countered this with an explanation of my circumstances and that I was at the time *on the dole*. I told them, furthermore, that I would be only too delighted to accept, provided I could have a dispensation to allow me to continue my visits to the Labour Exchange every Thursday for a couple of hours, in order to be able to live. There was an astonished silence for a moment or two and I was asked to wait outside. Evidently my outrageous request, much to my surprise, amused them enough actually to grant it and I was duly enrolled as a student at RADA, where I began my studies almost at once. There I remained for a full year, before King and Country summoned me to the colours.

It was fortunate that I was not found any suitable employment by the Labour Exchange during that year as that would have upset the apple cart rather more than somewhat. Apart from the voice training, which was excellent, and the opportunity to play such diverse roles as Bottom and Richard the Third, to reinforce my confidence, I had found the curriculum itself surprisingly old-fashioned and disappointing. It did, however provide opportunities to sow a few more wild oats, which helped considerably to enliven the situation.

When the time came for my departure, I was told that my course of a further year, could be completed after the war, provided, of course, I managed to survive the conflict. However, this was an offer which I privately decided not to take up.

I did return many years later, but in the situation of an occasional director of student productions there, whenever I was playing in the theatre in the evenings. Sir Kenneth still held sway and things were still being run on much the same lines as in my student days, a situation which I was largely unable to alter and so I did not stay long in my tutorial capacity either. I was then invited to perform similar activities in the recently-formed and more go-ahead London Academy of Music and Dramatic Art (LAMDA), under the dynamic leadership of Michael McCowan, himself a distinguished theatre director, where I was much happier. The going was modern and run on professional lines, and rather less like a snobbish finishing-school for young ladies.

Mabel and I corresponded until the war swallowed us up and, unfed by proximity, alas, the whole thing gradually petered out. I saw her only once again, many years later, when she came round to my dressing-room at the theatre. She was middle-aged but still very attractive and had married one of the draughtsmen at Seeley and Paget's, by now a full-blown architect, who had for years worshipped her from afar.

I still feel much gratitude to her for the delightful furtherance of my education.

4

On His Majesty's Service

War had broken out and Seeley and Paget were gallantly flying their Barrage Balloons and I was living in my comfortable *digs* in Highgate with my two kind ladies and a student at RADA. Here I first met Elizabeth Melville, who many years later was to become my lovely wife, a marriage which was to last for 25 years.

When I received my summons to serve King and Country, it was decided, as I had had *architectural experience*, coupled presumably with the mysterious report from Harley Street, that I should be sent to be trained at the Royal Artillery School of Survey at Larkhill, a bleak and wind-swept situation on the Salisbury Plain. Theodolites and working out mathematical problems with maps, while high explosive shells rained down, appeared my ticket for the foreseeable future.

After six months of that, much of the time in uncomfortably arctic conditions, having shown little aptitude for the job in hand and quite possibly to get rid of an unpromising artillery surveyor, it was decided to recommend me for a commission. Accordingly, still dogged by my mathematical illiteracy, I found myself at the 122 Field Artillery Officers Cadet Training Unit, still on the Salisbury Plain, and still flummoxed by the *sums*.

I reached the nadir of my military career in the Intermediate Gunnery examination, when I achieved the distinction of getting my guns pointing 180 degrees in the wrong direction.

As this could have had somewhat serious repercussions, possibly even to General HQ, I was hauled up before the Chief Gunnery Instructor, who confirmed what I had begun to suspect: that I was, perhaps, not Gunnery Officer timber. He offered me the alternative of RTU (returned to unit) or Anti-tank, in which branch of the artillery one did not open fire until one could see the whites of enemy eyes. He added that, in this branch of the Gunners, promotion was relatively rapid and that my fire-power would be less likely to take inconvenient directions.

Rapid promotion, of course, went hand-in-hand with a high casualty list but, as I thought it better to be dead than to endure another winter as a private soldier, I decided to transfer to this rather more direct branch of the Royal Artillery. Not, perhaps, quite the right attitude, but then I was hardly cut out for a military life.

I was eventually commissioned with one brand new shining pip on each shoulder and shunted off to a dismal Holding Unit in Hitchen in Hertfordshire, with very little better to do than sow a few more wild oats. There I languished for several months.

Eventually, I was offered a posting as troop commander in the 1st West African Anti-tank Battery, to be commanded by the Senior Major of the British Army. He had achieved this status, as I later discovered, by being promoted to Field Rank (major upwards) in a *Dad's Army* style Territorial unit in a remote and undemanding part of Scotland long before the war and was allowed no further promotion ever again. He ended an inglorious military career as, I believe, Town Major of Bombay and still presumably the senior major in the British Army.

Under his command, we sailed to West Africa, at that time still enjoying its well-deserved reputation as *The White Man's Grave*.

We were six officers and some 20 British NCOs, shipped off in a very slow convoy, enjoying the considerable interest each night of enemy submarines, in our leisurely voyage to Nigeria. It was always of some interest, before coming on deck in the morning, to guess how many ships had been lost in the night.

In Nigeria, we were to pick up native troops to be trained in the art of anti-tank warfare. We were then to lead them in the Burmese jungle against the Japanese. This, in practical terms, turned out to be easier said than done as the Nigerian soldier, while being in many ways an endearing individual, and, especially in the case of the northerners, often conspicuously brave, was not, generally speaking, overly quick on the uptake. There was also a considerable language problem.

The battery was to consist of one-third Hausa-speaking men from the north and two-thirds from the semi-literate southern and coastal regions.

In peacetime, the RWAFF (Royal West African Frontier Force) was recruited only from the Hausa-speaking north, the southerners then being considered unsuitable military material. The exigencies of war decided the powers-that-be to water down the northern element, the traditionally warrior material, in each troop of the battery with two-thirds of men of considerably less military promise. Unfortunately, those from the north had great difficulty in communicating with the European officers and NCOs who, in peacetime, had always been obliged to learn Hausa. However, the ruling from on high was that Hausa was no longer to be the language of training.

My brother officers would flop dejectedly in the mess after a hard day struggling with lingo difficulties and, whenever one of them complained of the impossibility of getting through to a particular soldier, I would offer him one of my *savvy* southerners, in exchange. I had privately decided to go against orders and learn Hausa, as quickly as possible, gradually siphoning off the tall, strapping northern warriors into my own C troop, which arrangement seemed to make everyone happier.

I suppose there are those who would consider this hardly ethical but at least I managed to get together a force of potential fighting troops with an *esprit de corps* and a possible capacity for facing a fiercely-determined enemy.

How A and B Troops fared later on in action in Burma is open to conjecture. I felt pretty sure that they would never have made the grade and, recognised as unreliable by even the dimmest of *Top Brass*, would have escaped any serious combat. However, before Burma, we had another little expedition to make. This was to defend the small Crown Colony of Gambia from a threatened attack by Vichy French forces in Senegal.

Churchill had ordered the invasion and occupation of French Madagascar where our former allies, ever since the fall of France, had been regularly fuelling and supplying aid to a fleet of German U-boats, thus enabling the enemy to maintain a serious submarine threat in the South Atlantic and Indian Oceans. In retaliation, the French were preparing an attack on Gambia, our tiny colony, surrounded on three sides by French Senegal, a place of little strategic importance and therefore virtually undefended.

Upon our arrival at Bathurst, the small port at the mouth of the River Gambia, the battery commander was ordered to deploy his strongest troop of guns to support the First Battalion of the Gold Coast Regiment, which had taken up a sparsely-defended position in the bush along the north bank of the river. The remainder of the battery was to join the second and third battalions in reserve on the south bank.

Reports had been received of movements of French troops towards our line of defence and that they were cutting a way through the bush for their tanks to advance from St Louis. The First Gold Coast, a seasoned body of men and veterans of the victorious campaign in East Africa, and my troop of anti-tank guns were to be the sole defence against a considerably stronger French force supported by two or three squadrons of tanks and batteries of field guns, which would, almost certainly, be covered by air support from Dakar. We had none of these comforting aids.

We had an hour's stand-to at dawn and at dusk, and I had chaps up the trees, listening for sounds of movement, mechanised or otherwise. Our main source of intelligence was from the almost incessant nocturnal drumming of messages by the border natives who were conducting a brisk trade, mostly in misinformation across the northern border.

Just as we were braced to receive the onslaught of the French, the Anglo-American forces invaded Vichy-controlled North Africa and the French, overnight, were once again our glorious allies.

I really feel that I owe my life to that invasion as I believe the French would have gone through us like the proverbial hot knife and butter.

Meantime, it was ordained that the First Gold Coast and C troop were to remain on the north bank for another two or three months, just in case coats were turned yet again. This campaign, that nearly was, has been tactfully buried and forgotten by both sides, but certainly not by me.

During our time in Gambia, food supplies, on the north bank at least, were in very short supply and I was in the habit, after the threat of invasion was over, in taking a 15cwt. truck, with my batman (a delightful individual, with a face and body, tattooed all over with snakes and scorpions and teeth filed to points) into the wretched villages to buy any tiny tomatoes or scrawny chickens we could find. In these villages, there was a high rate of TB, almost certainly from malnutrition, and I was unlucky enough to fall victim to it myself. I had had some five or six bouts of malaria which reduced my resistance somewhat.

However, before this, and following a series of tiresome bothers from the infantry CO, I had managed to extricate C troop and myself from the battalion's immediate vicinity to build a camp on our own. Freed from continual interference, we were all much happier and better able to get on with the job. On one occasion I had taken a section of the troop on a recce into the bush and when we stopped for a rest one of the men let out a howl of pain. He had been struck on the hand by a scorpion. My batman, who was with me, was reputed to have power over snakes and scorpions (hence all the tattoos). He ran to him at once and, seizing his stricken hand, he breathed on it, muttering almost silently.

Almost at once, and to my astonishment, the victim's distress subsided completely and we were able to continue our march.

Some form of hypnosis, no doubt, but I once saw my witchdoctor/batman remove his headgear and there, sitting on top of his shaven head, was a small live black scorpion. What possible explanation there could have been for this, I never discovered, but he told me that all the men in his tribe had this power.

Soon after this, I became unwell and had to say goodbye to my beloved C troop for ever. I was in a military hospital in Sierra Leone for six months, undiagnosed, and the Brigade went off to Burma without me. I was at last sent home to a civilian hospital where they knew what they were doing and I was invalided out of the army altogether.

In spite of all that, I would not have missed the experience.

I really loved my African soldiers and, some considerable time after, when a contingent of the RWAFF was sent over for the Victory Parade, I was walking down Kensington Gore and was recognised by a bunch of them, doing the sights, from the other side of the road. Uttering loud whoops of joy and, regardless of life and limb, they ran across through the traffic to embrace me.

I later heard that my lot had been in action against the Japanese enemy and had acquitted themselves very well.

5

Early Stages

Upon my return from West Africa sometime in 1945, I received the news, from the International Red Cross, of my mother's death in the Japanese internment camp in Hong Kong. Although we had had our difficulties, it was a shock nonetheless and I felt greatly saddened by it. I also felt tremendous sympathy for my poor father, now alone in his incarceration which continued for another year.

In the meantime, I had had to report to the Royal Northern Hospital in London where I was at last in the hands of those who knew what they were doing. Here I was examined by a celebrated surgeon called Kenneth Walker who, in about five minutes flat, diagnosed my condition as surgical TB of the epididymus, which he reassured me was perfectly curable with the appropriate surgery. He said it was not before time and that he proposed to operate within a day or so. He also put the original infection down to my low state of health and the prevalence of the disease in West Africa.

Unfortunately, the condition had spread, which occasioned a second operation a fortnight later. This, I was told, would not affect my potency, but would certainly put paid to any future I might have had as a father.

After a few weeks, having been invalided out of the army, I was pronounced well enough to leave the hospital and Walker recommended that I find myself a billet in the country, preferably on a farm, where I could have access to such aids to recovery as butter, eggs and milk. Rationing was still very stringent and he suggested Devon or Cornwall, where the winters would be less severe, as, owing to the war, Switzerland was out of the question.

I advertised for just such a situation and found myself on a farm near Perranporth where matters were not all that one would hope for. The farmer had just had his health certificate for his dairy products withdrawn. The farm itself was not quite what I expected. It was extremely primitive and far from clean, as were the owners. It would have made a perfect location for a film of that hilarious novel, *Cold Comfort Farm*, but was hardly the ticket for convalescence. Here I became ill again after a month or so of trying to make the best of it and was obliged to return to London for further hospital treatment.

In time, I was out again and, looking less far afield, found a kind, motherly lady in Bournemouth in a reasonably comfortable suburban situation and who was happy to take me in. This was more like, if not quite, what the doctor ordered and a vast improvement on the farm. Here, as in Cornwall, I was obliged to report for weekly check-ups with a GP, who weighed me and generally sounded me out. Although it was winter, with kind and motherly treatment, and sea air, I was soon able to take the short walk to the Front, where, with a rug over my knees, I could sit with a book, enjoying the gentle sunshine and taking deep breaths of sea air.

Even though it was February, I lost my West African pallor and became really quite brown. Things were looking up and I began to find my enforced inactivity somewhat irksome. As the army had no further use for me, I wished to get on with my life and began to pester the doc to give me the OK, to that end. Each time I saw him, I put the question to him but his answer was always the same. "I think, not quite yet."

In time I started frequenting a club theatre in the town, in which touring companies frequently performed and where, every so often, amateurs of a surprisingly high standard also put on plays. One day I noticed that The Malvern Company, a touring theatre ensemble, was to appear with Noel Coward's *Blithe Spirit* and I went to a matinée. To my delight, I saw in the cast that my old friend from RADA days, Elizabeth Melville, was to appear. So, after the performance I went round to the stage door to surprise her. We had lost touch because of the war but she seemed pleased to see me.

We were never what is now known as an *item*, but we had had a good many interests in common and had always got on very well. I seem to remember that on one occasion, when we were students, she even invited me to stay with her family, in the house they took every summer at Bolney, in Sussex. For some reason or other, I do not think I ever actually went, in all likelihood because my attentions at the time were focussed less worthily elsewhere.

At all events, here we were in Bournemouth after a three-year gap, so there was much catching-up to do. From the slightly gangling girl I remembered, she had, somewhat naturally, developed into a young woman. Her character, however, was unchanged. She was sensitive to the feelings of others, she was cheerful, with a great sense of humour, extremely intelligent and quick to take a point in discussion.

We were on the same wavelength and, to me, long starved of really compatible companionship, she was manna in the wilderness.

We saw a lot of each other during that time. On one occasion, we were going for a late stroll along the promenade after her evening performance, reminiscing about the days at RADA, when she suddenly said to me, laughingly, "I don't think you realised, did you, that I was madly in love with you in those days?" adding hastily, "But it's all right now. You've really no need to worry."

In a blinding flash I knew I wanted, more than anything else in the world: for this girl to be my wife. I told her so, but she laughed it off. I think my startlingly precipitous proposal had somewhat taken her off-guard.

I left her that night, determined to return to the attack next day. She was not to be easily persuaded, being convinced, as she was, that I still had a *roving eye* and that I would not be a faithful husband. Alas, poor darling, she was more clairvoyant than me; but I would not take no for an answer and kept up my eager pursuit. I was convinced that she need have no worry on the score of my fidelity.

She then raised the question of children as I had, of course, told her of my sterility. I began to see at last that she was beginning to give way and told her that if she really wanted children, we could adopt them. That finally moved her and she confessed that she still loved me and always would. She said she would have to tackle her parents, with whom she was still living and whom I had yet to meet, and that would probably be difficult.

It was more than difficult. They were stunned when she told them. They had given way to her *whim* of wanting to go on the stage, but they had envisaged it as a sort of gap-year and her soon *getting over* such fancies, making a suitable marriage and settling down with a family. To that end, she had been put through Queen Charlotte's Debutante's Ball.

However, to actually *marry an actor*!

Her father required to see me, while her mother went into hysterics, wailing over and over again, "It's the death-blow! It's the death-blow!"

I could see their point. After all, I was no great catch. I was still a semi-invalid and forbidden to work. I was of no proven abilities and without any visible prospects. I had not even got one foot on the ladder of my chosen career, a precarious one in any case. Also, I was unable to sire a child. When Liz was next in London, I, saddled with all these disqualifications, went up to see her parents in Kensington. They were very much *establishment*, especially her father, who was a retired senior officer in the Indian Civil Service.

I liked him at once and could see in him many of Liz's best traits. He was straightforward and gave me a very fair hearing at the end of which he said that, if we were to consider ourselves engaged, then he thought it should be for at least a year, starting from the time when I would be fit for work. Then, if we were still of the same mind, we could consider it.

I was able to get on with my putative mother-in-law, once she had recovered from the shock, by finding she had a strongly developed, if peculiar, sense of humour. I found I could make her laugh. I thought she was eccentric, verging on slightly bonkers, and never had any occasion later to revise my opinion. On the whole, our meeting had got off to a promising start, far better than we had dared to hope.

By this time, Liz had finished with the Malvern lot and had been taken on, playing principal roles, by the Rugby repertory company under the management of the, at that time, notorious Yvonne Le Dain, commonly known in the business as *Yvonne Le Drain*.

I had decided to ignore the doctor's advice and to try my hand at my chosen profession. Armed with Liz's recommendation, I applied to be taken on by the lovely Miss Le Dain. A meeting was arranged, during which the lady eyed me as if she was buying a horse. She then told me she had a full complement in the company, but if I was willing to fill in with bits and bobs, she would take me on as a supernumerary at a salary of £10 a week, to which I agreed with alacrity.

I bade my kind lady in Bournemouth a fond and grateful farewell and went to join Liz in Rugby to start my career in the theatre. I managed to find the most wonderful *digs* there with a most charming Swiss lady, who spoilt me, while Liz stayed with the Lyons at the School, where Hugh Lyon was headmaster. I think he was rather smitten with her. They certainly remained friends for years, in fact, right up to the time of his death.

The work was hard. It was weekly rep, which meant rehearsing for the second week, during the day, while playing the current production in the evenings. In other words, it was pretty much of a treadmill. My first play was to be *The Barratts of Wimpole Street*, in which Miss Le D. was to play Elizabeth Barratt Browning herself. Hardly type-casting, I felt, and I was given the role of the romantic lead in the character of Robert Browning who, from his first entrance in the piece, never stops talking. In other words, it was a highly responsible role.

I felt this was hardly a *bit and bob supernumerary*. Well, never mind, perhaps Miss Le D. wanted to see what I could do, but I felt she was taking a bit of a risk starting me off with Browning.

The next item on the agenda was *Trilby*, by Gerald du Maurier, in which Liz was a lovely Trilby and I was cast in the male lead, as Svengali, a highly complex and difficult role, comprising a tricky tightrope of near farcical comedy and formidable menace.

So, when I was told that in the third week I was to undertake the leading role in *Quality Street*, I took myself to the lady and told her that if she could not afford me a salary of at least as much as the other members of the company, then she could not afford a leading man, in which case I would feel obliged to retire from her service forthwith. I also reminded her that I had not tried to conceal the facts of my not over-blooming state of health and that perhaps she had overlooked this. I suggested that she might occasionally consider casting one of the others in a leading role and give me a bit of a breather in something less weighty.

After a lot of flannel about how brilliant I was, *Totty*, she agreed to ease the pressure and to double my salary.

She called every one of us, possibly to save herself the bother of remembering our names. She really was the most extraordinary woman. She had boundless energy, the hide of a rhinoceros and was as stingy as *cat's water*, not only over salaries, but in every other direction: sets, props, anything she could get for nothing. She would scrimp, browbeating antique dealers into lending her their furniture to adorn her plays, with a compensatory mention in the programme. She was always bawling at her actors and threatening them with the sack.

A good story was related, probably quite apocryphal, that she had once taken one of her company to bed and that, after the deed was done, she had lain back with a seraphic smile, and was heard to murmur, "I'll *have* to sack you now, *Totty*".

Nearly at the end of the season, she was producing a version of *Pickwick*, in which I was to play the part of Jingle, and I was stricken down and obliged to take to my bed with an unpleasant attack of jaundice. There was, of course, no understudy so, without turning a hair, she donned my clothes and played the part herself. I was told she wasn't half bad, either. It probably suited her rather better than Elizabeth Barratt Browning. What the audience made of it, the Lord alone knows. But one had to admire her *chutzpah*.

Liz and I stuck it out in Rugby for another half season, with a short spell in Huddersfield where I was to discover the sheer delight of eating true Yorkshire pudding, the like of which I have never seen before or since. We both left the company at the same time and came back to London, Liz going back to her home to prepare for the wedding to which the Melvilles had finally become resigned.

Almost at once I was lucky enough somehow to be successfully interviewed for my next assignment by Basil Langton, who ran a company called TRT, the Travelling Repertory Theatre. He had actually been one of my tutors at RADA so that may have had something to do with it. What he instructed us in was actually make-up.

This was altogether a very different affair from the Rep at Rugby and a very decided step up.

We were to do a set of plays, *Romeo and Juliet*, *Saint Joan*, and two new plays, *The Wise Have Not Spoken*, by Paul Vincent Carroll, a rather turgid piece concerned with the sorrows of Ireland, and also a Greek tragedy, the *Electra*, plus a play about President Wilson, the title of which escapes me. The company was to include many distinguished players, such as Dame Sybil Thorndike and her husband, Sir Lewis Casson, Esmond Knight (a splendid Fluellen in Olivier's film of *Henry* V) and Renee Asherson, who had just given an enchanting performance as the French princess in the same film.

We were to open at the delightful 18th century Theatre Royal, Bristol with a pre-London production of the Irish play in which I was to play opposite Renee, before performing it, with the other plays, at the King's Theatre, Hammersmith.

I was cast in the part I really wanted, as Tybalt in *Romeo and Juliet* and to *double* as Bluebeard and D'Estivet, the prosecutor, in *St. Joan*. Basil Langton was to appear as Romeo and the leading character in the Irish play and Brother Martin in *St. Joan*. Sir Lewis was to direct and to play the Bishop of Beauvais and later President Wilson. Esmond Knight was to give his spirited rendering of Mercutio in *Romeo and Juliet*.

Life had certainly looked up, professionally speaking, and I had just had the news, Japan having unconditionally surrendered, of my father's release from the prison camp, alive, if not well.

Rehearsals for *Romeo* were on the stage of the rather grand King's Theatre, so we had the advantage of getting used to the acoustics and situation in which we were in fact to perform. Then there was the duel scene between Mercutio and Tybalt to think about. To those old enough to remember, Esmond Knight had been completely blinded during the war, in the naval engagement between the battleships, *The Prince of Wales* and *The Bismarck*. He had been told that he would never act in his life again, a situation he resolutely refused to accept.

I assumed that, because of this, the sword fight between us would be inevitably short and sharp. A few *dings and dongs* and then the coup de grâce. At that time I did not know my opponent. Esmond, or Ted, as he was generally known, flatly refused to make any concessions to himself. Not only did he insist on the full *works* with the rapier but, to my apprehensive dismay, he demanded the added complications of the left-hand dagger as well.

As no-one could talk him out of it, a long and most complex sword and dagger fight was arranged by Gabriel Toyne, who was then the authentic expert in such matters. This meant that night after night, after rehearsals, Ted and I would go for a couple of hours with Toyne to the upper room at the Red Cow pub and practice the routine, over and over again until it became almost like clockwork. Without this, it would have been decidedly dangerous. Ted never once put a foot wrong. The only mishap, during the entire run of the play, was my fault when I mistimed a riposte and stabbed him in the rump, while he was doing a *spin-round* lunge at me. He did not hold it against me. In fact, we became firm friends. Blood brothers, you might say.

I have never known a man so undaunted by adversity. This he carried through for the rest of his life, during which I enjoyed the benefit of his example and the pleasure of his friendship.

Later on in 1948 we shared a dressing-room at Stratford-on-Avon, when I used to while away the lulls in rehearsals, by reading to him *War and Peace* in its entirety. I think we also managed most, if not all, of *David Copperfield.* At one point, he handed me, for some reason or other, an old copy of a *Temple* edition of one of the Shakespeare plays we were working on. I was greatly struck by a most spirited drawing in colour in the fly-leaf of a marching gonfalonier, in 15ᵗʰ century costume holding a streaming banner. When I asked him about it - I had to describe it of course - he said it was probably something he had done before the war.

Whereupon I suggested that he could do something like it again. He could still make out vague shapes and colours. I told him of a painter I knew of who produced even better work after almost total blindness.

He laughed at the idea. But that very afternoon, he went out and bought himself a child's paint box and tried his hand at some skyscapes. They were splashy, of course, and loosely done, but they showed he had not lost his touch.

He stuck at it and later he went on to oils and began to sell his work very well. Every year he had a show of his larger paintings at Cookham-on-Thames and sold practically all of them. By way of thanks, he presented me with a fine, entirely imaginary scene of Venice in the renaissance, with banners flying, rather in the manner of the small drawing that started it all. It hangs on the wall above me now, as I write, but dear old Ted, alas, has long gone to his ancestors.

Typically he died, as he had lived, in harness to the last: a brave and wonderful friend.

He had told me that when he was filming in *Henry V,* he could not tell night from day. He was completely blind and did the whole thing by numbers. Olivier had to direct him with instructions, such as, "Take three paces to the left, Ted, and then say the line as you turn". It was very much to Olivier's credit that he was prepared to take so much extra trouble and such a chance with an actor who was totally blind in such an important role and in such an important film. It certainly paid off. Ted gave an excellent and incredibly spontaneous performance.

But to return to TRT and the final result of our labours in rehearsal. Ken Tynan hit the nail on the head, when he described our leading actor as "smug". Basil C. Langton had a manner, which can only be described as aloof and self-satisfied. This was most apparent in his dealings with his company, with whom he was loftily distant. Unhappily, he was unable to lose this manner in his performance on stage. He had been a man, gifted with extreme good looks but which, possibly without him realising it, had just begun to wane. He had also put on a morsel of weight. None of this was to stand him in good stead as Romeo, in which he appeared as a man in love certainly but, unfortunately, as a man in love with *himself.*

His Romeo was unlikeable. On the first night, as he raised one parti-coloured leg over the balustrade, in his descent from Juliet's balcony, his tights parted company from his waist, revealing the cleavage of an inappropriately plump pair of buttocks. This was greeted for a moment with an amazed silence, followed by a gale of laughter.

I believe the audience, on the first night at least, understandably, found difficulty in empathising with Romeo's subsequent tragic plight. It was really very bad luck. It was even worse luck for Renee, who managed to keep the play going, with a most delightful portrayal of Juliet and Sir Lewis was a splendid Friar Lawrence. But it does strike me as odd that an actor of Langton's experience should not have been *belt and braces* over such an important detail.

St. Joan was directed in his most dictatorial vein, by dear old Sir Lewis who, being a Welshman, conducted, quite literally, the whole play as if it was a piece of music. He was obsessed by the tune of it and the rhythm of the lines.

"No, no, no," he would shout, "I've *told* you how it must go. *Dum* dee dee dum dum *dum.*"

For those of us who were unfortunately not Welsh, this method of going about things could be disconcerting. As he was also acting in the play, any transgression of his strict orchestration, even during the actual performance, would be met with a fierce glare and a perfectly audible snarl, such as, "Get on with it!"

I had cause to be pleased that his forthcoming production of *Electra* was to be my play *out* and I did not envy his daughter, Ann, who was to bear the burden of the title role. We readily forgave the old bear, as he was such a really lovable old man, kind and honourable and totally devoted to his principles.

On the first night of the Wilson play, in which I had a very small part, I found myself in the gloom of the wings with Dame Sybil, who was nervously pacing up and down, waiting to make her first entrance. She was playing the

President's wife. After a few minutes of this, I went up to her and asked her if I could get her a chair, "No, no, no, thank you," she muttered, took a couple more turns up and down, then, seizing my arm in the gloom, she hissed, "I hold out no hope for you, my dear boy. None whatsoever. It gets worse as you get older!"

I often had occasion, in the course of my acting career, to remember those fateful words.

The remainder of the season passed, as far as I was concerned, without any memorable incident.

There remained the little matter of our marriage. This took place at Holy Trinity, Prince Consort Road, and was altogether, considering the stringencies of the time, quite a smart sort of affair. We all dressed up for the occasion: I, by courtesy of Messrs. Moss Bros. Liz looked lovely in her bridal dress. I had made for her a coronet of large fake pearls, on a wreath of twisted light blue and silver.

Many of Liz's grander relations turned up, including her Norton cousins, through whom I discovered she was related to Caroline Norton, the Victorian beauty associated with Lord Melbourne, and also to Richard Brinsley Sheridan, which was quite a thought. The head of the Nortons also came. He was a distinctly racy individual, called Richard Brinsley Grantley, who was, I believe, the Chairman of Pinewood Film Studios where he was once seen using a urinal while conversing with a colleague. Happening to notice the pencilled remark on the wall, "Richard Norton is a bastard," while still continuing his conversation, he took out a pencil and crossed out *Norton* substituting *Grantley*, the peerage he had just inherited.

Representing me was my grandmother, *dolled-up to the nines* and also, looking painfully thin and drawn, my poor father, who had just come back from New Zealand where he had been sent to recuperate after his release from the prison camp. Teddy Knight also came with his lovely wife, the well-known actress Nora Swinburne, plus Liz's oldest and closest friend, Bunny, who really merits a chapter on her own. There was most of the family of Champernowne, Liz's cousins, of Dartington Hall. And last, but by no means least, Liz's rich and very formidable Aunt Hermione Calvocoressi, who resided in Victorian splendour with her two maiden sisters in Wilton Crescent where the reception was to be held.

In spite of my forebodings, it all went surprisingly well. The only remark Aunt Hermione made to me during the reception was, "You know where it is, don't you?" This was a reference, I after discovered, to the whereabouts of the loo: apparently a great preoccupation with the older Melville ladies.

Our wedding night was spent at the Savoy Hotel, where we could at last relax on our own, from whence we repaired to a tiny one-bedroomed flat, which we had found in Charlotte Street, opposite the Scala Theatre, in the Bohemian heart of *Fitzrovia*, with Soho nearby.

It was an area, in those days before it was totally ruined, full of continental atmosphere: French, Italian and German restaurants, delicatessens, and small individual shops and businesses, full of charm and character. It was also the haunt of painters and writers and where that celebrated *stately homo of England, The Naked Civil Servant,* Quentin Crisp, was often to be seen in full sail cruising down the street in bell-bottomed trousers and lurid make-up. This, of course, was long before he was famous and almost before the dreadful word *celebrity*, in its present context, was even thought of.

Liz was working in a play with Robert Morley called *The First Gentleman* at the Savoy Theatre, which was reasonably close by. She was playing a small part, Lady Hertford, and understudying Wendy Hiller. I was still rehearsing in Hammersmith.

We adored our little flat and were blissfully happy there for a couple of years.

6

Redgrave's Macbeth

In 1947, for whatever reason, I was approached and asked to present myself at the august offices of H.M. Tennant, which lurked on the top floor of the Globe Theatre, reached by way of a claustrophobic, coffin-sized lift. This was where I was to be interviewed by no less a personage than Michael Redgrave, with a view to possible casting in his forthcoming production of what is superstitiously always referred to in the profession as *The Scottish Play* and which I will, with some boldness, entitle *Macbeth*.

I was duly shown into a small room where there was a good-sized desk, behind which sat a very large Michael Redgrave and a rather small American who, it appeared, was to direct the play. We had some sort of conversation, the gist of which was that they would like me to be in the production and would let me know very soon in what capacity. An odd approach, I remember thinking, and dismissed it from my mind.

The next morning I had a call from my agent who said, rather to my astonishment, that they would like me to play one of the witches! And how did I feel about that? I began to wonder quite what sort of impression I could have made on them. A witch! For heaven's sake!

I expressed my astonishment, with which he concurred, adding that it was, after all, Michael Redgrave and, "He is pretty odd". I did not realise until later, just quite *how* odd.

I said I would like to think it over and I would let him know.

Well, I thought long and hard and I began to be rather intrigued by the idea. It would certainly be a departure from anything I had ever done before or, for that matter, would ever be likely to do again. I was, after all, young in the business and I could chalk it up to experience. So, putting any misgivings aside, I said I would do it.

Some time after, I had an invitation to a pre-rehearsal drinks' party at the Redgrave house on Chiswick Mall. I went to what appeared to be a most delightful Queen Anne family home, called, I seem to remember, Bedford House. There seemed to be a great press of people and a very high volume of chatter. Strangely enough, I have no recall of seeing Redgrave there. I met his charming wife, Rachel Kempson, and there were, I think, two or three children, presumably Vanessa and siblings, and the other members of the cast, some of whom I already knew. My old friend from RADA, John Blatchley, was to be the Porter and Michael Goodliffe was to play Banquo. He had been Benvolio in the King's Theatre, Hammersmith, production, of *Romeo and Juliet*, in which I had played Tybalt. Not being over fond of large gatherings, I did not linger and, being unable to find my host, I took my leave of his wife and departed.

A day or so later, we all met for the first read through and I was somewhat astonished to find that there were to be no less than six witches, three of whom were women and three were to be men, who were to stand in a row, upstage at the back, encased in canvas, or hessian, tubes, surmounted with an enormous head of papier mâché, a sort of gargoyle completely obliterating the actor, who was to intone the odd witch's line now and again. The witches themselves were to be the usual conventional crones.

What purpose this was supposed to serve, the Lord, Michael Redgrave and the director alone presumably knew. We humbler mortals were not, so far as I can remember, let into the secret at all.

As can be imagined, I felt rather as if I had been got there under a misapprehension and certainly intended to have no part of it. I could hardly wait for the coffee break, when I went up to Redgrave, who was also in reality, of course, the director, and told him that I had clearly misunderstood the original offer to play the witch and that, under the present circumstances, I would like to withdraw from the production entirely, thank you very much.

He appeared flabbergasted at this and asked me to stay to the end of the reading as he would like me to consider it further. I agreed to do so, but without the smallest intention of changing my mind.

At the end of the session, he asked me to sleep on it and to telephone him in the morning. It was perfectly clear to me that it was not my peculiar talents that inspired his insistence so much as his objection to being thwarted. At all events, I called him in the morning and was about to reiterate my resolve of the previous day when he cut me short by asking me if I would agree to play Lennox instead. As there were no particular peculiar strings attached to this that I could see and I was at least to be visible, I agreed to do it. Apart from his aberration regarding the witches, it seemed it was to be a conventional *hair and horns* production of the play.

Rehearsals got under way and it soon became apparent that all was not quite well.

Ena Burrell, an actress of great power, was clearly not happy with what a critic of the time described as, "Michael Redgrave's manipulative direction" of her performance as Lady Mac. The actor playing Macduff had an odd manner of delivering the verse in short staccato bursts, while Redgrave himself seemed to have great difficulty in coming to terms with a notoriously arduous role and one which, without any independent and experienced direction, could be deemed almost impossible.

The putative director was not, as it may be surmised, possessed of such qualifications, being merely, so far as I can recall, not much more than a cipher. He had had little experience, if any, of professional directing, being an academic whom Redgrave, as I understood it, had met in a bar in America. A great deal of time in rehearsal was spent in researching the inner meanings of the text, with constant scholarly discussions on this or that authority. I recall that at one point Redgrave, coming back from the lunch-break, having just heard that Professor Dover Wilson had produced a very recent and hot-off-the-press commentary on the play, and flushed with excitement at the news, suspended all rehearsals while a messenger was despatched to Foyle's bookshop immediately to procure a copy.

I was on more than one occasion reminded that he had been at one time a schoolmaster. It is probably apparent to the reader that the prospect of success was not a rosy one.

Apart from those I already knew, there was in the cast a most amusingly camp character whose racy conversation did rather more than somewhat to enliven the longuers of the day. His name, I think, was Paul Stephenson. He was tall and willowy, and had been cast, rather implausibly, as it seemed to me, as the rugged Duncan, King of Scotland.

I will never forget his account of how he wangled himself out of the RAF during the war. To me, it ranks alongside the very similar and oft-repeated anecdote of Lytton Strachey in almost the same situation during the previous conflict. Paul had decided that the colour of the uniform hardly suited his complexion and he therefore determined to behave in as outrageous a manner as possible, in order to attract the attention of his superiors to the same point of view. His success in this enterprise was crowned with an interview before the CO, followed rapidly by a course with a psychiatrist who told him that in time he would begin to notice that his unnatural orientations would gradually be transferred to him. Whereupon, Paul replied in the following salty terms:

"Don't flatter yourself, ducky. I like 'em big and I like 'em black!"

His discharge from the RAF was almost immediate.

Paul certainly provided us with some of the brighter moments in what was beginning to appear otherwise as a pretty depressing experience. The play itself is not a very cheery one at the best of times and is generally regarded with some unease by many thespians, having a curiously long history attached to it of mishaps and disasters, some of them, believe it or not, actually fatal. And this particular set-up was beginning to appear quite definitely outside the category of *best of times*.

Eventually the tour started, in Glasgow or perhaps Edinburgh, anyway one of the Scottish number one dates, to somewhat mixed notices from which their majesties did not emerge too well. After the first night, Michael, as I now called him, arrived at the theatre the next morning for correctional notes, sporting a very fine black eye. How this was acquired, history, alas, does not relate. Curiously, he was to appear on a subsequent occasion bearing similar signs of being involved in some sort of affray.

We duly received our notes and matters were meddled about a bit, on a fairly regular basis. And so we went on with the tour, taking frequent notes from on high with instructions and counter-instructions, a few to some purpose and others to none whatsoever. However, it was my first proper experience of a number one tour and I was beginning to thoroughly enjoy the changes from London. I was lucky in my choice of theatrical *digs*, having done my researches and found ones of good repute where one was guaranteed a comfortable bed, a hot supper after the performance, a roaring fire and a doting landlady, some of whom enjoyed a considerable reputation in thespian circles.

There were framed photographs of their regular favourites, such as Ivor Novello, and I even seem to remember an early one of Noel Coward, all affectionately signed. These ladies never advertised but enjoyed their reputations entirely by word of mouth and their would-be lodgers frequently vied with each other to get in first to make sure of their applications. Such a one was a Mrs. Macdonald of Edinburgh, who could pick and choose. She was the great *star* in the landlady firmament and her digs were always fought over. This wonderful arrangement is, alas, no more. Nowadays actors have to make do with characterless hotels, that is, those intrepid enough to undertake touring the provinces, where salaries have to be high indeed in order to pay for the simplest of accommodation.

Dan Massey once said to me many years later, "You know, Doug, you really wouldn't enjoy it nowadays. It's not a gent's profession any more. It's all money, bloody money."

An extreme view, perhaps, but one I think, fairly expressive of the views of the *Old Timer*, like myself. He was referring, not of course to the demise of the landlady, but to conditions in the *business* in general.

But I digress. A bad habit of mine. So, *revenons à nos moutons.*

The grand tour completed, we opened with a fanfare of trumpets at the Aldwych Theatre in London and, if my memory serves me correctly, to a barrage of highly critical reviews, the focus of which appeared to be on the two leading roles and the production itself. Redgrave kept any mortification he may have felt very much to himself. It betrayed itself only as an increase of general irascibility towards his cast, never a particularly warm relationship at best, together with a most noticeable increase in his intake of alcohol.

His dresser was instructed to stand in the wings with a bottle of Champagne, so that whenever he made an exit from the stage he could be handed a glass of the wine, with which he first would gargle and then swallow. He had certainly had trouble with his voice but I have never heard of champers as a specific for a sore throat.

As the production ran on, so Redgrave's behaviour on stage became more and more erratic.

On one occasion, during the banquet scene, just after the ghost of Banquo had occupied Macbeth's chair, I, in the person of Lennox, invited him thus,

"May it please your highness sit?" to which Macbeth is supposed to reply, "The table's full". Instead of which, he fixed me with a glassy stare and started swaying and tottering towards me saying nothing at all. After what seemed an age, he appeared to recover. I do not know if he took a prompt or quite how we got out of it, but I do remember the embarrassment of those on stage at the time and, less forgivably, that of the audience.

When, the scene was over Michael saw me in the semi-darkness of the wings and I thought he was about to apologise. He laid a heavy hand on my shoulder and, with a look of the greatest reproach, and to my complete astonishment, said, "I never thought *you* would let me down".

I stared at him and asked him in what way I was supposed to have done so.

"Your underplaying of the line. You completely threw me," he said.

"Do you mean, 'May it please your highness sit?'" I asked. It was not, I felt, exactly a line calling for high histrionics.

"Yes," he said. "You completely threw me."

I had no idea what to say so I told him if it was my fault then I could only apologise and we left it at that.

There were other occasions, but one particularly sticks in my memory. We were playing a matinée to schoolchildren and, much to Michael's quite understandable annoyance, they had clearly decided that he was the comic relief. All his moments of high histrionics were greeted with gales of mirth. He was half-way through one of his soliloquies when he broke off and, clutching his enormous battle-mace, all six foot three of him lumbered hugely downstage to the front and bawled, "BE QUIET! WHEN YOU'RE QUIET, I'LL GO ON."

There was most certainly a stunned silence, followed by the more usual subdued murmur, normal with most children's performances. He continued to glower at them for what seemed an eternity and then lumbered back upstage and continued his performance. The stage director and most of the cast were furious with him for highly unprofessional conduct and a report of his misdemeanour was entered into the diary and sent to H.M. Tennant, the head office.

For once, he did rather have my sneaking sympathy. The poor man had been battling for some time before he finally snapped and, bearing in mind the high opinion in which he held himself, he must have found the experience doubly galling. Privately, I felt it was the sort of thing which I, in an unguarded moment, might well have done myself.

The production, which could well have served as a model for the TV show, *Hairy Bikers*, finally came to a welcome and merciful end.

7

Antony and Cleopatra

In 1946, an ambitious production of Shakespeare's *Antony and Cleopatra* was put on by H.M. Tennant at the Piccadilly Theatre, the two principal roles being played by Godfrey Tearle and Edith Evans.

Binkie Beaumont, the then all-powerful uncrowned *Queen* of the West End theatre circuit, had offered Glen Byam Shaw, who had been convalescing from some unfortunate war-time disability, a production of any play he chose to direct. So Glennie chose *Antony and Cleopatra* and, for some extraordinary reason, offered it to Edith Evans, who, although a sublime actress in the right role, was 56 and by no means everyone's idea of the character anyway.

When asked why he had done so, he replied inexplicably, that she was, "the only woman in England who could touch it".

I was offered the unrewarding role of Ventidius with Euphronius which, being a young actor and new to the West End, I was happy to accept, particularly as I had two or three scenes with Godfrey Tearle, whom I idolised.

As rehearsals got under way, it became painfully clear that Dame Edith, whilst handling the verse magnificently, was, as a sex-pot, pretty much of a dead duck.

Also, many felt that Godfrey was rather miscast, in spite of his effortlessly commanding presence. He certainly seemed somewhat lukewarm in his passion for Cleo. He was not keen playing opposite her, I know. Once, when I was standing next to him in the wings, watching Dame Edith, he said to me, with what I thought was a rather uncharacteristic lack of gallantry, "How on earth can I make love to a woman with a face like that?"

Later on I was to realise, when I was playing the King in *Hamlet*, what a considerable handicap it is to be obliged to simulate sexual desire for a woman no longer anywhere within the plausible bracket of nubility.

Godfrey, however, though in real life in a laid-back sort of way a reputed *squire of dames*, was not really able to portray the reckless libertine required by Shakespeare's passionate Antony, but I am sure he could have made a more serious shot at it with a more probable Cleo. I remember one rehearsal, when the suitability of one of Edith's costumes was in question, Godfrey's jovial interjection, "What we need isn't a new costume: it's a new Dame" and, pretty amazingly, everyone including Edith laughed. Only Godfrey, with his lazy bonhomie, could have got away with it. How he did, I still do not know. Perhaps it was his amazing natural warmth which somehow took the sting out of such a remark. He certainly had a most endearing personality, totally devoid of pretence of intellectual depth or any form of grandeur. He had a natural grandiosity of personality which somehow spoke for itself and of which, I am sure, he was largely unaware.

While we were on tour, one Sunday evening, Mark Dignam and I happened to go into the local Grand Hotel for a drink and bumped into Godfrey, who was coming down the stairs, dressed for dinner, which we were most certainly not. He immediately hailed us and invited us to dine with him, which we did, and most enjoyably.

An example of his lack of pretension: he was relating how someone had sent him a play by Charles Morgan, called *The Flashing Stream*, recommending it to him on the grounds of its intellectual depth. Godfrey, having read it, said he didn't know about that, but he thought it "a damned fine melodrama" and was more than happy to do it as such. And do it, he did, with some considerable success, somehow or other by-passing the considerable intellectual pretensions of the piece, as written by the author.

On one occasion I was waiting in the wings to make an entrance with him and he was hardly able to contain his mirth. He was the possessor of a magnificently rich and effortlessly powerful voice, and he told me he had just opened a fan letter, which described him as having, in the writer's opinion, "The finest organ in the English theatre".

At the first dress rehearsal, when Godfrey, who was still far from word-perfect in the role, was being hoisted up on to Cleopatra's monument, in a state near to death, his voice rang out, "I am dying, Egypt, dying," as he came into view, lying on a litter and reading his lines from a small *Temple* edition of the play.

Dame Edith, whom we lesser beings never addressed without the *Dame*, was a very different proposition, maintaining her august distance throughout from everyone except Glennie and Godfrey. I could never make up my mind what she was really like. She was certainly not friendly or warm and sometimes, despite her reputation for wit, seemed really rather stupid. She was certainly ill-advised to take on the highly unsuitably difficult role of Cleopatra.

I can remember one very good piece of advice that she once gave me, regarding the playing of Restoration comedy. "Always tackle the lines in long bites. It's the only way you will make sense of it."

This was some years later, when I was having some difficulty playing Pinchwife, opposite Joan Plowright in a radio production of *The Country Wife*, in which Edith gave one of her superb comedy performances. She certainly knew her stuff in that very difficult line of theatre, being justly celebrated for her definitive performances in so many of the plays of Congreve, Wycherly and Vanbrugh. She was also greatly famous for her appearances in the plays of Oscar Wilde, most notably, of course, as Lady Bracknell, a creation which, for comic individuality, has made life extremely difficult for anyone else assaying the role thereafter.

Both she and Godfrey were forced on this particular occasion, to rely on their absolute mastery of classical Shakespearian playing, creating, in a way, their own convention of presentation of the two roles rather than making any attempt at more realistically obvious sexuality or flirtatiousness. I think in this way they managed to get away with it ... just.

This device, however, failed to convince a young critic called Ken Tynan, who described Dame Edith's performance as, "Lady Bracknell, cruelly deprived of her cucumber sandwiches".

Alec Guinness, who I am sure was not present, relates in his *Memoirs* a story, which I am certain he got from me, concerning an enormous black man, playing the attendant's memorable line, "Soundly, my lord," in reply to Antony's, "Is he whipped?"

This most amusing man had ample leisure during the first very slow stop-start dress rehearsal to sit in the stalls, watching the progress of the scenes he was not in. He happened to sit himself down, immediately in front of Binkie Beaumont and a cohort of top-brass from Tennant's who were watching, I imagine with some dismay, the pretty shambolic dress rehearsal.

Not having the faintest idea who they were, he turned round to them and cheerily observed, "My, my. Mistuh Tuhl and that ol' lady must have an awful lotta money to put this show on!"

8

Stratford-upon-Avon 1948

Some time in 1947 Anthony Quayle, a youngish and very ambitious actor/ director, happened to meet Robert Helpman and Michael Benthall at a drinks' party. During the course of conversation, Quayle asked what they were up to. They told him that they had been invited by Sir Barry Jackson to direct, in Benthall's case, and to perform a certain number of leading parts, in Helpman's, the following year at Stratford-on-Avon.

These were to consist of *Shylock*, *King John* and *Hamlet*, which last role Helpman was to alternate with Paul Scofield, a young actor of great promise who had already made a name for himself there. These three plays were to be directed by Benthall, as well as *Taming of the* Shrew, and they would get someone else to direct the remainder, which were to be *The Winter's Tale* and *Troilus and Cressida*. Their aim was to transform the Stratford season from something of middling quality into an event of some theatrical importance. Towards the end of the season, they would also put on *Othello*, for which they had in mind Godfrey Tearle.

Hearing this, Tony Quayle eagerly offered his services. He would be only too happy to join them, to direct two of the plays and, otherwise to play the leading parts, not already set aside for Helpman or Scofield.

Benthall and Helpman promised to think it over and then perhaps submit the idea to Sir Barry who, although about to retire, was still in effect the Director. This they did and Sir Barry, in turn, submitted the idea to Fordham Flower, the all-powerful Chairman of the Memorial Theatre and of Flower's Brewery, and therefore, by consequence, a pretty big cheese in Stratford-upon-Avon.

It so happened that Tony had just directed a production of *The Relapse*. This was a little-known, but highly salacious Restoration comedy by Vanbrugh, which was being played with much romping gusto and enjoying a considerable

53

succès de scandale at the Lyric, Hammersmith. The *permissive society* had, after all, not yet arrived. Flower went to see it and, encouraged by the full houses which were drawn by the production, gave his immediate approval to Tony's appointment, to direct *Troilus* and *Winter's Tale*. The overall Director, of course, was still nominally Sir Barry Jackson. (I was not, of course, directly privy to this, hearing it all much later from Bobby Helpman himself.)

The two directors then set about the task of casting.

They invited Diana Wynyard to play Desdemona, Portia and Kate in *The Shrew*. Bobby Helpman had already picked the plums of Hamlet, King John and Shylock. Esmond Knight, who had been in Tony's *Relapse*, was to play Leontes in *Winter's Tale*, Thersites, in *Troilus* and Sly in *The Shrew*. Later in the season, Godfrey Tearle would do *Othello*. Tony Quayle had Claudius in *Hamlet*, Faulconbridge in *King John* and Petruchio in *The Shrew* - not a bad little personal haul. They also managed to pull in some reasonable names for the lesser roles.

Tony, in conjunction with Benthall, invited me to join them, offering Antonio, a boring part, albeit the title role, in *The Merchant of Venice* and the very much better part of Achilles in *Troilus*. There was also the dreadful part of Count Melun in *King John*, Guildenstern in *Hamlet*, not great either, with Lodovico, a nonentity, in *Othello*. Antonio eventually slipped down to Salanio, a role of no interest to me at all.

Young in the profession, though I undoubtedly was, the thought of tying myself down to such a repertoire for so long bored and depressed me, and the more I thought about it, the less inviting the prospect appeared. I rang Tony and told him. He seemed astonished and asked what, as a young actor, did I expect? I replied that, at least, to be interested in what I was doing. For some extraordinary reason, my reluctance seemed to challenge him in some way and he appeared determined to have me.

He told me that this season was merely a doorway to greater things to come and further twisted my arm, telling me that he would like to have Liz in the company, as well. Foolishly, as it turned out, I allowed myself to be swayed.

Before very long, I was to learn that he had a genius for persuading actors into accepting roles, in which they were *under-parted*. This he did by offering one comparative *plum*, together with a parcel of dross. He eventually became notorious for it in the profession. He was thereby able to cast all the roles of any consequence with the best actor he could get. This was, of course, not only for the greater glory of Stratford, but also the greater glory of Quayle. He would offer the same role to more than one actor, to stimulate interest, and then gradually *whittle* down the offer to one of much lesser importance.

There was a story, which became legend, how two actors, returning to London, in the same railway compartment, discovered that they had *both* been offered the role of Macduff, the following season.

But to return to 1948. When I came to studying the roles, I felt I could do a lot with Achilles. Salanio was, of course, a chore, Guildenstern not much better and I believed I had *The Shrew* as my play *out*. Melun consisted of staggering, from the battlefield, "wounded unto death", delivering an improbably lengthy speech, at the end of which he expires on stage. Difficult, but not too onerous, I thought.

I was to discover, however, that not only did the wretched Melun have to do this, but he was also destined, in Benthall's production, to stand on, for much of the play, as silent *stage-dressing*, clad in chain mail and lugging a large iron shield of unbelievable weight before finally lurching on to deliver his long and improbable speech of expiry. It always felt as if part of the scenery had unbelievably acquired the gift of tongues.

I grew to dread the performances of *King John*.

My play *out*, I was to learn, was nothing of the sort. I soon discovered that I had to understudy Baptista, which meant I had to watch all the rehearsals of *The Shrew* and learn a role of monumental tedium which I was, mercifully, never called upon to perform. I had not been apprised of the two latter developments, before I agreed to sign on for the season.

Meantime, I recall Bobby Helpman telling me that he and Michael had begun to notice that Quayle was inviting Fordham Flower rather often to lunch or dinner at the Garrick Club and that he was generally making a reasonable job of cultivating the other Governors. The penny eventually dropped when, a month or so later, and without any warning, a note appeared on the notice board outside the Green Room door to the effect that, on Sir Barry Jackson's retirement at the end of the season, the Governors would appoint Anthony Quayle, as Director of the Memorial Theatre.

Quayle then sent for Michael Benthall, according to Bobby, and said to him, "You realise, of course, that our positions are now relatively different".

What Benthall said in reply, I really cannot imagine.

Soon after this, I and about half a dozen others of the company had letters from Tony, as heir-apparent, which ran, "I would like to let you know that it is my definite intention to ask you back next season and with an offer of parts, which I feel sure you will be happy to play. I will very soon be in a position to say which parts and to make you a firm offer."

In my case he made it clear that Liz, who had played Dorcas, in *Winter's Tale* and other bits and bobs, was also included. I read his letter with mixed feelings. I was not enjoying the season very much, mainly because I was engaged in parts which I was *not* "happy to play". Also I was in love neither with Stratford, nor its ethos of heavily commercialised Shakespeare. Some hotels, which had been happy to accommodate many of us during our rehearsal period, had the gall to put up their prices as soon as the Season actually started. As the Company's work was their principal *raison d'être*, we thought this *a bit rich*. It did not affect Liz and me as we had comfortable digs in a nearby village with a kindly old soul who smoked her own bacon. We cycled in and out each day.

I visited Stratford with some friends, a year or so ago, to see *Othello*. After the long car journey, I had need of a loo. I found one for the disabled in the enormous car park. It was locked. There was a notice, which read, "Persons wishing to use this convenience may *purchase a key* from..." and named some office or other in the town. Some things do not change.

But I digress, as usual.

One very definite plus to the season was the company of my old chum, Teddy Knight, with whom I shared a dressing-room. As I have described elsewhere, I used to read to him, during our breaks. I also had to make him up, as he could not see well enough to do so himself. We used sticks of greasepaint in those days, far more than is customary now.

One day, when I was *slapping* it on him, I felt something sharp on the end of his nose. When I drew his attention to it, he said, "Oh yes, that's most likely a bit of armour-plating from *The Prince of Wales* ... either that or a bit of shrapnel from *Bismarck*. There are dozens of bits of them in me and, every so often, one erupts."

Incredibly, the three of us used to go for bike rides in the country. How on earth Teddy managed it, Heaven alone knows. He was just as keen to get away from the town as we were. The country lanes were much quieter then, so we probably rode three abreast. We would describe the charming Warwickshire countryside to him as we rode and he seemed to enjoy this almost as much as if he could have actually seen it. He also seemed to have an extraordinary facility for the enjoyment of paintings: again, largely, from their descriptions. In fact, he bought quite a few, including a very fine Cotman water-colour of an actor in a heroic attitude with drawn sword on stage. It could well have been a portrait of himself. I am sure he could not actually *see* it, but, by some curious provision of nature, he somehow seemed to be able to *know* it. He never whinged or felt sorry for himself.

His plum role that season was Leontes in *Winter's Tale*, an extremely difficult one, with which he would need a great deal of help from direction. I thought it a curious piece of casting as the brooding and bitter character was the complete antithesis of Teddy's own nature and I felt it was going to be a *tall order* for him, but hoped for the best.

As rehearsals got under way, I watched him, working with Quayle, who was directing the play, and encouraging him, for some reason best known to himself, to shout and bellow his lines. It was exhausting to listen to but Ted, being dear old lovable Ted, took it as gospel. I well remember one of Quayle's directions to him, as he was shouting his lines. "That's it, Teddy boy, that's it. Think Hitler! It's Hitler!"

Tony was obsessed with World War II, in which he had achieved the dizzy rank of major. To those of us who had been in the war, and I believe most of us had, he never failed to enquire what rank we had reached. He referred to himself as, "When I was a humble major..." in a speech he made to the company.

We had a quietly efficient and altogether delightful production manager called Paddy Donnell, who had been in the paratroops, but was most reticent about it. Tony, putting on his best bluff military manner, said to him one day, "Paddy, I hear you were in the paras," followed by the inevitable, "What rank were you?"

"Brigadier" was the laconic reply.

In fairness to Tony, he apparently did do something extremely dangerous, I believe, in Greece and to do with special services, which was never exactly a picnic. But we were all so fed up with his warrior preoccupations, that I forget just what it was. When he was directing Bill Squire, as Ulysses in *Troilus*, he said to him, by way of enlightenment, "This is the kind of chap, who could be military commander of the Allied Zone in Berlin, who could wake up in the morning and say to the Russians, 'No, I don't think so'." What that was supposed to mean, Heaven knows. Bill certainly did not and very sensibly ignored it as nonsense, eventually turning in a fine performance as the wily Ulysses.

Tony, for some reason, had decided that all the Greeks were to be dressed as quasi-American paratroops. At one point in the play, just after the death of Patroclus, the boyfriend of Achilles, the latter comes on stage, drawn sword in hand, in a murderous rage to avenge his death. Tony directed me to make this entry, springing on to the stage, like a panther, shouting the line, "Where is this Hector?"

I felt instinctively that this was a bad idea, but Tony insisted and that was how we rehearsed it over and over again. On the first night in performance, I sprang, as directed, to be greeted with an embarrassed laugh from the audience, who had been startled by the sudden appearance of a snarling GI, drawn sword in hand, leaping on to the stage. My instinct had been right and I felt discomfited by it. After the performance, I spoke to Tony about it and he said, "Well, you know why *that* was. It was because you leapt on to the stage like the *Demon King*."

Exactly! But I simply had not the heart to pursue it.

The season continued its course and, as time went by, none of us, eight weeks after receiving the letters of Tony's "definite intention", had heard another word about it. I decided to go and see him. His manner was evasive. He said it was gradually sorting itself out. It depended on this and that, but how would I feel about Don John in *Much Ado*. It was more than one up on most of this season's parts, but certainly not as good as Achilles, so I said it would do for a start, but I would wait to see what else he had up his sleeve.

"Don't worry," he said, with a reassuring wink. "It'll all sort itself out. You'll see."

Much Ado was to be directed by John Gielgud, who was coming down the following week, to give us all *the once-over*, and he would like me to meet him. And meet him I did. Sir John was very pleasant and talked vaguely about the play, without giving any indication of the direction he was proposing to take. He then asked my views on Don John. I had had a good look at the role, which had seemed pretty straight-forward. I outlined what I felt it was about. He seemed interested.

There was a longish pause, presumably for thought, and then he startled me with, "I think you should play him with a withered arm". I wondered if that was really necessary, and tentatively asked him why?

"Well," said Sir John, "he's got to have some *reason* for being so nasty." I modestly offered the view that perhaps it was the stigma of bastardy that appeared to be troubling him.

Sir John pondered on this for a moment and then smiling brightly, he said, "Yes. Yes. But I *still* think you should play him with a withered arm."

I have to confess to a slight feeling of disappointment, when I left and perhaps also of disillusion about one whose many great performances I had, for so long, admired. I continued to do so, of course, but it did rather confirm my view that to be a really great actor requires no very great intellect. Indeed it sometimes seems almost a hindrance.

But back to sunny Stratford. I had made another unsuccessful attempt to find out about next season. Apart from the everlasting Don John, he remained evasive, talking some nonsense about the glorious future awaiting us next season, adding cryptically, "once we've got rid of the queers". I remember wondering how he was going to square that with Sir John. By this time I was beginning to have serious doubts about Mr. Q.

On the very last night of the season, I happened to find him in the backstage gents, so I tackled him yet again. After a conspiratorial glance round the loo, he invited me to come into his office. There he said, "Well, it's Don John and probably Lysander in *The Dream*. The rest, as yet, undecided, but perhaps less important." Hmmm, most likely, I thought, remembering the dreaded Count Melun. He asked my reaction. I said that for Don John and Lysander I would probably come, making a private reservation, until the other parts were named.

"Splendid," he said. Then he added, after a moment's cogitation, "Supposing, just supposing Lysander didn't *quite* work out. How would you feel about that?"

Not for one moment was I going to consider a repeat of the present season, so I said that with a guarantee of Don John alone, he would have to count me out. Whereupon with eyes, blazing with sincerity, he hastened to reassure me. "I'm sure it *will* all work out. I'm absolutely determined to have you and darling Liz in the company next season. You know that."

He then told me that he was off to Paris in a couple of days, to confer with a designer there, and that he would be fixing up things after that. In the meantime, here was his address and phone number in Paris. He begged me not to accept any other offer of work without talking to him first, suggesting that I intimate as much to my agent. He then offered me his hand, with a manly grip. The next day, we left Stratford for London and home.

I never heard another word from him about it.

Many years later, after a successful first night in London, there was a knock on my dressing-room door and there he was, advancing on me with outstretched arms.

"Doug!" he said, emotionally gripping my arms, "Doug!"

Then, almost with tears in his eyes and as if I was some sort of racehorse he had trained, "You were *marvellous!*" he said. "*Bloody marvellous!*"

And that was the last time I ever saw him.

9

The Old Vic 1951/2

The year 1951 was that of the Festival of Britain and I was with the Old Vic which, in contrast to the season at Stratford, I greatly enjoyed.

I joined the company for George Devine's rumbustious production of *Bartholomew Fair* at the Edinburgh Festival, playing the smallish, but amusing part of *Captain Whit, a bawd*. Esmond Knight was also in the company, playing Tom Quarlous. When the company moved to London, he had to leave the production for some reason or other, probably a previous film commitment, and I was promoted to his role. This was a more important one and certainly of much more interest.

I was sorry that Ted Knight had to go as he was a great friend but, for me, it was not an entirely ill-wind. In fact, when we opened in London, it provided a decided boost to my personal progress. I also played the demented King of France in Glen Byam Shaw's production of *Henry V*, which earned me the praise of Ken Tynan in an article, headed *The Young Lions*.

I followed this with a personal success in *Captain Brassbound's Conversion*, an otherwise dismally slated production with Roger Livesey and Ursula Jeans, in which I played Redbrook. I had a very good season, in fact.

I was invited to stay on for the following season in 1952, to play Demetrius in the *The Midsummer Night's Dream* in which, for a change, the *lovers* got all the notices and in which I had the added bonus of working with the great Tyrone Guthrie.

This was followed by *Othello*, in which I played the comedy role of Roderigo. Added to this list was an uninspiring piece, called *The Other Heart*, a modern play about Francois Villon, which was played for more than it's worth by Alan Badel and in which I was cast as Renee de Montigny, a poor man's version of Shakespeare's Mercutio.

With these three plays, though with Badel unfortunately replaced as Villon, plus an indifferent production of *Macbeth*, we took off on a most enjoyable South African tour, marred only by the most noticeable and disturbing element of apartheid. We were allowed to play only to *Whites* and were told that *Blacks* were not allowed to enter the theatre; so we arranged to play on Sundays, taking the entire productions, minus scenery, to the township slums of Johannesburg, where we received a most enthusiastic reception. We played to full-houses everywhere but those township performances I recall with particular warmth. The *sell-out* success of the others, we all felt, was largely due to the fact that it had become very much the *thing to do*.

We were fêted everywhere we went, which eventually became really wearisome. One could certainly not fault the South Africans on the score of hospitality. The country had great natural beauty and a few of us were able, somehow, to visit the Kruger National Park, an experience I shall never forget; but we had spent almost six months there and I was quite glad to come home.

10

Sir Tyrone Guthrie 1952

It has been my fortunate lot, in a long and not uneventful life, to have met a number of interesting people. These encounters, as I have often been told, warrant some form of record. In my account of events and conversations, I have recounted what actually happened and what was said to me, face to face. Such recollections are entirely personal to me. I have tried to avoid the commonplace, which would be of no interest, either to me or to anyone else.

It sometimes occurs to me that these random memories have become something of a catalogue of incompetence and strife, while records of excellence seem, comparatively, all too few. It may well appear from this that my life has been far from charmed and that I must indeed have suffered a miserable existence in my chosen profession. I would like to say, therefore, that this is not the case.

I believe, in fact, that I have been very fortunate in my contacts in life which, even when less than agreeable, have been of some retrospective interest, even if only to me.

I would like to put on record that I have, for the most part, enjoyed a comfortable working rapport with most of my fellow actors, many of whom I am honoured to call my friends. I have enjoyed working also with many directors, of varying degrees of excellence, and have even, in many cases, received their written plaudits and thanks, letters which I have kept ever since. I have also worked less happily with others. A certain degree of professional competence should be taken as read, so I have not chosen to record the merely run-of-the-mill as to do so would be of no interest.

It is true that I have encountered a surprising lack of judgement and professional ability in directors of some renown. But then, to err is human and clearly no-one can be 100% all of the time. Occasionally one may be fortunate enough to meet with actual brilliance, such as in the case of Jonathan Miller or Tyrone Guthrie, under whose direction mere work becomes a real delight of creativity. Unfortunately such gifted souls are rare.

In some cases, I may be accused of detraction and even iconoclasm. So, in case these pages appear to be mainly a catalogue of professional gripes and groans, perhaps it is timely to introduce a personage for whom I had total admiration, verging on reverence.

My first encounter with Tyrone Guthrie occurred at The Old Vic theatre in 1952.

He was a remarkable man in many ways. In appearance, he was bony and of an extraordinary height, with a curious, ungainly flapping manner of movement. He had an eccentric mode of speech, with a most colourful turn of phrase. He was original and amusing, and his rehearsals were never dull or merely repetitive, as he brought something fresh each time to the actor's performance, keeping it alive and receptive. There was never any hurry about anything to develop. Possessing natural authority, he was never authoritarian and always open to someone else's point of view. His wit, which was considerable, was never deliberately hurtful, demeaning or unkind. He had the gift of keeping his actors happy and treated the least among us with the same consideration as he did the leading players. We were at ease with him and we loved him for it.

He had an uncanny genius for detecting an actor's potential, however miniscule, and somehow developing it to a level of performance, without appearing to have imposed his own will in any way. It used to be said that Tony Guthrie could find a way to capitalise, even on a really bad performance.

I went to see him when he was casting *Midsummer Night's Dream*, for the next season at The Vic, when he told me that he had no idea what I should do.

"What about Flute?" he suggested.

I rejected that idea and said I would like to play Demetrius.

"Demetrius!" He looked astonished. "Why *on earth* would you want to do that?"

I outlined my ideas on the character and how it could be played to become substantially more interesting than was usual and have a comic life of its own. He listened to what I had to say, without a word, never taking his eyes off my face. When I had finished, he smiled and pointed a long bony finger at me.

"Demetrius," was all he said.

This of course was at a very early stage, when he had not made up his mind how to tackle the various other aspects of the play.

"What *does* one do about the fairies?" he thought aloud. "We really *can't* have all those dreadful little Conti's, simply *bursting* out of their jock-straps." He was referring to the almost traditional use of little boys, generally cockneys, from The Italia Conti School of acting, a juvenile academy, providing children, often unusually precocious, in more ways than one.

In the event he decided on girls, one of whom was Joan Plowright, who sang the fairy song with a very sweet voice. I think she was Mustard Seed.

I remember Tony (he was never called Tyrone) regaling us with anecdotes, one of which referred to his recent production of *Salome* at the Metropolitan Opera House in New York. The part of Salome was to be sung by Lubja Welitsch, a wonderful singer, but a lady of considerable bulk. He had wondered quite how she was going to manage the Dance of the Seven Veils. She, however, had no such qualms, apparently, launching into it with complete *elan* and producing, at the dress rehearsal, what Tony described as "dreadful little ten-cent scarves", while she capered about, shedding small beads, which rolled all over the stage. He had been puzzled by a curious noise, which he described as "plip-plap, plip-plap", which he was later to discover was the sound of "*madam's buttocks*".

At the Vic we had a young actor in the company, blessed with extraordinary good looks, called Edmund Purdom. He was a nice enough young man, but almost unbelievably lacking in discipline, turning up sometimes at least an hour or so late for rehearsals and sometimes, even, not at all. He had received several tickings-off and warnings from the stage manager. One day, he strolled in to rehearsal very late as usual and Tony, who was sitting at the side of the stage, stopped the rehearsal for a moment. "Purdom," he said and beckoned him over. Purdom strolled nonchalantly over to him and Tony smiled kindly at him.

"Purdom, I'm going to sack you. *Hope* you don't mind."

And fired he was, only to be summoned to Hollywood, where he enjoyed a brief, but meteoric career as a film-star, thus fulfilling Robert Helpman's prediction of him at Stratford. "That boy will either do nothing at all, or he will end up as a film-star." I suppose, in a way, Purdom did both.

With Tony, as may be gathered, rehearsals were really a joy to which one could look forward with pleasurable anticipation. He was always relaxed and open to suggestion and, as I have said, he treated everyone alike, almost as a benevolent father-figure but whose ultimate decision was law.

Donald Wolfit was being directed by him in Marlowe's *Tamburlaine*. This was also at The Vic and Wolfit, if he felt he was not being given due deference, was apt to come the "I'm the King of the Castle" stuff, from time to time. At one such point, he interrupted a rehearsal to make a fuss about something or other and Guthrie's voice came from the back of the stalls. "Now come along, Donald," he said, clapping his hands in admonition. "Let's just get on with it, shall we!"

As he had been his own boss, as actor-manager, for so many years, Wolfit was so taken aback, to be treated like anyone else, that he *did* just get on with it, eventually giving a splendid performance in a fiendishly difficult play.

Guthrie's unforgettably sumptuous production was breath-taking, in excitement and spectacle. So much so, that I felt fired to direct and at the end of the season I wrote to Tony, to ask him if I could work with him, as an unpaid assistant, presumably in the hope that some of the *genius* might *rub off* on me.

I have before me his long-hand letter in reply, in which he said after a preamble:

"I would love to work with you again as an actor and hope we shall do so. But I don't think it's at all a good idea to skivvy for someone else. If you want to tie knots in string, it's absolutely hopeless (at least so I find) to watch someone else tying knots. The only way is to get a bit of string and work away. Ditto with production. The only way is to get a group of actors and *produce* them. You *do* appreciate, don't you, that this isn't to imply that I wouldn't like to work with *you* - certainly I would. But if you were my assistant (virtually unpaid) I would feel continually fussed that you were wasting your time. It always seems to me that, if the stage manager knows his job, there's very little for an asst. producer to do. And I can't cope with minions who take notes and fetch dainty cups of tea and anyway, you're much too *advanced* for that. I'd like to think there was a likelihood of our working together soon. I enjoyed our association at The Vic very much and wish we'd had more continuous work together. But

my plans are all in foreign parts next year, with the exception of
Henry VIII at The Vic," and so on and so forth.

Tony ends his letter typically, on a frivolous note. "I do hope you can read
this. I'm writing with one of those simple items *[sic, presumably a ball-point
pen]* and for some reason it makes my round girlish hand - usually so clear -
into something I can hardly read myself. I've tried writing bigger - smaller,
faster, slower - but it's all equally illegible. Ah, science!"

What he meant by "Ah, science!" I can only surmise is a reference to the
wonders of science, as exemplified by the ball-point pen.

As it turned out, I took over the part of Cranmer in *Henry VIII*, much later
on.

He could be very direct, which sometimes took people aback. When he was
setting up Stratford, Ontario, he was on a pre-season lecture visit, giving talks
on the treats in store and in the question-time, at the end, one woman asked
what they should do about accommodation, as she pointed out that was a
shortage of suitable hotels in the town. With a touch of, perhaps, unreasonable
asperity, Guthrie replied, "Madam, for the privilege of seeing the plays of
William Shakespeare, we should be prepared to sleep in a ditch".

He could also be a touch off-hand and perfunctory, especially in his dealings
with officialdom. After the 1952 season at The Vic, we did a tour of the plays
in repertory in South Africa, as mentioned. This was to be preceded by another
such tour of lectures by Guthrie. All the arrangements were in place for this
and Tony was eagerly awaited, much like the Second Coming. At the last
minute, he sent the South African powers-that-be a cable which simply read,
"Sorry, can't come. Guthrie".

As elaborate preparations had been made, I believe they were not over-
pleased. Eccentricity can sometimes have its less attractive moments.

Tony lived with his equally-imposing wife, Judy, in a flat in one of the Inns
of Court and there is a possibly apocryphal story of an actor going there for
an appointment and Judy leaving him alone as Tony was late. Apparently he
picked up a magazine while he waited and when he opened it, he swore he
found a *fried egg* inside it!

The notices for *The Dream*, apart from the lovers (Irene Worth, Jane
Wenham, Robert Shaw and myself, who had occupied Tony's main interest)
were unfortunately not good. Tony, who never kicked against a bad press,

called us all together and cheerfully apologised to us. "Sorry to have made such a nonsense of it," he said.

I suppose even a near-genius can have his *off* moments. But he more than made up for it with *Tamburlaine* and simply by being himself.

11

Sir Donald Wolfit

I have been asked if I knew Donald Wolfit.

I had a slight acquaintanceship with him, having acted with him in a TV play when we played opposing barristers in a courtroom drama. This was rehearsed in Twickenham and, for some reason or other, he rather cottoned on to me, inviting me to accompany him to the pub for a drink and lunch. Quite why this was I cannot imagine as I found him in no way an engaging personality. However, one cannot be rude, or perhaps one should be.

At all events, I always went with him, during the couple of weeks of rehearsal. At the bar, there was always the same procedure. He would order a large gin and tonic for himself without ever once asking me what I would have. There is no reason why he should have bought me a drink, I suppose, but I have to confess that, contrasted with his otherwise over-friendly demeanour, I found it rather chilling that he never so much as offered.

Some time later on, when Laurence Naismith proposed me for the Garrick Club, I was dismayed to learn that Wolfit had come forward to second me.

I then received a letter from him, asking where I had been to school, what my father did for his bread and cheese and a few more details, which I felt were pretty irrelevant to joining a club originally formed as a milieu "to enable actors to meet gentlemen". He then went on to say that it would increase my chances of successful election, if I were to "meet a few men in the club" and suggested that we should meet at the Garrick, to be introduced to them. I knew quite a few of them anyway and the idea of being touted round the Club by Wolfit frankly appalled me, so I at once rang Larry Naismith and told him of this letter I had had. I added that if it was necessary to comply with these conditions, then I would prefer to withdraw my name.

Larry made a few uncomplimentary remarks about Wolfit's pomp and self-importance. "The old bugger's only seconding you, for heaven's sake." He told me to take no notice. So I wrote him a short note, ignoring the request for details of my background, thanking him for his kind offer, but declining on the grounds that I would be out of the country until after the ballot.

A whopping lie, but I could hardly tell him the truth. I got in anyway.

Regrettably, perhaps, whenever I used the Club later on, I did my best to avoid him. Fortunately the wine waiter, an extraordinary character in his own right, called Barker, who was heavily stage-struck, nearly always let me know that, "Sir Donald is in the bar, sir. Shall I tell him you are here?" I would always hastily assure him that I was in need of a bit of a rest and that I would be going up to the library for a few moments' quiet and would he be so good as to bring me up a pint of the Club's excellent Flower's bitter? I would come down to the bar quite soon."

This formula was always the same. Innocent that he was, Barker never seemed to twig that I could possibly be avoiding Sir Donald at almost any price. But he never did let on that I was there. The discretion of club servants is of course legendary.

On the rare occasions when I did bump into Sir Donald, he treated me as if I was his personal property. He clearly thought this was only right and proper. After all, had he not bestowed upon me the honour of seconding my election?

There are many stories told of his antics, both on and off-stage, not all of them particularly complimentary.

During rehearsals for Ibsen's *Ghosts*, the director John Fernald placed him and Flora Robson in what Wolfit considered an unfavourable position on stage, favouring the maid, Regina, who had to deliver a long speech, which was actually one of the expository key-stones of the plot and therefore of considerable importance. Wolfit interrupted the rehearsal, objecting to this, saying, if it can be believed, "Perhaps you have forgotten, John, that Dame Flora and I are two titled people of the theatre".

He was only really happy when in absolute command himself with no-one to tell him what to do. This was an unfortunate circumstance for him as he was by no means a supreme arbiter of taste. He also tended, in his own touring companies, to surround himself with inferior talents, not only in his actors, but also in tatty costuming and décor, all of which greatly lowered the standard of his productions. Perhaps he thought it made him appear as a whale among minnows.

No memory of Wolfit would be complete without reference to his curtain calls. These performances alone were well worth the price of admission to the theatre. He would appear alone from between the drapes, clutching them with one hand, as if for support, with every appearance of utter exhaustion, as if to say: "I have given my all to my adoring public. As you see, I can do no more." This masquerade was apparently carried out as a ritual, regardless of whether the performance was in fact a taxing one or not.

He certainly felt out of his element with us at The Old Vic, surrounded as he was by first-rate performances. After falling out with Guthrie and also his fellow actors, who strenuously objected to his attention-drawing tricks, he left the company as soon as he could find a convenient loophole in his contract. Before he left, he gave a fine performance of Lord Ogleby in *The Clandestine Marriage*. His early departure was an event, largely unmourned by one and all.

At that time, Guthrie was running a policy of having two separate companies at The Vic. These would perform alternate seasons in London, either with tours of the provinces, South Africa or the principal European cities, or even a two or three week break from performing at all. I was fortunate enough to be in the other company, so never had to bear the brunt of Wolfit's poor behaviour myself. It was sad that a man, capable of such truly great performances, could be so self-destructive.

He went back into the only way of theatre life he felt at home in, the old-fashioned role of actor-manager, where he could, no matter how limited his horizons, at least be monarch of all he surveyed.

12

Bunny And J. Paul Getty

I referred very briefly in the account of our nuptials to a very close friend of Liz's, called Bunny, who was to figure much in our lives. Her proper name was Penelope but to all her close friends, she was Bunny. She and Liz had been children together at a school in South Kensington, called for some reason Glendower, and remained firm friends ever since, a state of affairs that remained up to the time of Liz's demise.

They were, in some ways, almost like two halves of the same person, giving each other identical nicknames. Their voices and manner were also almost identical. On the telephone I could not tell them apart. They both went on to RADA, which was where I first came across them.

There was otherwise a great deal of difference between them.

Liz was of a spiritual turn of mind, passionately into literature and poetry, and, without being in any way shy, of a naturally quiet and reticent disposition. She had also surprisingly deep religious feelings, of which she seldom spoke, and which I, at the time, did not share. She was unusually perceptive and sensitive towards others and frequently warned me against those who, because of my outspoken nature, secretly bore me ill will. She was also possessed of an indefinable charm: a good listener, a faithful friend and everyone found her adorable.

It all sounds too good to be true, but that is what she was like.

As her closest friend, Bunny was often in evidence, as they had many chums in common, and we saw a lot of her. During the war, and against her parents' wishes, she had married a naval officer, whom she had met whilst doing her war-work at the Admiralty. He had been appointed as naval attaché in Washington so Bunny was living with her parents in Prince's Gate, Knightsbridge. He soon wrote to her, saying he had met someone else in Washington and wanted a divorce.

Poor Bun was devastated, but postponed telling her parents, and went off for the week-end to some friends in the country. When she returned to London, she went straight to the office in the Admiralty where she tried to telephone her home. As she could not get through, she concluded that the telephone lines were down as the Blitz was still at its height. At the end of her working day, she went home and found it a smoking pile of rubble. The house had received a direct hit and her mother, father and grandmother were all dead.

Almost in the space of a day Bunny, still in her early 20s, had lost her husband, her mother and father, her Granny, her home and all her possessions. The resulting trauma hardly bears thinking about.

She came to Liz at once, of course, who must have provided her with some comfort, and the two of them later went back to the ruins in an effort to salvage whatever remained.

All this happened while I was in Africa, well before I was to meet either of them again. Liz related the terrible story to me much later. I never heard Bunny refer to it. By the time I arrived on the scene, Bun had thrown herself, hardly surprisingly, into the mad social world of war-time London. It was a "hail and farewell for tomorrow we die" atmosphere, with all-night dancing in exclusive clubs, like the 400, with glamorous young officers on leave. And all that went with it.

Her whole world had gone up in smoke and the poor girl must have badly needed some sort of distraction, not to say anaesthesia from a terrible sense of insecurity. But Bun, being Bun, managed to survive more-or-less intact.

One day she told us she had made a conquest of a young major in the Grenadiers who was "wildly attractive" and also otherwise highly eligible. He had extensive estates in Cornwall, with a fine Elizabethan manor house, a deer shoot in the Highlands, somewhere near Glencoe, and more than ample means for their upkeep. In short, he was very well-heeled, was crazy about her and wanted to marry her as soon as may be. His name was Robert Kitson.

We met him. He was very tall, slimly elegant, but facially gaunt, with a curiously haunted expression. He would not have been everyone's idea of an Adonis, but he seemed diffidently willing to be friendly, without going overboard to appear so. He had an unusual charm about him and one could see that, in an off-beat way, he could be considered attractive. We both liked him.

They were married very soon after and Bunny was whisked off to Cornwall. I think that the war was virtually over and Robert had left the Guards. Bunny was at last in her element and had clearly recovered her equilibrium, and lost no time in firmly establishing herself, as châtelaine of Morval, which was the name of the house. Liz and I went down for Christmas and on several later occasions. The house was certainly a very fine example of a stone Elizabethan manor, which would have done very well as *Manderlay* in a film of Daphne du Maurier's *Rebecca*, and Bunny was putting her stamp on it and making all sorts of improvements, not all of them to Robert's liking, as was becoming very apparent.

Socially, also, she began to exercise her sway, making great strides in the County and joining all manner of committees. I believe Robert was beginning to feel like *Mrs. Robert Kitson's husband*. He had begun to disassociate himself more and more from her, making sardonic remarks and gloomily drinking too much. He had already told me that she saw herself as "the Queen of the bloody County" and himself as "the kitchen maid". She had, however, on the credit side, managed to produce three children, one of them a boy and much-needed heir. Liz was godmother to one of the girls.

Robert had always hoped to be chosen as a JP when the next vacancy occurred. However, it was Bun who was approached for this distinction. Knowing his modest ambitions in that direction, it would have been tactful, perhaps, to decline and suggest approaching her husband. But this she neglected to do. She accepted and that was the final crunch.

Robert exploded and said he wanted a divorce. He got his way at last and they were indeed divorced. As part of the marriage settlement, he bought her a splendid house on Campden Hill, just round the corner from us. Her solicitor, however, omitted to notice in the document that the gift of the house was subject to the phrase *dum casta*, meaning *while chaste*, an extremely dangerous oversight, as it later transpired.

So Bunny was free of her marital entanglements and free to do pretty well as she liked. Or was she?

She threw herself back into the social whirl of London and, after a very short time, came to see us and announced that an American multi-millionaire had fallen for her and that, furthermore, he was reputed to be "the richest man in the world". He was also "terribly sweet".

His name was J. Paul Getty. No-one had ever heard of him.

In what seemed a very short space of time, Bunny became what the media would describe as his "close friend" and artistic adviser, redesigning, of all things, the captains' living quarters on his oil-tankers. She also began the habit of launching new ones for him. When he later began buying palaces and castles in England and in Italy, she was commissioned to redesign those as well. In the meantime, he appeared to have no permanent place of residence, living in a room at the London Ritz or the Georges V in Paris, wherever he happened to be.

We met him long before he settled in England. He was a strange-looking man. He appeared to have undergone more than one face-lift, which had done very little to improve his features, which were decidedly and unevenly *saggy*, giving him a more-than-ordinarily depressed expression. Beside Bunny, at least, he seemed short and insignificant, with *gingerish* improbable hair. His manner, for a *captain of industry*, was remarkably diffident and uneasy. His voice, when he could be induced to say anything at all, was monotonous and mournful.

All in all, he was not a man who suggested either fabulous wealth or everyone's idea of a powerful oil mogul. That he was "terribly sweet", we had to take on trust, as there was very little to suggest such a quality. He did, however, seem totally besotted with Bunny, following with hang-dog looks her every move and gesture.

He had asked her to marry him on many occasions but, very wisely, Bunny held off. She would have been his sixth wife. The others had all been impossibly young as well so perhaps she guessed that he was not good matrimonial timber. As I heard the parish priest say to him at dinner in Sutton Place many years later, "Well Paul, you only need one more wife to equal the record of Henry VIII". An observation that produced not so much as a twitch of a smile from his host.

Sutton Place was the Jacobean house and estate that he bought from the Duke of Sutherland when, doubtless influenced by his infatuation with Bunny, Paul finally decided to settle in England. Prior to this, he had led an almost nomadic existence, occupying one room in the grandest hotels wherever he happened to be.

The house was very large and oppressive, with seemingly endless galleries and huge grand rooms. I found it had no atmosphere whatsoever and, like its new owner, was rather depressing. It was more of a museum than a home. Bunny had, of course, given it the *works* to all the rooms and Paul had filled it with medieval tapestries, Aubussons and other rare carpets, and the walls were hung with some of the greatest paintings in the world. But I can recall nothing painted much after the end of the 17th century. I did once see a large and very fine Bonnard, from the series of *Woman standing in a bath*, but it was hanging in a spare bathroom in an obscure part of the house. I asked him once why he never bought anything modern and received some sort of non-committal reply.

There was, about 10 minutes walk from the main house, a large, disused cricket pavilion, which Getty had made over to Bunny for life. Refurbished, with no expense spared, she converted it into a comfortable and charming second home, where Liz and I stayed very often. From here she was able to run most things up at the house and once again she was very much *riding high*.

Then she became, in some ways, a bit careless. She decided to take Paul up to Scotland to show him her erstwhile estates. Here they booked into a hotel. Early next morning Robert Kitson's brother, who was living on the estate, finding himself short of cigarettes, went to the hotel to buy some. He was just in time to see his former sister-in-law coming down the stairs with Paul Getty. After a quick look at the register, he made a call to his brother and *wham!*, the all-but-forgotten *dum casta* was invoked.

Poor Bun came round to us in a state and told us what had happened. In law, her house was no longer hers. The only hope was Paul. But would he cough up? He was notoriously stingy, even over the smallest details and she now had to pin her hopes on persuading him to buy the house from Robert and re-instate her in her ownership. She seemed to be able to do anything she liked with the man, but this was a pretty hefty item and she did not seem too happy about it. However, cough up indeed he did. So with a huge sigh of relief, Bunny quickly recovered her customary *sang-froid* and continued to walk the tight-rope between staving him off as a suitor and still keeping him, if not on the boil, at least on a manageable simmer.

One Saturday in Christmas week, she rang to say she was bringing Paul that evening to a play at the Savoy Theatre, in which I was playing the lead and could Liz bear to see it again? It would help to "leaven the lump" of an evening alone with him, and Paul would take us all out to dinner afterwards.

I asked if we could not have dinner at the Savoy Grill just upstairs as, after two performances, I would be pretty weary. She said she would do what she could.

I told my dresser to expect them after the evening show and, while I was changing, to open a bottle of wine. We then went to Paul's car and he told the chauffeur to drive, first of all, on a grand tour of the West End Christmas lights, then on to Annabel's, a noisy and fashionable night club. I groaned inwardly, but Liz said I had to put up with it. As we cruised endlessly round the *lights of London*, Paul, round-eyed as a child, would draw Bun's attention to the most particularly garish examples.

"Look, dear. There's Santa Claus and look at the reindeer's eyes! Look, they go round and round!"

At last we arrived at Annabel's, where, as he never drank anything but rum and coke or water, he told me to choose the wine. I was tired and irritated, and the band was loud so that conversation was almost impossible. Perhaps reprehensibly, I chose one of the most expensive wines on the list, which was so splendid that it almost made up for the rest.

And that was just for starters.

Paul sat gloomily, taking no part in any possible conversation, munching something frugal and health-giving, no doubt, and sipping his dreadful drink. I said, "Paul, you really must try this wine. It's magnificent." Rather unwillingly, he took one cautious sip, and, after a moment's consideration he admitted, "Yes, that's smooth. Yes, that's real smooth," adding, after another moment for thought, "If I may say so, Douglas, that wine is smoother than the wine you gave me in your dressing-room."

I told him that the wine in my dressing room had cost me all of six shillings and sixpence in a Soho deli, whereas he might be surprised at the price of the wine on his bill for the dinner.

One day when we were at Sutton, Bunny, wanting to have half an hour or so alone with Liz, suggested that Paul might like to take me round the galleries in the house and show me some of the paintings and other *objets d'art*. I had, of course, seen many of them before, but thought it might be interesting to prowl round them again, on a conducted tour, alone with the man himself. Off we went, Paul pausing before each painting and telling me how much he had paid for it and the present insurance value. As to any aesthetic considerations, they never seemed to enter his head. But, who knows, perhaps he thought they spoke for themselves and, apart from the price, needed no comment from him.

He did exactly the same, as we crossed over seemingly endless Aubusson carpets and past priceless pieces of furniture; but nothing, of course, was without its actual price in the Getty scheme of things.

I remember how we stood before a wonderful *Madonna and Child*, by Raphael, and him telling me that there were several versions of it, in various parts of the world, but that Agnews had assessed his as quite definitely "the only authentic one". I wondered how it would have fared, had its owner not been Paul Getty!

As Bunny by this time was virtually his *lady of the house*, Bullimore, the butler, begged her to get Paul to *up* the allowance he had set per head for each guest, some of whom were royalty, many of them dukes, duchesses and other nabobs. He said he was not accustomed to such parsimony and felt it was *infra dig* and hurtful to his pride to serve up such meagre fare. So up the allowance went, to Bullimore's mollification. Paul, nevertheless, at a later date, asked an astonished Duke of Bedford how much per capita he allowed for his guests at Woburn. The Duke said he had not the faintest idea.

His own habits, however, remained determinedly frugal. He would sit, hunched up, at the head of his mile-long table, eyes down, munching like a slow-motion squirrel while his guests, on social occasions, at least, dined and wined like kings and queens.

On one such occasion, I was on his left while one of his quondam ladies, Marie Tessier, sat on his right. She still occupied a distant part of the house, from which he had, for some reason unknown, been unable to dislodge her, when she ceased to be *maîtresse en titre*. Her mood from the start was decidedly grumpy and did not improve as the meal went on. As the excellent claret went down, so the level of Marie's resentment rose. Addressing anyone who cared to listen, and me in particular, her grumbles directed at Paul grew more and more strident. He totally ignored her and barely glanced in her direction. I do not think he addressed a single remark to me either. But I was used to his silence.

At one point, before the dinner came to a merciful end, she turned in her chair and, flinging an outstretched arm, pointed to a painting behind her of a beauteous young woman by Annigoni. "*That* is what I was like when I met Paul and *see* what he has made of me!"

It was indeed just recognisable as a portrait of Marie Tessier, but clearly painted long, long ago. It bore not too much resemblance to the plump and, by this time, tousled and tearful lady before me. Paul did not twitch a muscle or say one word in his own defence. He could as well have been carved in stone.

Somewhat later, I had an assignment, involving two or three months on film location in Spain. At the time we owned a very long and rather spectacular car, a 1952 Mulliner Park Ward Bentley Continental, which was too long for our garage, so it had to be kept in the street outside the house. It was an eye-catcher, in two-tone black and white. Liz never drove it, so it would be left unmoved for the whole time I was away and likely to attract the wrong sort of attention. The cult of vandalism was not yet in full swing, but by no means was it unknown. I asked Bunny if I could leave it at Sutton Place, in one of the many empty mews garages there. She said she was sure that there would be no difficulty, but she would mention it to Paul, as a matter of form. My relief was short-lived as I had an anxious message from Paul, who wanted to see me.

So over to Sutton I went to be confronted by a seemingly most agitated Getty. "You understand, I take no responsibility for your car, if I let you leave it here?" he said.

I replied that I was sure it would be perfectly safe, locked up in a garage, adjacent to the house in the middle of an estate secured by electric gates and with guard dogs roaming at night. He then embarked on a rambling saga about his son.

"My son had a big house in Florence and a man asked him if he could store some valuable furniture in it for a few months, while my son was away. Waall, my son agreed to store it, but as you may know, they had some bad floods in Florence, which affected this furniture. Why, that man sued my son. After all, my son is not a pantechnicon. So I want it understood, that I accept no responsibility for your car or for whatever might happen to it, while it's here." I did my best to reassure him and duly stored the car in perfect safety at Sutton, as planned. I suppose he was right, in a way, but his agitation, I felt, was a little unnecessary.

At about that time, Harold Wilson came out with his notorious disclaimer of "The pound in your pocket..." which I thought Paul could perhaps elucidate. Feeling somewhat anxious about this, I asked him what it really meant for the economy and, after a long silence for consideration, all he said was, "Waal, it certainly won't affect Getty Oil".

On one occasion Bun drove Paul and me over to the Royal Horticultural Gardens at Wisley. Liz had dipped out, pleading a headache. As we were wandering round, some people recognised us, and we heard one woman say, "Oh, look, there's Paul Getty with Sherlock Holmes!" which seemed to please him in some way. He managed, at least, to twitch some sort of a smile. By this time his face was quite well-known. And once seen, not easily forgotten.

On the way back to the car, I quietly suggested to Bun, that, instead of dropping him off at the house, she might ask him to stay for a drink at the Pavilion, which she rather reluctantly did. He immediately looked very nervous and asked if we would stop at the house first to pick up Shaun, his own personal guard-dog. This was an enormous, very shaggy old Alsatian, of uncertain temper which he always took with him for protection, when walking alone on the estate. This Bunny flatly refused to do, saying she would not have that smelly brute in her brand new car, which was, incidentally, a recent present from Paul. By this time he was really agitated, torn between wanting to be with Bunny and his fear of being set upon on his way home.

When she refused again, I said to him, "I'll walk back with you, Paul," adding half-jokingly, "You'll be perfectly all right with me. After all, people know that you've got Sherlock Holmes staying with you."

He looked back at me, over his shoulder and then after a moment, he muttered, "Yes, yes, that's right" and he seemed totally reassured.

I could hardly believe that a world-sized financier, controlling billions, could in some ways seem to have the mental age of a child of four. But then he was a most peculiar man and fearful of his own shadow. He had once had a slightly unpleasant experience, flying. Who has not? But he flatly refused to fly ever again. I wonder how he got to the middle-east, or to the magnificent castle that he bought in Italy, overlooking the sea.

Apropos these guard dogs, he had some half-dozen of these savage beasts, which were kept in a cage by day and, soon after dark, let loose to roam the estate at will. Their cage bore a threatening warning, "Danger! These dogs are trained to regard all strangers as Enemies."

One day, when we were staying at the Pavilion for the weekend, one of Bun's Norwich terriers was on heat, a matter, which had not gone unnoticed among the guard-dogs, which were snuffling and whining in force, outside and surrounding the house. This was awkward as Liz and I had, as usual, deposited our things for the night in the little annexe-out-house, where we always slept, which lay a few yards away. After dinner that evening, when the time for us to retire for the night arrived, we were unable to do so. Bun telephoned Mr. Pete, the dog handler, telling him of the problem and asking him to come and collect the dogs. This he refused to do, saying that the last time he had been called out at night, one of the brutes had attacked him and he had nearly lost an ear. So Bunny, as ever resourceful, took the bitch to just inside the front door, thus concentrating the attentions of her would-be suitors, as we hoped and prayed, to one spot at the front of the house, while Liz and I made a quick dive out of the back door, to our nearby haven of rest.

The afore-mentioned Shaun, Paul's personal guard dog, eventually became very ill with a noticeable cancer of the rectum. The animal was obviously suffering, as well as looking very unattractive, and Bun told Paul that he should really have him put down. This, he resolutely refused to do, saying, in his flat, doleful voice, "That dawg really loves me and I'm not going to have him killed". I felt it was rather pathetic. I think he probably suspected that he was *loved* for reasons mainly material and the dog, at least, could hardly be aware of those. But it was rather hard on the dog.

Getty never seemed to enjoy his wealth. He was so mean over such trifles. There was, for the use of his guests, the notorious pay-phone booth, which he had had installed at the foot of the main staircase of the house, bearing the legend, writ large, "YOU MAY PHONE FROM HERE". If I had not seen it with my own eyes, I would hardly have believed it.

Before he bought Sutton when he and Bun, in their earlier days, were living at the Georges V Hotel, in Paris, he apparently never took her out anywhere, having meals sent up to their suite, until she, in a fit of claustrophobic desperation, insisted they go for a weekend to Nice; whereupon he asked her to pack everything up, as he had no intention of paying for their suite, while they were away.

After years of living with these eccentricities, Bunny, of course, inevitably met someone else. He was a man called Patrick de Laszlo, and Bunny and he decided to marry. Bun had to bite the bullet and tell Paul. So, out of his will, she popped. That marriage did not last too long and they parted. The problem now was how to pop back into the will.

Bunny came to see us and told us she was going to Sutton to the Pavilion and she was going to see Paul and do what she could to effect this process. I thought she would have her work cut out and said so. She also wanted us there "for moral support". For the life of me now, I cannot think why or how. But I remember that is what she said. She asked us to be there in time for lunch, which would give her the morning free, to *work the oracle* with Paul. So, just before lunch-time we arrived at the Pavilion to find Bunny looking intensely relieved and Paul Getty in a state of emotional disarray.

I believe she told him that her marriage to de Laszlo had all been a great mistake, which may, of course, have been perfectly true, and that she had found she could not live without Paul, and had, more-or-less, given the man his marching orders. Whereupon Paul, overcome with emotion, announced his intention of making love to her on the spot. Our arrival, it seems, was just in time. She was *saved by the bell*, as it were. But it had been, in more ways than one, a pretty *near-run thing*.

In the fullness of time, Paul Getty died in his favourite chair. Fearful of his impending death, like Queen Elizabeth I, he had refused to take to his bed.

His fortune was variously distributed. Large amounts went to his various progeny by four of his five different wives. One son was disinherited because of a grudge against his mother. Large sums went to various ladies who had pleased him. Even Marie Tessier, despite her noisy upbraiding, came in for a tidy amount.

For Bunny, the long vigil was over. She had the largest dollop of all the ladies-in-waiting and eventually married a lord, who died fairly soon after. She was known by the press as Penelope Kitson. To me, of course, she was always Bunny, a truly amazing woman.

Indigestion? Not quite. The onset of Svengali's terminal heart attack in *Trilby*, by George Du Maurier, in the second week of my professional career, in Rugby weekly repertory in 1945, after being invalided out of the army. We were putting on a fresh production each week, dress-rehearsing on Sundays for the next week's offering, having just had rehearsals every morning and, as I recall, in the afternoons as well. I was playing Robert Browning in the evenings, while I rehearsed and learned the part of Svengali during the day. That was my baptism of fire and introduction to the acting profession. I must have loved it

Eyeing up Trilby, charmingly played by Elizabeth Melville, who later became my wife. She was a great favourite with the faithful regular audiences, having performed leading roles the previous season. It was she who introduced me to the management because I had never acted before, except as a RADA student. I was pushed in at the deep end but was lucky enough to get away with only a year in repertory, before working in London. at the King's Theatre, Hammersmith

Above: As the young hero in Alexandre Dumas' *Black Tulip*, BBC TV, circa 1950. It was an adventure serial, made for Children's TV at a time when programmes made for the young were compared very favourably by many of the critics with the adult drama productions. For some reason many of the best directors, such as Sean Sutton, seemed to be clustered in that department

Above left: As the King of France in *Henry V* at the Old Vic Theatre in London with Alec Clunes as Henry and Dorothy Tutin as the Princess of France, in 1951, as part of the Festival of Britain. Ken Tynan liked my performance enough to single it out in his notice

Left: In my dashing vein, as Tom Quarlous in Ben Jonson's *Bartholomew Fair*, with Alec Clunes and Dorothy Tutin at the Old Vic in the same season of 1951. The play had to be performed with much energy on everyone's part. It was first tried out at the Edinburgh Festival with an excellent production by George Devine, I being promoted from a smaller part to Quarlous, a much more showy one, when it came to London

Right: As Robert Beauchamp, Earl of Warwick in Shaw's *St Joan*, with Siobhan McKenna and Kenneth Williams. An original drawing done for *Punch* by Emwood in 1954, which is still in my possession. Siobhan was a definitive St Joan and Kenneth was an hilarious Dauphin. I greatly enjoyed playing such a tremendously rewarding role as Warwick

Left: The Oliviers in 1954. Sir Laurence is cracking a joke with my wife, Liz, on the Mayor of Garda's private launch on our jaunt on the Lake. This was on the very first day we met and the start of a long association. On the boat he told me a lot about his next project: the film *Richard III*

Right: Vivien Leigh, not in the best of spirits, is seen in the background, with Olivier and Liz. I later heard that Vivien had just come out of a nursing home where she had undergone shock therapy. I felt very sorry for her

Below: Liz, back to camera, with Sir Laurence on our protracted conducted tour of Gabriele D'Annuncio's enormous villa on the shores of Lake Garda. I am lurking in the background, talking to the wife of a French playwright, a friend of the Oliviers. On the left is Ginette Spanier, the Paris Directrice of Balmain, who was also of their party

Viewed in context, old man, and properly captioned, I really feel this is a still you should have.

Left: Exhausted after a hard day in the saddle on the battlefield in *El Cid*, waiting for Charlton Heston's car to take us out to dinner. Chuck had a lively sense of humour! He needed it. He and I had to be up at 5am every morning, ready for a 50-mile drive to Peniscola where the battles were all filmed

"BUT THIS IS REALLY A FINE PART FOR YOU, MR. WILMER! THERE'S ONE TERRIBLY FUNNY SCENE WHERE YOU LOSE YOUR TROUSERS, AND..."

Below: As Moutamin, Emir of Saragossa, conferring the honorific title of El Cid on Heston, as Rodrigo de Bivar, after he had spared Moutamin's life. Henceforth, he was always known as El Cid. The Moorish prince was an actual historical character and occurs in the anonymous Spanish epic poem El Cid, later dramatised by Corneille

As Sherlock Holmes in the mid-sixties BBC
television series that brought me a measure
of fame for a while. Holmes, typically, is
showing scant interest in an article in *The
Times*, pointed out by Nigel Stock, who
played the doughty Dr. Watson. The making
of the series was not without certain trials and
tribulations, as described in the text

"Hmm. Interesting, Watson." If I remember
rightly, I am seen here, examining the sole of
a foot for traces of something or other, but
for the life me I cannot be certain which of
the stories it came from or why I found the
foot so absorbing!

A self-portrait painted in water-colour. It was used as the jacket for the set of two audio tapes of the SH stories, commissioned by Philip Porter and produced by him in conjunction with the eminent Holmesian, Richard Lancelyn Green. We were stuck for a jacket cover and thought this a reasonably good way out of our difficulty. So, I set to and painted it

13

Dame Peggy Ashcroft

I first met Peggy Ashcroft in 1948 while Liz was understudying and playing a small part in Robert Morley's play, *Edward My Son*, in which Peggy was giving a much-acclaimed performance as Robert's wife.

She had taken a liking to Liz who, after the play had been on for a time, used to go to her dressing-room for a chat before the show. As I used to call at the theatre every evening to bring Liz home, I often met her as well. She seemed a warm and friendly soul, with no *side* to her whatsoever. Later in the same year, when Liz and I were both at Stratford-on-Avon, she attended a matinée, coming round after the show to see Liz and we all three went and had tea somewhere in the town.

In the Old Vic season in 1952, Peggy joined the company to play Mistress Page in *The Merry Wives of Windsor*, in which I was playing Pistol. She was, as ever, her usual friendly self and we used quite often to go, after a matinée and before the evening show, to Scott's in the Strand, for tea and the most wonderful herring roes on toast to which Peggy, as I remember, was much addicted.

There was another play in the theatre in 1953, called *Blind Man's Buff*, which was put on by Frances Day, with two or three interesting legal parts. I played the barrister, Theobald Thin, who, although convinced of his client's guilt, was acting for the defence of a doctor accused of poisoning his wife but who was, in fact, innocent. I enjoyed that because it was an interesting situation of a barrister with an aversion to the man he was defending. The accused was played by Denis Price. The only fly in the ointment was that poor Denis, a film actor of some considerable ability, on this occasion was experiencing difficulty in familiarising himself with the lines. This was liable to gum up the works and a hiatus could be expected at any time.

I had to play two long scenes with him: one, a private examination prior to the trial and another, a long examination in the court itself. I spent many hours, between the matinée and evening show, in his dressing-room hearing his lines over and over again. I do not know how much good it did but, as an actor, I knew only too well the horror of *drying* on stage and he had my deepest sympathy.

In 1954, Peggy Ashcroft had another great success, as Hedda Gabler, at the Lyric, Hammersmith, where it had a preliminary run, before it was due to transfer to the rather grander Westminster Theatre in the West End. She was playing opposite my old friend, Alan Badel, who was Eilert Loevborg. Shortly after they had opened at the Lyric, the film company, who had a lien on Alan, unexpectedly exercised their contract rights, requiring his services. This meant that he would be able to complete the run in Hammersmith but would not be available for the transfer to the Westminster.

H.M. Tennant began casting for somebody else, who could take Alan's place. Peggy had the right of yea or nay to any possible successor. Fortunately there was a three or four week interim before the Westminster became available, during which Peggy took her children to Whitley Bay on holiday. She later told me that it was while she was playing with them on the beach that, for some reason, my face had flashed into her mind, as a possible Loevborg. She told Binkie Beaumont of Tennant's, who was very relieved that she had, at last, come to some conclusion on the matter. I was contacted through my agent and invited by Peter Ashmore, the director, to his house in Hampstead to have tea with Peggy who lived in Frognal nearby.

So up to Hampstead I went and it was really the oddest experience. A transformation seemed to have come over her. She hardly uttered a word and left all the *going* to Peter and me. Then towards the end, looking hard at me, she suddenly said, "Of course, you're awfully English," which struck me as a very odd thing to come out with.

I said, "Well, I suppose I am, but then, so are you".

As she had seen me in a number of roles, in which I had *not* been "awfully English," I was somewhat taken aback. She then asked me if I would *like* to play Loevborg. I thought to myself, "Well I would hardly be here otherwise," so I laughed and said I would like nothing more. After a pause, she then said that she had not *quite* made up her mind and that there was one other actor, whom she had never actually met but whom she had promised to see. They would be letting me know very soon.

Feeling naturally somewhat deflated and, by this time, rather less sure that I wanted to do it at all, I rang my agent to tell him what had transpired. He tried to reassure me, by telling me who "the other actor" was. It was Donald Houston, a hefty Welsh rugby-playing type, who could hardly have been more wrong for the alcohol-haunted literary genius, Loevborg. It so happened that we both had the same agent and that was how he knew. Added to his unsuitability, Houston had also just been offered a remunerative film role, which he could ill afford to turn down, so the part was as good as mine.

The next day or so, I had a call from my agent who flabbergastedly told me that she had offered the role to Houston. He had been through *tea routine* and Peggy had asked him the same question: whether he would *like* to play Loevborg. Upon him explaining the film situation, she had promptly offered it to him. Felix, my agent, then went on to say that Houston was certain to choose the film, so the part would be mine in the end. In the meantime, however, he had had an offer of Warwick for me in *St. Joan*, with Siobhan McKenna. I told him to accept it. He suggested that I wait a day or two, before I made up my mind and I told him I had already done so. I would do Warwick.

The call came a day later from Tennant's asking me to play Loevborg. Felix had been right, but I stuck to my guns and was very happy with Warwick. I would have been delighted to play opposite Peggy but, as she had shown herself so very uncertain, I had gone rather cold on the notion. This left *Hedda* back at square one, with both Houston and myself out of play.

Two or three days later, I was in a pub in Highgate, *The Flask*, with Liz where we bumped into Michael Warre to whom I related the story. He said he would give his eye-teeth for the part, so I said to him, "Why don't you go after it?" With time running out, it seemed to me *up for grabs*. So that is just what he did and, what is more, he landed the part. I went into *St. Joan*, which I greatly enjoyed. It was a considerable success and transferred to the St. Martin's, where it had a decently long run. Siobhan McKenna had rave reviews and I did pretty well on that score, myself.

As matinées of *St. Joan* and *Hedda* fell on different days of the week, Liz and I decided to go to one of Peggy's performances and pay her a visit after the show. This we did and, although we thought Peggy was splendid, I knew that I was happier with the light-hearted role of Warwick than I would have been in the heavily oppressive gloom of Ibsen. After the performance, we went round and asked the stage-door keeper if we could see Dame Peggy. He took our names and spoke on the phone. The message came back that Dame Peggy was having a rest and could see no-one.

There was a strange epilogue to all this.

Sometime later, after both plays had ended, I met Michael Warre and, in the course of conversation, I mentioned our meeting at *The Flask* and its fortunate outcome with *Hedda*. He looked at me blankly. He, quite clearly, had not the slightest recollection of what I was talking about.

14

Kenneth Williams

Some years ago I received a letter from a man who was writing a book about Kenneth Williams, asking me for any recollections I may have had of him. Kenneth and I had worked together in John Fernald's production of *St. Joan* with, as recounted, the wonderful Siobhan McKenna in the title role. Kenneth was the Dauphin and I was the Earl of Warwick, two magnificent roles.

I was sorry to have to say that, from the word go, I had not greatly taken to him and, as I told his biographer, as time went on, I found him more and more difficult to like. He seemed arrogant, constantly showing off as an attention-seeking *enfant terrible*, snorting his nostrils and putting on camp *comic* voices. What the real person was like, behind this ever-changing masquerade, was quite impossible to know. He never seemed to be able to let up.

Towards the end of rehearsals, he surprised me by asking how I thought his performance as the Dauphin was shaping. Assuming from this that he really wanted to know, I told him that the undoubted brilliance of his sense of comedy was, perhaps, in danger of losing the actual heart of the character he was portraying. In other words, he was sacrificing the human ingredient of pathos, which I felt was an important aspect of the role, but that what he was doing was certainly extremely funny.

This was a mistake on my part. What Kenneth required of me, as I very quickly discovered, was not constructive criticism, but unstinting praise. He went white with rage and shrieked abuse at me.

His performance, as rehearsals progressed, showed no sign of any consideration of my opinions and I would clearly have done better to have kept them to myself. I gave them because I thought that he could have given a truly great performance, instead of merely an extremely effective comedy turn, which appeared to please the director and which, in the event, certainly amused the audience.

He certainly showed at that early stage of his career a strong stage presence and was, I felt sure, a star performer, as was later borne out by his great success in the *Carry On* series of films. He had a highly original talent for comedy which, doubtless, made up for any deficiencies in other directions. He received a very good press and kept audiences rocking with laughter.

In my own role as Warwick, I had no scenes with him so I am unable to assess what he was like to *play* with but from external observation I would have thought not easy. However, I never once heard Siobhan, who shared many scenes with him, utter a word of complaint on that score.

Naturally, after such a reaction, I was not asked for an opinion again and, apart from ordinary politeness, I was able to avoid him as far as possible. During the run of the play, which transferred to the St. Martin's Theatre, Siobhan began to feel increasingly the tremendous burden of playing the arduous and exhausting role of Joan. This was particularly the case on matinée days, when she would try to snatch an hour's sleep in her dressing room between the two performances. Her room was next to mine on the ground floor. Kenneth's room was on the next floor, immediately above hers, which he shared with two other young actors in the cast. In between the shows, Kenneth would hold court to his lesser brethren in the dressing room, entertaining them with noisy impersonations, accompanied with much shouting and stamping on the floor.

One day after a matinée, I noticed that this was worse than usual and poor Siobhan came to my room and told me that it was quite impossible to sleep with the noise our Ken was making and she had tried to find someone on stage management to quieten things down but they had all gone out. Would I be an angel, as she was desperate for a nap, and ask him to be a bit quieter?

Not relishing the idea at all and feeling uncomfortably like the head prefect, I went up to Kenneth's room where he was giving his private performance to half a dozen admirers and asked him, in as conciliatory a manner as I could muster, to dampen it down a bit, as Siobhan badly needed a nap before the evening show. His reaction was as before. Fury.

The noise went on for a short time and then indeed quietened down to a reasonable level.

Siobhan gave the definitive performance of Joan, which for sheer power of conviction and spirituality, combined with sudden flashes of impish humour, would be difficult to surpass or even equal. She was sublime and I admired her more than I can say. Off-stage she was totally without pretension or airs of the *prima donna*. She was a real trouper, always giving of her best. She also loved a pint of Guinness after the show.

I counted the production as one of the highlights of my career. Kenneth Williams very soon found his niche, as is well known, starring with brilliance in the *Carry On* films, in which his brand of humour was able to find its true element. After *Joan* I had no occasion to meet him again.

15

Laurence Olivier 1955

My old friend, Esmond Knight, had given splendid performances in at least two of Olivier's Shakespearian films, *Henry V* and *Hamlet*. He was about to take part in a third, namely *Richard III*. He was clearly part of Olivier's *pool* of actors, from which he cast his films. He was also an old personal friend.

Esmond, or Ted, as I prefer to call him, told me that he had often suggested my name to Olivier, when he was casting, as indeed had his own ADC, Tony Bushell. Olivier was conservative in such matters and so their efforts on my behalf had been in vain. Nothing had ever come of it and it looked as if it never would.

However, in the summer of 1955, Liz and I went on a three-week holiday to Torre del Benaco, on the lovely shores of Lake Garda. The weather was perfect and we always had lunch on the long balcony of the hotel, overlooking the sleepy fishing harbour.

On one such occasion, we were surprised by the arrival of a large black limousine, which pulled up just below us. The chauffeur opened the door and, to compound our surprise, out stepped Vivien Leigh and Laurence Olivier, who then came up to the balcony for lunch. They sat at a table nearby, on the otherwise empty balcony. Lake Garda was nothing like as frequented then as it is now.

As they ate their lunch, it became apparent that all was not well with them, as the meal progressed in stony silence. She, though still ravishingly lovely, did not look at all well. When we had finished our lunch, on an impulse that later amazed me, I rose from the table and went across to them. In the light of their obvious malaise, I summoned the nerve to ask them if, after their lunch, they would do us the honour of having a drink with us.

After a momentary look of surprise, instead of a well-earned rebuff, they both seemed delighted at the idea so Liz and I went downstairs to a table outside to await them. I felt pretty aghast at what I had just done but told myself I really had nothing to lose.

Well, join us they did and Larry seemed thoroughly relieved to have someone to talk to. Happily the gods were kind and I was on reasonable form. They both seemed highly amused by my account of a hilariously bad production of *Romeo and Juliet*, which we had just seen a few nights before in Verona, at the Roman Theatre. Vivien actually laughed and Larry was relaxed and easy to talk to.

After about half an hour, he looked at his watch and told us that they were due to be picked up at San Vigilio, where they were staying, for an afternoon on the lake in the Mayor of Garda's private launch. This was to include a tour of the Villa Vittoriali, which had been Gabriele d'Annuncio's vast home, now a shrine to the dead hero, on the other side of the lake. Would we like to come with them?

We certainly did like, so we all piled into the limo and tootled over to San Vigilio, where we were joined by some of their friends. There was Ginette Spanier, *directrice* of Balmain in Paris, Paul Emil, her husband, a Parisian consultant physician, Didine Spanier, her sister, who ran interior design in Peter Jones, and a French playwright, whose name escapes me, and his wife. They were all staying together at this small, but exclusive hotel, tucked away on the shores of the lake.

Off we all went on the boat, cruising along the shoreline of the lake, past castles, private villas and churches, all very spectacular. Olivier and I sat in one corner of the cockpit, as we seemed to have plenty to talk about, while Liz seemed to be doing very well with Vivien. But then Liz was always charming, especially in one-to-one conversation. Olivier was much preoccupied with the forthcoming film of *Richard III*, which he was about to make, and seemed pleased to discuss his plans.

We went ashore, as arranged, at Gardone Riviera, for the conducted tour of d'Annuncio's villa, which appeared to be dauntingly extensive. It was a pretentiously rambling complex, which had been presented to him by Mussolini, in recognition of his heroic role in the annexing of Fiume into Italy, plus his eminence in literature. It consisted of an endless series of rooms, halls and galleries, each one named after an Italian victory. I had had no idea that Italy had so many victories to celebrate.

It was all very Fascist and tiring, but we plodded politely round most of it, until Larry suddenly said that he had, "had enough of this effing place" and we all thankfully went back to the boat, Larry remarking on the way, that the Italians seemed to know how to honour their heroes. He added that Eleanora Duse, the great actress and d'Annuncio's mistress, having died abroad, was brought back to Italy in a warship.

"Could you imagine the British Government sending a battleship for Edith?" (Dame Edith Evans) A rhetorical question, accompanied by one of his quirky looks.

Once back in the boat his spirits seemed to revive on our way back to San Vigilio. He invited us to dinner that night, in their hotel, which had been one of Winston Churchill's frequent painting haunts.

I can well remember him, skimming his hat over the lake, to be retrieved by an obliging skipper and then clapping it on to his head, like a schoolboy, with the wet running down his face, helpless with laughter.

This was a Laurence Olivier, I would later find hard to believe I had seen. I worked with him and met him quite often thereafter, but I never once saw him again as he was on that day. He was, literally, *happy as Larry*. He could have been an entirely different man.

We were asked to dinner so the car took us back to Torri, where we changed and then brought us back again to the party. There was a very good dinner - San Vigilio was well-known for cuisine and cellar - and a most animated and sparkling evening. After dinner Larry told us that he had tickets, as guests of honour, for the first night of the opera, *Norma*, in the huge Roman arena in Verona, the next day. He and Vivien were unfortunately unable to go as, suddenly, for some reason or other, they had to go back to London in the morning. Would Liz and I like to go in their place? The car could take us there and bring us back.

Well, we did not refuse and so the next evening the car came for us at Torri and drove us to Verona for the first night of the opera. We were led with the deference due to representatives of the Oliviers, to the Emperor's box, bang centre, facing the stage.

We were very struck by the charming custom of every member of the audience being given a candle, to be lit when the lights went down. The overture began and, as the lights were dimmed, the thousands of little candles were lit and then the opera began. After a short time, an enormously fat woman sailed on to the stage, dressed, most unsuitably in billowing white, but the moment she opened her mouth and sang the first few notes, we were electrified. I had never heard such a voice. It was sublime. I peered at the programme and the name meant nothing to me.

It was Maria Menighini Callas.

The remainder of our time in Torri was spent basking in the memories, of those two amazingly eventful days.

When we had been back in London a few days, the telephone rang and it was Tony Bushell (LO's ADC), who had suggested me, without success, for various ventures, including *Richard III*. He said, "I hear you met the *Guv'nor* in Italy. It was good of you not to pester him for a part in the film."

I said, "Tony, for heaven's sake! You know I wouldn't do that."

"Well, a lot of people *would* have done. Anyway, we've cleared a part for you; Dorset, with one or two other characters, rolled into it, to make it a bit more substantial."

"Lovely," I said, "But what do you mean, 'cleared a part for me'?"

"Just that. Don't ask too many questions," he said.

It later transpired that Brian Nissan, who had already been cast as Dorset, had been summarily evicted from the role and demoted to a messenger, entirely, so far as could be seen, on a whim of Larry's. I did not feel too easy about it but, of course, I accepted. I could hardly do otherwise.

Eventually the great day arrived, when we were all gathered together for a reading of the script. We were all sitting, ranged round the room, like so many wallflowers at a ball, in Korda's offices, at Number 2, Hyde Park, George VI's old home, when he was Duke of York. Many of the *great* were there: Gielgud, Richardson, Cedric Hardwick - three theatrical Knights, for *starters*. Larry walked slowly round the room to shake hands with his cast and, as he reached me, he murmured, *sotto voce*, "Up the Italian holiday-makers".

We then read the script and as Gielgud, who was to play Clarence, started with that wonderful voice in full Shakespearian bleat, I saw Larry sizing him up over his horn-rims and I could guess pretty much what he was thinking, "Lovely, Johnnie, lovely. But HALF!"

Of course, Gielgud gave a splendid and hauntingly lyrical performance, but much toned down by Larry. Clarence is a wonderful part and one which I have always had a hankering to play myself. Larry gave a very muted rendition of Richard at that first reading, leaving out the long soliloquies altogether. But then he had played the role in the theatre, with resounding success, so he knew exactly what he was doing and what he *intended* to do in performance. He knew that anything more than the merest sketch, at that early stage, would have daunted the rest of us.

Then there were the costume fittings. I had two or three changes of costume, but when I saw the design that Roger Furze had made for Dorset's most significant scene, my heart sank to my boots. A reddish, bobbed wig and a very short tunic indeed and white tights, topped with a clown's white flower-pot hat. I thought to myself that perhaps Brian Nissan might have looked all right in it, but with my saturnine cast of countenance, I would most decidedly not. It was also a classic case of, "Does my bum look big in this?"

I was hardly in a position to object but I have to admit to extreme dismay at the time. When I eventually saw the film, my worst fears were very much realised. I looked ridiculous: a fact brought home to me by relations and friends, who greet my appearance, whenever it is shown on TV, with uncontrollable hoots of mirth. Not quite the effect for which I had strived.

Nevertheless, it was a fascinating and wonderful experience, and I would not have missed a moment of it.

During the progress of the film, Olivier seemed almost to grow into the character of Richard, appearing ruthless, hard and sometimes sadistic. We were all, I believe, afraid of him. The exigencies of his triple situation of director, producer (i.e. financial responsibility), as well as bearing the weight of the principal role, must have weighed heavily upon him. I remember John Gielgud saying how much he admired Larry and he did not know how he did it.

He was directing one particular scene, in which he, himself, did not appear, set in *the Tower of London*. He was setting positions for Claire Bloom, Mary Kerridge, Helen Haye and Larry Naismith, with much pondering, and was grimly monosyllabic. I was also in the scene, but had not yet been placed. I helpfully and foolishly stood in the only vacant part of the set and piped up, "Shall I stand here, sir?"

I remember, as if it were yesterday, the slow, deliberate turn of the head, to regard me with the most baleful glare for what seemed an eternity, until he snapped, through gritted teeth, "I don't know ... YET!"

Withering, but it taught me a lesson about how not to be *helpful*.

In another scene, when Clarence's death was announced by Richard, Larry wanted to make a point that suspicion fell on Buckingham. He told me to make a slow circle round him, looking searchingly at his face, while Buckingham stood, like a maypole, in silence. Ralph Richardson, not surprisingly, was not too keen on this piece of direction and said so. "Larry, I don't think this is a very good idea."

Larry looked at him and, after a moment, said, "Oh, don't you, Ralphie? I think his intention is perfectly clear." And, so far as I remember, that is how it was; but 'Ralphie' did not like it at all.

For a young actor, it was a most exciting experience, but it was certainly not without considerable difficulties. The strain of directing, and the financial responsibilities, to say nothing of a most exacting role, increasingly took their toll and Larry had become really rather a frightening man to be with. When things went wrong, he would scream with rage at whoever was the cause and he could be very cruel. He had an old retainer, called Kelly, who acted as his dresser, valet and factotum. She was the widow of a naval officer and had for many years been completely devoted to Olivier, nannying him and attending to his every want. He was her whole life. She adored him.

After one particularly trying day, he flopped into the chair in his dressing-room and Kelly tried to jolly him into life, saying, "Now come along, don't make too much of it. After all, it's not as if you were playing a *really* demanding role."

Not tactful, perhaps, and I can well imagine the slow turn of the head and the stony glare, having had a taste of it myself. Larry did not say a word to her in the car, remaining grimly silent, all the way back to Durham Cottage, in Chelsea, where he and Vivien were living. He then curtly demanded Kelly's key to the house, turned on his heel and slammed the door in her face. She was fired from that moment. He never spoke to her again.

The poor woman was distraught. I believe she never recovered from the blow. I know all this because, a few years later, dear old Kelly became my dresser when I was playing at the Savoy. She was still totally obsessed with him, which did sometimes become a touch trying.

When I went with Liz to Lord Olivier's Memorial Service in Westminster Abbey, and Alec Guinness, in his eulogy, said that, "Wherever Larry was, there was always a strong element of danger", this and other incidents came to mind.

I always felt that element of danger with him: except for that extraordinary day in Italy.

It may seem, perhaps, a strange thing to say, but in all my contacts with him, despite his towering reputation, I never once had the impression of a consistent character. Without a role to play, he seemed, in some extraordinary way, to be curiously empty. No-one at home, so to speak. I feel sure that there are many who knew him much better than I did, who would dispute this, but that is how he always struck me. As a consequence, I felt it was impossible to know him at all ... I mean *really* to know him. I sometimes wondered if he knew himself?

He was, in his way, loyal to those who served him well, tending to use actors, such as Esmond Knight, over and over again. He was also kind enough to write to me, after *Richard III*, to thank me for my "contribution to the success of the film". So it looked as if I, too, was now admitted to the band of the elite. But perhaps he wrote to every one of us, I do not know. However, it was kind and civil of him. After all, Dorset was hardly going to make or break matters and he need not have bothered; but he did, which, I must say, pleasantly surprised me.

In extenuation of what I have truthfully recorded of much of his behaviour on the film set, the man must have been at the end of his tether with exhaustion. I can well remember, during an interval for lighting, seeing him, slumped in his director's chair, eyes closed, chin on chest and motionless. After a few minutes, the assistant-director went up to him and said, very quietly, "We are ready for you now, sir". He slowly opened his eyes, abruptly slapped his hands on his thighs and stood bolt-upright. He then strode purposefully on to the set and filmed a brilliant and very long soliloquy of Richard's, without a trace of difficulty or the slightest *fluff*. His willpower and concentration were incredible. The difficulty was that he expected the same high standards from those around him.

He was particularly intolerant of *fluffs* or *dries*, which made the lives of us lesser mortals - who had not, of course, had the benefit of having already played our roles many times in the theatre - somewhat tense, to say the least.

On occasion he could appear perfectly affable and would chat briefly during a break. On one such occasion, he surprised me with a sudden and unexpected burst of confidence. He had just been down to Eton to take his son out to tea. He looked at me, almost wistfully, and said, "You know, he was really very sweet to me," as if he somehow felt he did not deserve it. But one never knew what to expect. It was like being approached by an uncertain dog, unsure whether to wag its tail or bite. To describe him, therefore, as a man, not only of many talents, but also of many moods, would be, on both counts, something of an understatement.

One of the most likeable people on the film was Sir Cedric Hardwick: at his age, really a touch past playing with credibility the role of the lusty Edward IV. I was sitting next to him in the *rushes* theatre, watching the results of the previous day's work, which was the death scene of the king, with Cedric being not quite up to the mark. We left the theatre at the end of the showing and he trudged through the rain puddles in glum silence, back to the studio, when he suddenly said, "You know, there ought to be a law passed, prohibiting me from trying to play Shakespeare," then adding with a sigh, "or anything else, for that matter".

I remember two of his witticisms, related to me by Teddy Knight, who had filmed with him on *Helen of Troy*, for which role, the producers had secured the services, ill advisedly, of an unknown Italian actress of undeniable pulchritude, but rather less talent. She also experienced some difficulty in remembering her lines. After a number of unsuccessful attempts, Cedric, in the role of Agamemnon, was heard to murmur, "If at first you don't succeed, troy, troy and troy again".

And later, "Is this the face, that lunched off fish and chips?"

Olivier's next project, which concerned me, was *The Prince and the Showgirl* with Marilyn Monroe. Larry was to direct and repeat his role in the theatre, as the Grand Duke. There were a number of small parts, normally filled by extras, but for which Larry wanted actors, because a bit more was required of them. He had a number of his usual faithfuls contacted with many apologies that it was not much to write home about, but explaining why he needed us, and if we had nothing much on and would like to pick up a few quid, then it was ours for the taking.

Well, the money was not peanuts and I assumed it would amount to two or three days at the most, and that would be that. He wanted me for the leading man of the theatrical company, of which Marilyn's role was a member. I had not reckoned, however, on Miss Monroe's eccentric behaviour.

Neither, I imagine, had Larry. She led us all a terrible dance.

I was kept hanging around on full salary for weeks which, though it was *money for jam*, became very awkward, as I was already committed to John Clements, for his star-studded production of *The Way of the World*, in which I was to play the excellent part of Fainall. I was already late for the first few days of rehearsals and John was getting impatient.

Finally, I asked Larry if he had any idea when we would be able to finish what we had started. He replied grimly, jerking his thumb in the direction of Marilyn's caravan changing-room, "Look, chum, you'd better go and ask *her*! Like you, I'm only a hired man in this outfit."

Marilyn had recently married Arthur Miller and he was rather more in evidence than was agreeable to Larry. He was prone to comment adversely on some of the clothes that had been designed for her and also, worse still, on some of Larry's direction, which caused more disruption and delays. In fact, she seemed to be almost totally un-directable and made little or no attempt to follow her director's requirements.

For reasons, often undivulged, she would walk off the set and shut herself in her caravan dressing-room, totally deaf to entreaties to come out and finish what she was doing. There she would stay, often for several hours, either ensconced with Miller, getting up to heaven knows what, or with another thorn in Larry's flesh in the shape of Mrs. Lee Strasburg, her private *dialogue coach* and also the wife of the founder of the notorious *Method* school of acting. This tenacious lady was permanently at Marilyn's side, clutching an enormous folder, each page devoted to one of Marilyn's lines, accompanied by copious analytical notes, in the style of the *Method*.

These notes, delivered in a hoarse and confidential whisper, were constantly being fed to Marilyn, to whom she represented the Delphic Oracle. As many of these were clearly in contravention of Larry's direction, his views on this particular bugbear were explicit and totally unprintable. The fact the film was ever finished constitutes a major miracle.

Sometimes Marilyn would fail to appear for days at a time, with no reason given.

One assistant-director actually got her to the phone and was bold enough to ask why she had not turned up for her morning call. She apparently snarled in reply, "I got the Curse! Don't you have that over here?" and slammed the receiver down.

On another occasion, we were scheduled to film the procession to the Abbey, through the streets of London, for the coronation of George V. Marilyn was to ride in an open carriage, seated next to Larry, as the Grand Duke, receiving the plaudits of the populace. Sybil Thorndike, as the Dowager Duchess, was to ride in the carriage behind them. Our *calls* required a very early start, as there was an enormous amount of preparation to be made, a large number of extras to be made-up and organised: all the principals, such as Larry, Dame Sybil and, of course, Marilyn herself and also the rest of us. There was a large detachment from the actual Brigade of Guards, who were to line the route.

If the shooting of this difficult and highly complex sequence was to be completed in one day, we all had to be ready, made-up and dressed in full costume and with every logistic organised, by eight am sharp. Larry was ready, long before that, fully clad in his tight dress-uniform, dripping with orders and medals. Sybil was encased in her robes, with an immense train lined with ermine. Eight o'clock, nine and then 10 arrived, but not a sign of Miss Monroe. Larry was grinding his teeth in fury.

By this time, the sun was well up and it had begun to get swelteringly hot. From the comparative comfort of the roofed-in seats (thoughtfully arranged, for us *theatricals* by the Grand Duke), I could see the *crowd* getting restless. One or two of the Guardsmen in their scarlet and bearskins were beginning to sway on their feet.

Marilyn arrived soon after 11 and sauntered on to the set, cool as a cucumber, in white blouse and cotton trousers. Larry expostulated with her, "At least you might go and apologise to Dame Sybil".

Marilyn was outraged at the suggestion.

"Apahlagise!" she spat out. But, after a few moments consideration, she did take herself over to where Sybil was sitting and muttered some sort of apology.

Sybil's reply was exquisitely reassuring. "That's perfectly all right, my dear. I'm sure you had some very good reason and we're all the more pleased to see you, now you *have* come."

There was no sarcasm in what she said: she really meant it. But then, she was a very great lady.

It has often been said of Marilyn, that "the camera loved her" but to what considerable extent, I would not have believed possible without the evidence of my own eyes. At the first read-through, as was Larry's civilised custom, he introduced to each other, those whom we did not already know and someone ushered in a plumpish young woman in a wraparound, with her hair tied up in a headscarf and this we learned was Miss Monroe. Without make-up of any kind whatsoever, she looked unbelievably ordinary. She could have walked down Oxford Street quite safely and no-one would have had the slightest idea who she was.

Her build was decidedly chubby, with a round undistinguished face and a small but unusual nose, which was *retroussé*, until, just before the end, when it changed course into a small round blob: a defect, which was clearly remediable in the make-up chair, with a touch of judicious shading. In some stills, it is just visible, and then only when knowingly looked for. It certainly never seemed to show on film and I have watched her a number of times with the greatest enjoyment. Neither did she ever look plump. Voluptuous and, perhaps, a touch full-blown, but only desirably so.

I can see her now, as I walked behind her and noticed that, in her tight lacy dress, her bottom looked decidedly large. But it certainly did not on film. Indeed, the camera loved her.

On one occasion she fluffed her lines, over and over again and, when she did it again, for the umpteenth time, Larry exploded, "Marilyn! FOR FUCK'S SAKE!"

She looked at him, round-eyed and said, "Oh, d'you have that word over here too?"

But she was quite impervious to his fury. By this time they were, quite certainly, not each other's favourite person.

Sybil Thorndike, who was playing Larry's mother remonstrated with him. "For goodness sake, Larry, leave her alone. You are wasting your breath. Just let her get on with it, in her own way, and she will be fine." But Larry was not used to that sort of thing, so the result was an unholy deadlock, from a battle of wills, which she almost invariably won.

I think it must have aged him somewhat. It was certainly good for his humility.

Many years ago, when Larry played Iago to Richardson's Othello, he performed the most outrageous antics behind Othello's back, which did much to make the blacked-up Ralph Richardson appear an idiot for being so easily taken in. It seems to me very much to the latter's credit that their friendship survived.

Olivier is reported to have said that he would never play Othello, unless he had "a complete lemon", to play Iago. Well, Frank Finlay was certainly no *lemon*, but a very fine and powerful actor. Larry had him as Iago. Someone certainly saw to it that there was always plenty of light on Othello, but Iago spent most of the time in comparative darkness, and in most of their scenes together, firmly downstage. He was, thereby, reduced to *a lemon*, and a well squeezed one at that.

It was really pretty shameful and Frank was most unhappy about it, as he later told me, adding that it was during that production, that his hair turned white. The whole balance of the play was, of course, destroyed. When it was later made into a film, Frank came very much to the fore. There were close-ups, in which what he was doing and thinking were perfectly apparent. His performance could now be seen and had become a different matter, altogether.

When the 100th anniversary of the birth of Laurence Olivier took place recently, there was remarkably little notice or celebration of it, which was all the more surprising as a great fuss was made of John Betjeman's 100th. But when I thought about it, I suppose this was because Betjeman had a firm place in the affections of the nation, which Larry, despite all his achievements, quite simply did not.

I read today, by a curious coincidence, an article from *The Times* of May 28th, 1987, by the critic, Benedict Nightingale, on great performances, in which he says of Larry's acting, "Was there not something calculating about it? While he might astound the eyes, boil the blood and freeze the backbone, he could not activate the lump in the throat," which rather sums up my feelings about him.

When I mentioned that he seemed strangely empty of centre, could it be that the missing area was the heart? I may be wrong but I felt that, despite the odd acts of kindness, there was nothing really lovable about him. Indeed he was often quite difficult to even *like*.

This is probably why I was unmoved by his Othello, Lear and Archie Rice. One could always admire the fireworks, but one did miss the heart of the matter.

In 1966, I was working with him on *Khartoum*, in which he appeared as the Mahdi, while he was also playing Othello at the Old Vic to packed houses, critical acclaim and public plaudits. I asked him if he could wangle me a ticket, somehow, for a Saturday matinée. This, in spite of being so busy, he managed to do. So I went to see it and as soon as Olivier walked on the stage, twirling that flower-shop rose and using that phoney *Rasta* voice, my heart sank. I knew that I was going to hate it.

I found it vulgar, externally showy and totally lacking in nobility. It was not Venice that I felt I was in so much as the Notting Hill Carnival.

How on earth was I going to face him and what was I going to say, which would not be a wallow of untruth? Larry was not a fool. He would see through any subterfuge on my part. So, in some trepidation, I went round after the performance and asked my old friend, Ernie, the stage-door keeper, if I could see Sir Laurence. Ernie said that Sir Laurence had left me a message. Would I excuse him, but as there was no evening performance of *Othello*, he had to get off all his body-make-up and catch a train back to Brighton? I beamed at Ernie with relief and was able to write Larry a carefully-worded letter of thanks with, I hope, not too many untruths, to which neither of us referred when I next saw him.

We both happened to frequent a place, euphemistically known as "the gym of the stars" in Holland Park, where a man called Edward something gave one-to-one sessions of individually tailored exercises. I used to bump into Larry there, from time to time, as he was preparing himself for *Othello* and proposed displaying rather more of himself, than was usual.

On one such occasion, I had arrived early at the changing-room to see a rather startlingly loud shirt and a very expensive-looking watch. In due course, out came Larry, whose property it was, and we had a brief conversation during which he surprised me by telling me how very little public applause now meant to him.

The hand-clapping of his tiny children (by Joan Plowright), when he returned home to his house in Brighton, was all the applause he now needed, which I found a little hard to swallow, in more ways than one.

A few weeks later, I was listening on the radio to the speeches at the Royal Academy dinner, at which Larry, as guest of honour, was to reply to the traditional *Toast to the Stage*. Towards the end of his speech, he again trotted out this improbably embarrassing statement, for which I had clearly been a rehearsal. Hmmm!

In another of our changing-room chats, he was talking about the National company and Alec Guinness's name cropped up. I asked Larry why he had never asked him to join the company. "Of course I bloody well have," he said. "He turned it down. That boy's out to make a million." I replied that I would have thought he was well into that already.

"Ohhh, no. A million takes a hell of a lot of making," was his reply.

A year or so later I was working with Alec on a film in Spain and I asked him why he had turned Larry's offer down? Alec smiled his quizzical smile, pursed his lips and then he said, "Did he tell you what the offer was?" I said not. "It was to play Antonio, in the *Merchant of Venice* (a really boring role: I know, because I've played it) and the rest was left open."

I could hardly believe it: to an actor of Alec's international stature. Larry could never have thought that Alec would accept such an offer. I could only assume that he made it to square his conscience. Had Alec been in the company (because of his world-famous portrayal of Fagin in the film of *Oliver Twist*), he would have been an obvious choice for Shylock, which Larry had earmarked for himself.

I have briefly mentioned the film *Khartoum*, in which Charlton Heston appeared, as General Gordon. Olivier had been approached to play the Mahdi, but had decided against it, owing to pressure of work. He felt unable to give such an undertaking the due thought and time required, and so the role was offered to Alec Guinness, who also said no and then to someone else - I forget who. Heston, with whom I had worked on *El Cid* (playing his Moorish friend and ally), told the film people that, as they had failed to get a big name for the Mahdi, then he would like to recommend someone less known for the part, namely, myself.

Before they would agree to this, they said they would have another go at Olivier, offering him a considerably larger fee, also a schedule, elastic enough and tailor-made to fit his timetable. In other words, it was an offer he could not refuse. He did not. The deal was clinched and I, swallowing my natural disappointment, accepted the offer of his ADC.

On the first day of shooting our sequences, I arrived on the set, suitably bearded and blacked-up and in flowing robes. Then, Larry appeared, also *as black as your hat*, and seeing me, advanced on me, arms outstretched, with that curious, side to side, head-nodding walk of his and clutched me to his manly bosom and said, by way of greeting, somewhat incongruously I thought, "Oh, my darling baby-boy!"

Accustomed as I was to thespian endearments, I did consider this a little *over the top*.

He then asked me to have lunch with him in the studio restaurant, so that I could instruct him in the Arabic pronunciation of such words as Khartoum, for instance. He knew that I had spent a few days, visiting the Sudanese Embassy, in order to familiarise myself with the necessary knowledge, which he had had no opportunity to do.

He also told me that his first shooting was to make a longish speech to his army, consisting of a rabble of blacked-up extras, and he asked me if I would help him by standing in the middle of the front rank, so that he could have "at least one intelligent face to address", which, of course, I did. At all events, they managed to shoot as much as they needed of his full-face shots, filling in with someone else's back of the head, wearing Larry's turban, to be voiced-over later by the great man himself.

This, at best, was a somewhat patch-work way of going about it and, in my view, as far as Larry's performance went, ended up in a patchy result. He had always given his work a great deal of time and careful thought and here his characterisation, deprived of these two essentials, was largely off the top of his head, disconcertingly inconsistent and lacking in dimension.

He also started off, using his Othello voice (as per his evening performances, playing the role) and gradually changing its timbre to a curiously sinister sort of whine. There was no real suggestion of the man's fanatical *spiritual* leadership, to counter-balance the corresponding element in General Gordon. One was left, therefore, apart from his powerful presence, with less interesting characteristics, such as sadism, portrayed in an unusually demonic way.

Perhaps he found it difficult, playing two different black men in the same day. Or perhaps he had simply not had time to give the matter thought.   .

I freely admit that this assessment of his performance is probably, to some extent, tinged with *sour grapes*. Having recently seen it again, though, I can look back upon it without much modification of my opinion at the time.

Heston, playing Gordon, a brave venture for an American, was excellent, giving an astonishingly convincing performance. I know that he regarded working with Olivier as an honour, as he himself told me, and that he did so with much trepidation. He need not have worried on that score at all, as it turned out. He had had ample time to give it full consideration and had done so, to some purpose.

He told me that he had been at some pains to acquire the authentic *Woolwich* accent, a reference to the Royal Military College at Woolwich, where Gordon had been a cadet. He, of course, possessed in his own character, many of the requisites for portraying Gordon. His intrinsic fortitude, courage, total obstinacy and an unspoken moral rectitude were all natural traits that had served him well in so many of his heroic filmic roles.

When they were setting the scene for Gordon's assassination, someone capable of throwing a spear with accuracy had been found, but as the man demanded rather more as a fee than was considered appropriate, it was decided to save money by dispensing with his services. The camera was set up at the top of the steps to the palace, from Gordon's point of view and facing the threatening mob below. A likely lad from among them had been selected to hurl the fatal spear.

When the director, Basil Dearden, a funny little man with sandy hair, called "action", the blacked-up crowd of extras approached the foot of the stairs and the javelin wallah hurled his spear. There was a loud curse from behind the camera. The spear had been thrown, not *just wide* of the camera, as instructed, but with deadly accuracy, straight at it. It had cracked the camera lens.

Basil Dearden popped his head up, like an outraged Jack-in-the-box, from behind the camera, demanding indignantly, "What did you do that for?" This was followed by a long wait, while the lens was changed, costing, I would imagine, a great deal more than the fee for the original javelin man. That was *Khartoum*, a film not otherwise crowded with incident: at least, not from my point of view.

I have a memory of Olivier, many years later, after his long and serious illness, during which he had been out of action for some time.

I was filming at Pinewood Studios and I knew that Larry was working again, playing Moriarty in *The Seven Per Cent Solution*, in the next studio. I was finishing an early lunch in the restaurant, when Larry appeared alone at the entrance. He looked very ill indeed, but somehow managed to make his way slowly down the few steps to the restaurant level, supporting himself on the balustrade and then on whatever piece of furniture came to hand. He seemed quite literally incapable of walking, or even standing up unaided. I was surprised that they had let him come in on his own but, knowing him, he probably insisted that he would be perfectly all right. He made a painful progress to the table, nearest to the entrance and, I am ashamed to say, I funked speaking to him, recalling our lunch together in the same restaurant, in his hale and hearty days of *Khartoum*.

As there was no other way out, eventually I had to pass his table. So, biting the bullet, I greeted him, saying how splendid it was to see him back, like a lion among us, or some such awkward hyperbole. Again, there was that slow turn of the head, eyeing me balefully and then, through gritted teeth, and, almost resentfully, he said, "Christ, you look well!"

I had difficulty in finding a suitable reply to that. I believe that was the last time I ever spoke to him, but he slowly made a remarkable recovery and remained a fighter to the last, many years later.

When I read through my memories of Laurence Olivier, it seems that my opinion of his character deteriorates. He does not sound a very pleasant person. But then, if I speak the truth, I have to say, that very often he was not. I have said that he inspired intense admiration and amazement, but not the warmer feelings. At least, not in me. His own rare moments of apparent warmth seemed, almost always, false and out of character. He had, in common with many of the very hard, a noticeable streak of sentimentality.

If these memories are to be a faithful record of the truth of what I have seen and heard, I must risk the accusation of detraction.

Bobby Helpman once told me that when he was staying for the week-end with Laurence and Vivien at Notley Abbey, as he often did, he woke up one Sunday morning, earlier than his hosts. Perusing the Sunday papers, he noticed a startling item. Taking the paper with him he went up to their bedroom, knocked and went in and said, "Larry, I'm afraid I've got some very bad news for you".

Larry smiled apprehensively, "All right, Bobby darling. Ha, ha. What is it?"
"Ralph's been knighted."

There was a stunned silence and then Larry said, "Oh jolly good. Of course I'm delighted."

Vivien was above pretence and she screamed, "What d'you mean, GOOD? It's BLOODY TERRIBLE! It should have been YOU! And it means 'Moo' will be Lady fucking Richardson! Get up, get out of bed and DO something!"

Wheels were put into motion and, not long after, Larry was knighted and Vivien, I feel sure, felt very much better about it.

I was able to feel rather more warmly towards her. Though in many ways a very tricky individual, she always seemed intrinsically more herself. Once, when I was playing at the Arts Theatre, it was the habit of the stage manager to come to my dressing-room to retrieve my props to be set ready for the next performance. There came the usual knock at the door. I called, "Come in", the door opened and there, like a flower, radiant in sables and diamonds, was Vivien.

I was taken aback, as I had removed my trousers and, whilst not revealing my all, it was more than enough. I apologised and reached for my dressing gown but she seemed highly amused and, after the mandatory compliments on my performance, she left.

The last time I saw her, was some years later at a drinks' party, given by John Standish and his wife, Jill Melford. She was with Jack Merivale and it was after Larry had left her. The change in her was heart-rending. She looked ill and very much older. She was drunk and reeking of a most powerful scent of lilies of the valley. Apropos of nothing at all, she reached into her handbag, producing the spray, which she directed at me, dousing me with it from top to toe, giggling like a mischievous child. It took three visits to the cleaners for my suit to be neutralised.

Not long after this, I was saddened to read that she had died, alone and uncared for. She was a woman not easily forgotten and I believe that Larry carried her ghost with him to the end of his life.

16

Badel, Belita And 'The Bin'

I have briefly mentioned already the brilliant Alan Badel, whose intervention in my life, albeit unwittingly, was to effect the course of it greatly.

He was an interesting character and I first made his acquaintance at RADA, when we were both students there, at the start of the war. He and I were, at one point, neck and neck competitors for the Academy poetry-speaking prize. He chose, unwisely I thought, "To be or not to be" and I, perhaps more bizarrely, Edith Sitwell's *Little ghost that died for Love*, which none of the judges knew, and which, in any event, was certainly designed for a woman. Anyway, I won; purely, I suspect, because I had made the more original choice.

We were also together in a touring student production of *The Merchant of Venice*, in which he played Bassanio and I the less rewarding role of Antonio, the Merchant himself. I remember him at that time as gentle, unassuming and easy to get on with.

We both went into the Army, I as already described elsewhere and he into the paratroops, where he had, in more senses than one, an extremely bloody war. I had no contact with him during that time but, meeting him very soon after, I was in for something of a shock. He looked haggard and haunted, seemingly preoccupied, when he talked at all, with stabbing knives, garotting with cheese-wires and other horrors of war. At times, he seemed almost mad, with unsmiling eyes and a strangely malevolent smile. He was unrecognisable as the same gentle soul of our student days. I found him uneasy and difficult to talk to. At all events, he went back to the pursuit of his former career, in which, despite many crossed-swords, he achieved considerable success.

He met, at some point, a man called Tony Furness, a shy but stage-struck peer, who admired him immensely. He had inherited ownership of the Furness Shipping Line and he was more than extremely well-to-do, in childhood bearing the enviable description of, "The richest little boy in England". He was also the son of Thelma Furness, sister to Gloria Vanderbilt and one-time American mistress of Edward VIII, before she ill-advisedly introduced him to Wallis Simpson.

But I digress.

Alan and Furness set up a theatre production company, called Furndel, where it seemed Alan was to have a free hand in control and his lordship to provide the wherewithal: as an *angel,* as he liked to be called. There was a degree of unwisdom in this. Alan was extravagant. He spent money as if it grew on the trees in his own back-garden. However, Furness was dazzled by his genius, almost obsessed, and seemed quite happy to cough up, while Alan spent lavishly on fast cars and other necessaries of management.

Their most prestigious venture was a production in the West End of James Joyce's *Ulysses in Night-town,* in which Alan was to play Stephen Dedelus, with Zero Mostel as Bloom. There was also a narrator, who stood uneasily with a music-stand at the side of the stage and launched into descriptive passages, from time to time, while the action on stage continued in mime. This was read by a fairly well-known (mainly) radio actor, whose name escapes me. I do not think it worked very well.

Mostel, however, was brilliant and gave a most powerful performance. The production was by Burgess Meredith and had received a mixed reception. After a limited run in London, it had been decided to take the production on a European tour of Brussels, Amsterdam, the Hague and Utrecht, finishing up at the Sarah Bernhardt Theatre in Paris. Alan rang me up and said that he would like me to replace the *Narrator,* who was unable to go on the tour, and would I come to see the show? I had a meeting with Alan beforehand, who told me Mostel was a bit of a handful, convinced of his own importance and prone to interfere with anyone's performance that might impinge on his own: pretty much of a trial, he said, with a wolfish grin.

I went to see the play, which I thought had much atmosphere. Mostel's performance was indeed a *tour de force,* but had little to do with James Joyce, tending to hog the limelight and bull-doze everyone else off the stage. I did not like the way the narrator was dealt with at all, shambling on through the curtain in an ordinary suit to take up his position at the music stand before the action started. It looked as if the stage manager was coming on to announce that an understudy was to appear as one of the principals was unwell. It was not, in any way, an integral part of the performance.

I decided that if I was to take it on this could be improved upon and I told Alan my thoughts on the matter. I suggested that I should appear, attired in period white tie and tails, seat myself comfortably in an armchair at the side of the stage, open the book and start reading, in a spotlight, which would fade out when the narrator was non-operative. There could even be a mock whisky and soda on a small occasional table. I felt it should be done with some style and be integrated into the body of the performance: not like a tin can, tied to a dog's tail.

Above all, I stipulated that I should never - and I meant *never* - be subjected to any unreasonable requirements by Mr. Mostel. Alan, scenting battle, rubbed his hands in anticipation and agreed to all my suggestions, without which, in some form or other, I told him I could not undertake it.

As Burgess Meredith, the original director, was no longer in evidence, having gone back to America, Alan had to assume his mantle. At the very first rehearsal, Mostel loudly stated his requirements, as to the pace of my reading: too quick here, too slow there. I referred him to the arbitration of Alan, who managed to calm him down. I also had trouble from a lady called Belita, a former ballerina and an Olympic skating star, who stated her own requirements. She proved very difficult and fixed her cat's eyes upon me in a baleful stare. I had noticed her in the performance, moving with athletic grace, in the doubling or trebling of the two or three roles that she portrayed. There was quite definitely *someone at home*. In other words, she had *star* quality. I felt it was a pity to have incurred her dislike. She made it pretty obvious that I had.

Once in Brussels, we were put into various hotels and, after two or three performances, I found myself alone in the bar one night, having a quiet drink after the show, when she came in to have one herself. She treated me, at some length, to a *piece of her mind*, leaving me in no doubt that she disliked me intensely. She considered me arrogant and gave me to understand that I had ideas above myself. I heard her out and then made a fatal suggestion. I asked her up to my room for a drink.

As may perhaps be surmised, after a few of those, I regret to confess, we ended up in bed. And that was the start of a long and destructive attraction, lasting over two years and causing a great deal of hurt all round. I left my lovely wife, hating myself as I did so, and moved in with Belita, in her flat in Onslow Square.

She really had me by the *proverbials*. I felt paralysed, trapped in an impossible situation. She soon made it clear that what she required from me was divorce from Liz, followed by marriage to herself; this I simply could not bring myself to do. There were endless scenes and the most terrible rows. She threatened to kill me and, on more than one occasion, actually menaced me with a knife.

I made my escape after two or three of these occurrences, telling myself, "Well, that's that". But mutual friends would tell me how "devastated" she was, not eating and a "shadow of her former self" and I would weakly go back to her, *on conditions*. These conditions were always meekly agreed to. Then, with her unerring instinct for trouble, we would be back to square one again; on one such occasion, she changed her name by deed-poll to mine, reverting almost at once, to full-blown replays of her old themes and demands.

It was during one of her periods of quiescence that I was asked to be in *El Cid*, with locations in Spain, and, instead of putting a few thousand miles between us, as I should have done, I rashly asked her to come with me. The result of this was a nightmare. We had transferred our situation to a location from which, tied by the film, I could in no way escape. I saw exactly how life, inextricably tied to her, would be and at last I had had more than enough. Back in England, after the film, after one big final bust-up, I decamped to Bill Franklin, who gave me much good advice and shelter from the storm.

I soon went to Liz and asked her if she would take me back, which, as we both thought I had probably learnt my lesson and we certainly loved each other, she very sweetly agreed to do. I knew that I had hurt her appallingly but, undeserving as I was, I believe she really forgave me. It had been a mad and obsessive attraction to this violent and passionate woman which I had found impossible to break for over two long years.

On my first night back home in Campden Street, when I went to draw the curtains, I saw her car parked on the opposite side of the road. She had somehow tracked me down and spent practically the whole night there: to what end God alone knows.

After some months, I heard that she had been given a job by her old friend, Michael Bentine, as his P.A., which, kind and gentle person though he was, he must have later regretted. He told me that she had talked incessantly about *us*, until he had finally agreed to speak to me about it. He asked me to meet him for lunch, which I did. He was very kind and well-meaning but I have no idea what he hoped to achieve. A recital of Belita's sufferings and her troubled state, much as I regretted them, was unlikely to alter my new-found freedom from her.

I told him so and why. He could not have been altogether surprised because, as I later heard, she had already antagonised many of his friends and theatrical contacts, and that most certainly had nothing to do with me.

My very last contact with her was a bill from her solicitor, Arnold Goodman (later, for some reason, created a Companion of Honour and awarded a peerage) for his fees for changing her name from mine back to her own. I paid up, but not without a wry smile.

Eventually she married an old flame and was, of all things, running a garden centre.

After the Belita episode, I should have learnt my lesson but unfortunately, with the best will in the world, the predicament in which we found ourselves remained much as before. My libido had remained all too intact, but, as I had unhappily come to regard Liz as a much-loved sister, it was unable to function in her direction.

It is perhaps easy from the side-lines to say that I should have been more in control of myself: I tried and failed, again and again. My resulting transgressions caused untold damage to poor Liz and indeed to both of us. Matters became worse so that, in a final effort to save my much valued marriage and on the advice of our friend and family GP, Stephen Sebag-Montefiori, I went to see a psychiatrist, a man called Dr. Ambrose.

I took myself to his rooms in Harley Street at vast expense but little noticeable difference, for two full years, finally agreeing to undergo a course of treatment with LSD, which, it seems, was *flavour of the month*, at that time in certain psychiatric circles. This involved weekly visits, for the entire night, to the St. Leonard's Clinic in Chelsea, for seven weeks on the trot. I was told to arrive at 6pm, when a nurse would take me to my room for the night.

I did so and was put to bed and a hypodermic plunged into my behind. I was then left alone to await results. They were not long in coming. After about half an hour, when the walls and ceiling of my room appeared to be bulging, undulating and assuming the most alarmingly unlikely colours, I was visited by a doctor I had not previously met, presumably an associate of Ambrose. He asked me how I felt and stayed with me for 10 or 20 minutes.

I cannot remember what we talked about, but I imagine it must have been pretty incoherent, on my part at least.

He would then leave me alone until in sailed Ambrose, looking, as I remember, sleek and prosperous. I did not like him one bit. He wished me good evening and sat himself down in smiling silence, looking, as it seemed to me, unbelievably smug.

I have total recall of our first exchange of words. "I suppose you've had a damned good dinner, a nice bottle of wine, a cigar and purred your way here in your Bentley?"

"Yes," he said, smiling. "I've had a good dinner, thank you. But what makes you think I have a Bentley?"

"You could bloody well afford one," I said. "Anyway I heard it when you drew up outside."

"Yes, I could afford a Bentley," he said, "but my psychiatrist tells me I don't need one." Hmmm. One up to Ambrose. I had, in point of fact, driven up to the clinic that evening in my own very beautiful Mulliner Park Ward Bentley, which was parked outside.

In between long silences, I remember attacking him on various fronts while he just sat there, deflecting my apparently nonsensical remarks. He would then pop out and the other fellow would come in again. I gathered later that they were supposed to represent my father and mother, Ambrose, of course, adopting the former role. What all this *boxing and coxing* was supposed to achieve, I never quite discovered but it went on, it always seemed, far into the night. At the end of it all, I would be plied with a couple of pills to put me to blessed sleep.

The next morning, after breakfast at the clinic, I would drive back home to face the same situation, Ambrose having told me that my attitude to Liz and sex was infantile and that, with further treatment, I would *grow up*. My libido, however, had remained as strong a compulsion as before and it was not difficult to find, in spite of strong feelings of guilt, outlets in a succession of other women. This guilt was always accompanied afterwards by extreme depression.

So in his optimistic prognosis, I fear, Dr. Ambrose was entirely wrong. The treatment continued, but so did the circumstances and symptoms likewise. In fact, my state of mind and consequent depression became so much worse that Ambrose recommended my voluntary admission to the Holloway Psychiatric Hospital (no relation to HM Prison!) at Virginia Water. Here, he said, I could have a complete rest under some mild form of sedation for a few weeks, completely away from any pressures of my domestic environment. This I agreed to do, provided I could have a room to myself, which apparently was not a difficulty.

So I drove up to the hospital, an enormous, Gormanghast-like, Gothic building, which had been purpose-built, as a lunatic asylum in the reign of Queen Victoria. On admission, I was examined by a Turkish doctor, who enquired of me if I was suicidal and I was able to reassure him that I was not. I remember thinking that, had I been so, I would hardly have forewarned him of the fact. But this was merely a formality to find out whether or not I was to have unsupervised access to my razor.

I was shown to my room, which was surprisingly bright and cheerful. After supper, which was served to a large number of the less unconventional patients in an enormous refectory, I was sedated and put to bed, eventually falling asleep. I was awakened the next morning by a male nurse who marched in, drew back the curtains and barked in mock Sergeant Majorial tones, "Good morning, Viscount Tenby, sir!" Upon my sitting up, he enquired, "Where's David?"

"David? Who's David?" I asked.

"David Lloyd George," came the improbable reply. I began to think that it was not only the patients in the place who might be a bit odd. It transpired, however, that the former occupant of the room, apparently accustomed to this bizarre form of reveille, had gone into considerable arrears with the fees and had consequently been evicted to accommodate me. Later, when I made his acquaintance, it was clear that he bore me no ill-will on that account, indeed, in his reticent way, seeming anxious to be friendly. He had, however, been transferred to a room he was to share with a pair of suicidal sailors, which he cannot have found too congenial.

Very soon we became friends. We had a lot in common and I found him highly intelligent and interesting, being, as I later discovered, an historian specialising in the American Civil War. He was also a barrister of the Inner Temple and an Honours MA of Jesus College, Cambridge. We talked a lot and I heard he had also been a Captain, at the end of the war, in my old Regiment, the Gunners. Wondering what had brought him to this pass, I asked him once why he could not have continued his career at the bar? He replied, with a sad smile, that Holloway Psychiatric Hospital was not a very suitable address, which was begging the question, of course, but I sensed his reticence and did not pursue it.

He was indeed called David Lloyd George, being a grandson of the Liberal Prime Minister, with the style of Viscount Tenby, a handle which in Holloway, at least, he felt it inappropriate to use and which he certainly never mentioned. I asked one of the male nurses what was the matter with him. He replied, cheerfully, "Nothing much - depressed. I suppose you'd call him an inadequate - but given 20,000 a year, Lord bless you, he'd be as right as rain".

I spent every morning in the hospital's very well-equipped Art Studio, where I did a number of pencil and charcoal portraits of David and other patients which I believe I still have somewhere. I found a few more congenial spirits in the studio. It was relaxing and therapeutic. I felt cocooned and away from my problems. There was one exceedingly comely young woman who seemed perfectly normal until, in the course of conversation, she revealed a passionate obsession for her brother with whom she had enjoyed incestuous relations from an early age. She had been there some considerable time but without making much noticeable headway. There seemed to be no psychotherapy department or, if there was, I saw no sign of it.

The patients all ate together, male and female, in the enormous refectory hall with walls covered with gigantic Pre-Raphaelite-looking murals, which were really very fine, if a touch oppressive. There were long refectory tables and at meal-times one did see a few pretty unconventional-looking citizens. One man wandered about with his mouth open, snapping at imaginary flies. There was another, a member of the peerage, with a permanently unlit cigar clamped in his Churchillian jowls who was allowed out only with a minder, to stop him from a disconcerting habit of buying up blocks of flats. He used to sit with a copy of the *Financial Times*, staring at it as if mesmerized. I once noticed him holding it upside down.

Weather permitting, I used to exercise myself, walking round the extensive grounds. There occasionally I would see crocodiles of the ultra-mentally disturbed, who were kept more strictly segregated from us. And they were really very odd indeed. I was told also that there was a surprising number of doctors, as patients.

Indeed, there was much material for study, useful to actors of what my old godfather, Ernest Milton, would refer to as the *journalistic* school, meaning those who based their characterisations from a store of observation of their fellow-humans, instead of relying, as he always did, on inward inspiration. He was disparaging of the former category, but I have known actors of his school of thought, capable of performances of near-genius and equally of those, which were atrocious.

It might be thought that I would have found such a milieu as Holloway depressing. The truth is far from it. I spent seven weeks there in blissful freedom from my responsibilities or any emotional demands, either real or imaginary. I had my car so I could get about. I often went with David for a meal in Egham or thereabouts, as the dietary regime in Holloway was perfectly adequate but hardly imaginative. I had accumulated a few hospital chums of both sexes among the patients and we had a little party most evenings, with wine smuggled into my room. We were obliged to sit on the floor for this, so as to be well below the eye-line of the spy hole in the door.

David would ask, in his gentle and diffident way, "Are you having your usual soirée this evening?" There was not a great deal in his life to enjoy and I think he really looked forward to it.

Then one day, after seven weeks of respite, I was told that my wife had rung up, wanting urgently to speak to me. When I called back, she told me that Julian Belfrage, my agent, had been agitating to get hold of me, as I was wanted for a film, called *Patton*. This was to play General Freddie de Guingand, Montgomery's Chief of Staff. It was nothing very onerous, but it entailed location work for several weeks in Spain. By this time, I felt well enough to do it. In fact, I was able to look forward to it, as an extension of my sequestration from the domestic situation, at the same time keeping me occupied and, as much to the point, earning my bread.

Once in Spain, matters certainly looked up. I had always enjoyed the country and life on location there and the change gave my morale a much-needed boost.

Fortunately, my role as a British staff officer came across George C. Scott, in the title role, hardly at all. He was not an easy man and a very hard drinker, who expected those around him to follow his example, in this latter respect, at least. Noticing that I did not welcome this, he found me stand-offish and referred to me, so I heard, as, "That bloody Englishman". I seem to have encountered a few noticeably hard-drinking leading actors, mainly in films: Harris, Burton, and now Scott, although Burton was never a nuisance and certainly never let it interfere with his work.

Scott, on the other hand, was sometimes so drunk that he had to be propped up to prevent him from falling flat on his face. On occasions, they had to shoot without him, someone else reading his lines, while they shot on Karl Maldon as General Bradley, who was ever reliable, a lovely fellow and a great film actor.

I cannot think how it was managed but when the film came out, it was a great success with none of Scott's shortcomings, in the smallest way, evident. His performance was, I have to say, quite magnificent and a tribute, I would guess, to the genius and infinite patience of Fleischer, the director.

When the filming was finished and I returned to England, I had to report back to Holloway for a check-up. I tried to find David, but was told that he had gone and no-one seemed to know where. Remembering that eviction from his institutional life had been his greatest dread, I was saddened not to find him there. However, I felt that he had moved on and would, quite possibly, not welcome pursuit by a former fellow-inmate of the *Bin*, as we used to call it. I never saw him again.

Briefly to return to Ambrose, I met him again quite by accident, many years after all this, in a restaurant in Suffolk. He was with someone who was certainly not his wife and I gathered his marriage was over and he was living with another woman. I was sorry to hear it, of course, but remembering my endurance of years of rabbinical finger-wagging, I could not help thinking, "Physician: heal thyself".

I was saddened to see Belita's obituary in *The Times* in 2007.

One of the more pleasant memories of her: I had never seen her dance (she had been one of Anton Dolin's principal dancers, in the Ballets Russes de Monte Carlo), nor had I seen her skate, which was, after all, her principal claim to fame. When I told her, more than once, how much I regretted this omission, she was always adamant. She had finished with it and, towards the end of her skating career, when she had been packing the Wembley Stadium, night after night, she had actually come to hate it.

One day, however, much to my surprise, she suddenly said, apropos of nothing, that she would take me to the Queen's Ice Rink in Bayswater and go through a few of her old routines. There we found several members of the Olympic Team, doing their training sessions. Belita took herself to the other end of the ice and slowly began a few figures. These gradually gathered momentum until the Olympic Team broke off their training and watched her, open-mouthed. She ended her performance with a spin at such speed that her whole body became a blur, which she broke off to the team's spontaneous applause, and glided towards me, extending her hands as she approached to show me the fine veins that had burst in this last manoeuvre. She had, of course, been the youngest ever member of the Olympic Team herself but, as she had not skated for years, it was a pretty astonishing performance.

This episode with Belita was, I am ashamed to say, not the beginning or end of my many regrettable transgressions. Liz, who had been superhumanly long-suffering, at last told me she would have to divorce me. She had quite definitely *not* felt like a sister and had suffered very much in consequence. It was with a heavy heart that I felt obliged to concur.

I love her still, although she is no longer of this world, and feel very badly about my behaviour to her. Now, in old age, I can feel with the late-George Melly who said, when asked how it feels to be impotent, "It's like being unchained from a lunatic".

17

El Cid 1960/1

This was a most ambitious venture, involving literally a *cast of thousands*. Almost half the Spanish Army was engaged as extras, earning no more than the pittance of their regular army pay. Charlton Heston was the eponymous hero and, opposite him, Sofia Loren was cast as Jimena. I had the role of Moutamin, Emir of Saragossa, an actual historical character who, after his life had been spared by Roderigo de Vivar, gave him the name and title, El Cid, by which he became known to Moors and Spaniards alike to this day.

A large number of well-known British and Italian actors played other prominent parts, as did the Americans. The film was lavishly dressed, with costumes made from specially-woven period fabrics from Florence. The sets were stupendously extravagant, designed and built with apparent total disregard of cost, which, even in those days, must have been colossal. However, as Sam Bronston, the producer, appeared to have a bottomless purse, it was hardly for us to worry.

Any member of the cast who might have a week or so free was flown home and back, if he so wished, first class; otherwise he or she could remain in Spain. The most generous expenses and salary were unaffected, either way. As I have mentioned elsewhere, I had taken Belita with me, which was a big mistake.

All the battle sequences were to be filmed at Peniscola, near Valencia. The fortress there was renovated, again at vast expense, and was substantial enough to appear for the siege of Valencia itself.

As the local hotels were deemed unworthy of us, the cast and crew were stationed in a much grander establishment in Castellion de la Plana, a good 50 miles away. This involved getting up well before sunrise and travelling in Heston's car, there and back, during which time he and I were able to take the world apart, including the film itself. There was no nonsense about him. I found him easy to talk to and we got on very well: so much so that seeming to wish to continue our converse, he would invite Belita and me to dinner with him and his wife, either in the hotel or, more usually, in one or other of the local restaurants.

As time went on, I began to feel the strain of the seemingly endless battles and very often felt more like going straight to bed. To compound my growing fatigue, there were almost as many domestic battles with Belita and I had begun to wish I had left her in England. The days were long and arduous, very much of the time in the saddle, either in cavalry charges led by the seemingly-indefatigable Heston, or beside him, in hand-to-hand sword fights. My role as his ally meant whenever Chuck was in the thick of the fighting, there I had to be also. As he insisted on doing everything without a double, so that the camera could come in close, my double was likewise almost unused. It had also begun to be very hot, which was not a help either.

The close shots of the fighting were, of course, very carefully orchestrated and much rehearsed. In charge of this department was a famous Italian sword-master, a delightful man called Enzo Museumeci-Greco. He put us all through our paces, over and over again. It would not have done to have had too many accidents, at least as far as the principals were concerned. Tony Mann, the director, was rather less particular with the *lesser mortals* and the horses, I noticed.

During the early part of the filming in the Madrid studios, there was, full-time on the pay-roll, an expert on medieval warfare. The moment we moved to the battle location, the director, about whom I was beginning to have some doubts, decided to dispense with his services and to run the whole show himself. The man was got rid of and sent back to England forthwith. Tony Mann presumably believed that his experience in the making of endless Westerns would now stand him in good stead.

It soon turned out he was wrong.

The battles appeared spectacular, certainly, but this was largely by sheer weight of the numbers involved, hundreds of horses and thousands of men; but as to any overall strategy, they were a total muddle. He would order a cavalry charge, usually involving Chuck and myself, followed almost at once by the discharge of enormous flights of arrows and, more unpleasantly, catapulted fire-balls of flaming tar which, owing to Mann's chaotic sense of timing, would rain down upon us as, quite literally, *friendly fire*.

It seemed quite the reverse at the time as I raced at full-gallop (it had to be always full-gallop) towards the enemy, cursing and swatting drops of hot tar from the back of my neck. These engagements were every bit as dangerous as they looked, largely due to our director's increasingly *gung-ho* attitude. He began taking unnecessary risks and, after each take, he would repeat it again and again.

After he had rejected the rubber tips to the levelled lances, bawling, "Take 'em away. I want steel," the ambulance men were kept pretty busy after each take, as was the veterinary department. After each of these repeated forays, the ground became more and more churned up, causing horses to fall with their riders, with inevitably dire results.

On one such occasion, when we were told to go yet again, we were working on swampy ground and the *going* had become increasingly heavy. I said to Chuck, "Why don't you tell him to stow it?"

Chuck looked at me grimly and said, "I guess he wants to get it right". I noticed after the take he rode over to the camera crane and said something to Mann, and we did not do it again.

By this time, I was beginning, understandably perhaps, to doubt our director's sanity. He was certainly a strange character, having an apparently great respect for the talents of the British actors, coupled with an irresistible desire to lose no opportunity for humiliating them. I saw him, on one or two occasions, dishing out this treatment, somewhat obliquely, even to Chuck who simply shrugged it off.

The only reason that I could see for the man's unacceptable conduct was that he had fairly recently married a well-known Spanish pop star, very much younger than himself. I understood that she had expected, as a result, to become a Hollywood star and when it dawned upon her that this was unlikely, the lady had *cut up decidedly rough* and, after giving him hell, had locked him out of their house in Madrid, causing him to take an apartment elsewhere. For whatever reason, I believe most of us found him difficult to like.

Finally an incident occurred which brought me not very much credit. In the curious way of film making, my first appearance in the film was the very last to be shot of me on the location. This was the scene where, having been captured on a church-burning raid, I and other Moors were brought before Heston in the person of Roderigo de Vivar, bloodied and bruised, with my arms tied to a heavy piece of timber, behind my head, like a yoke, in a travesty of a crucifixion. The crowd of extras, after stoning me, were baying for my death.

Roderigo, having accepted an oath from me, never again to attack Christians, granted me my life whereupon I gave him the honorific of *El Cid*, vowing my allegiance to him, should he have need of it.

Prior to the actual filming, a tip-truck had decanted a large load of hard balls, painted to resemble stones with which, when the assistant-director blew a whistle and called, "Action", the crowd were to pick up and *stone* me. They were quite hard enough, when thrown with force, as they were directed to do. This was a procedure which seemed to please Tony Mann greatly, as he ordered take after take to be made. This continued, off and on, for about two hours. I bore it, but with rising anger.

He then approached me and said, "Now I'm coming in real close and a rock is gonna hit you in the face and you don't blink or flinch, because you're a *prince*. Understand?"

I said, "Prince or no, he's still a human being and no-one can be hit in the face without some reaction."

"Why not?" he snarled, "You're supposed to be an ACTOR, aren't you?"

I had been temporarily released from my yoke. "Could *you* do it?" I said.

"Sure I could," he barked.

"Right then, DO it." I had picked up the nearest *stone* and I hurled it at him.

He leapt in the air, clapping his hand to his face, "CHRIST!" he yelled. "You got me right in the fuckin' eye!" Heston and all the others melted away, leaving me with Tony Mann, who was dancing with rage and screaming, "You'll never fuckin' work again. I'll have your name blackened all over!"

I was regretting my temporary loss of control, but a bit too late. The die, not to say the stone, was already cast.

I was clearly finished, not only in the film itself, but also in my entire career. One does not throw stones at a top Hollywood director and get away with it.

After an interval, while he presumably received first aid, and his rage abated somewhat, to my surprise, he approached me and said, "Now we're gonna do that shot".

The set-up completed, he came up close to me, just out of shot, and flipped the *stone* at my face with his own fair hand. Just one take: no repeats.

My career might be over but at least I felt I had made my point. Whether I flinched or not, I have no idea. Feeling pretty shattered and as that, fortunately, was my last scene to be shot in the film, I went to say goodbye to my fellow actors. They had heard about the dreadful incident and were absolutely delighted. They had all been longing to punch him in the face for months.

When I got back to London, Maud Spector, the all-powerful casting-director on the film, wanted to see me. I went, with not a little apprehension, to her office. She had certainly heard about it and, to my surprise, seemed much amused and wanted to hear more about it, straight from the horse's mouth, so to speak.

Later when Tony Mann had rough-cut the film, I was sent for. My presence was required at the sound studios in Soho for *post-synching*. He was there and when I enquired about the film, he replied, "It's a great picture, a great picture … or at any rate, a good one". No mention of my misdemeanour.

For his next film, *The Fall of the Roman Empire*, he chose only two actors from *El Cid*: Sofia Loren and, to my utter amazement, *me*!

I have not said very much about Sofia Loren, because my contacts with her were not numerous, but she always appeared good-humoured, witty and amusing, untemperamental and highly professional. I liked her and got to know her much better in Mann's next venture.

She did not enjoy playing opposite Heston. As she frankly told me, there was no *chemistry* between them and she had no direction from Mann. Everyone seemed to think it was enough to be Sofia Loren and to drift through the film, looking soulfully beautiful. She needed direction and she knew it. With good directors, like Da Sica and other top Italians, she could be wonderful, as she was in *The Women*, but with Mann she seemed listless and ineffectual, although always spectacular to look at.

Her very last shot in *El Cid* was a twosome, cross-cutting with Chuck. They first did the close-ups on her: the scene was supposed to be a tenderly touching farewell and he loyally spoke all his lines for her, off-screen and of course out of shot. This was a solo on her. Then when it came to the reverse solo on Chuck, it was assumed that she would do likewise for him. I was watching them and, much to my surprise, as soon as her own close-ups were finished, she turned on her heel and left. Poor Chuck was left to do all his emoting with a male Spanish assistant-director, inexpertly reading her lines.

In view of her usual high professional standards, I thought this unworthy of her. She went to her car and was driven back to her apartment in Madrid. As she got out of the car, she slipped and fell, unhappily breaking her wrist. I rang a day or so later, to ask how she was and spoke to a charming Italian, who turned out to be Carlo Ponti, her husband who had been summoned from Rome.

Her antipathy to Chuck was, of course, partly his fault. He never paid her the smallest attention. He and his wife Lydia never had her to a meal, never sent any flowers and, as far as he was concerned, off-screen she did not exist. I drew his attention to it more than once and he finally told me that he had made it a rule, never to *date* his leading ladies: or any ladies, for that matter. He told me that in his early days he had become seriously entangled with one of them and when Lydia found out about it, her reaction had been extreme and alarming. His determinations in that direction probably accounted for the sanitised lack of chemistry with Sofia.

The same problem beset him in his later brave attempt at Shakespeare's *Antony and Cleopatra*.

I finished work on *El Cid* with very mixed feelings. It had been exhausting and in many ways unnecessarily trying but I was genuinely sorry to say goodbye to the Hestons as I had become very fond of them both.

18

Charlton Heston

I had first met Charlton Heston on the set of *El Cid*, in Chamartin studios in Madrid and, as I got to know him very well, I have often been asked, usually by women, what he was like. I have always had difficulty in finding words to describe him, in brief, without sounding trite.

Over the months that I worked with him, on three different films, I have to say that I always had a good and companionable relationship with him, and counted him as a true and reliable friend. He was always most kind and generous to me in particular, and in very many different ways. He was always inviting me to dinner, with Lydia, his charming wife, after the day's shooting, or later on at the Dorchester whenever he came to London and refused any return, except when he came to dinner sometimes at our house in Campden Street.

He was also generous professionally, frequently telling me (as an actor young in films, as I was in *El Cid*) of Anthony Mann's plan for shooting a scene and how I could make the best of it, sometimes at his own expense. He once told me, as an instance of this, to edge my horse around, in a mounted two-shot of us both, "It's important for them to see your face at this point. Tony's not cross-cutting close-ups. They should know what *I* look like by now. This shot should favour you."

Not many big stars would do that, I believe.

He was punctilious and highly professional, taking endless trouble with foresightedness. When having a fitting for one of his costumes, he would make sure that it allowed him the necessary freedom of movement for the actions required in that particular sequence. I once told him that he was most *workman-like* in his approach, at which he did not look too happy, saying that the epithet implied dullness.

I told him that I had known only one actor, who was even more *workman-*

like and that was Laurence Olivier which delighted him, of course, as Larry was, in his eyes, almost greater than God. He had much respect for British actors, whom he considered, quite rightly, to be the best in the world, and in particular Larry himself.

It is true that Heston had a marked and almost puritanical streak, invaluable in his portrayals of men of heroic and sterling character but which seemed, in some curious way, to *sanitise* his love-scenes. He was cautious, but once he knew exactly what he was doing, he was as brave as a lion, insisting on doing practically all his own stunts, as he wanted to work close enough to the camera for it to be visibly him and not a stunt man, working the scene. This frequently caused me some anxiety, not only on his account, but also my own. All my work in *El Cid* was in close conjunction with him. Any situations of danger, and in that film there were many, I was obliged, willy-nilly, to share.

In spite of the confidence, borne of much successful experience and intrinsic in one in his situation, he had, in many ways, a most disarming humility. As a veteran in the business of epics, he would give a word or two of filmic advice, but always in a companionable way. In no way would he patronise. Indeed, with his great respect for traditional British acting, he was not above accepting the occasional word of advice himself. I could, for an instance, tell him that sticking his thumbs in his belt was, perhaps, not a good idea, as it did not look *period*, and he would accept it and, if he thought I was right, he would act on it.

During the filming of the battles, he once asked me if I had ever seen *The Ten Commandments*. I had to confess I had not, whereupon he told me he had heard it was on, dubbed into Spanish of course, at a flea-pit cinema in a neighbouring one-horse town and would I come with him to see it? When I demurred on the genuine grounds of exhaustion, he looked so disappointed that I felt I should make the effort and go with him. Also, I had heard it was very long and not totally lacking in tedium; however I kept that to myself. I did say, was it not a very long film and what about our beauty-sleep? We did, after all, have to get up well before dawn for the interminable *battles* next day.

He assured me that we would stay only for the first hour of the film so I agreed to go with him. We found the place after a fairly long drive and sat through the first hour, during which I had some little difficulty in staying awake. I nudged him and pointed to my watch but he was clearly enthralled, saying that there was just one more bit he would like me to see and then we could go. The *one more bit* came and went and still we sat on. After another half hour, I protested with rather more vehemence, so he tore himself away, put me into his car and told the driver to take me back to the hotel and then come back for him.

He obviously was determined to see the whole damned thing, which I thought a trifle inconsiderate to his most obliging Philipino driver. He did much the same thing when he came to our house in London, leaving his driver outside the house while he stayed chatting until really very late after dinner. These little acts of inconsideration, I found strangely out of character; but then, as has been said before, no-one is absolutely perfect.

Often, probably in an effort to save my own skin as much as anything else, I would remonstrate with him in his patience with Tony Mann's predilection for endless re-takes of dangerous sequences, but he remained loyally obstinate. It had to be right.

Mann took tremendous risks with him and, if anything had gone wrong, it would have shipwrecked the entire film; but then Tony Mann was not over-burdened with imagination.

The two of us always had long conversations in the car on the way to the battlefields and I remember more than once Chuck mentioning his ambition to play Antony in Shakespeare's *Antony and Cleopatra* on film, a role he was convinced that he was born to play. We all have our blind spots and, in my view, this was one of his. Almost everything about him radiated the reverse of Antony and all he represented: his clean-living, athletic appearance and his almost puritanical turn of mind.

Chuck was careful, almost frugal, whereas Antony is reckless and extravagantly self-indulgent. Antony is a louche voluptuary; Chuck was the picture of the model hero, who never seemed to look at any woman, other than his wife. All are admirable traits but hardly a personality recommendation for the role of Antony, a man undone by passion and his appetites. I have no idea where the financial backing came from but, eventually, in 1972 the opportunity to set it up occurred. His dream had at last come true.

So he approached his old friend Franklyn Schaffner and asked him to direct, which, for some reason, he was unable to do, suggesting that Chuck could direct it himself.

When Chuck questioned the wisdom of this, Schaffner had said, "Sure. Why not? Nothing to it".

Following the example of his idol, Olivier, in Shakespearian films, he approached Julian Glover, who was almost the same height as himself, with a view to directing him, as a sort of *alter ego*, and then taking his place for the actual shooting. He also offered him the role of Proculeius for himself. Julian learnt the part of Antony and all was ready for the *off*. I was far too old by then to play the part I would have liked, which was *the boy Caesar*, so I made do with the unrewarding role of Agrippa. It meant another location in my beloved Spain and I liked the opportunity of working with Heston again. Hildegard Neil, a strikingly attractive, if somewhat un-Mediterranean-looking actress, was cast as Cleopatra and my old friend Eric Porter, as Enobarbus.

Chuck had decided to keep all the sequences with Cleopatra to be filmed *en bloc* at the end, leaving him free to concentrate on all the Roman sequences first. This unfortunately meant that, for the weeks that we were out on location, Hildegard was left to her own devices in Almeria, not being used at all and pretty well alone. This was, from her point of view, not a good idea. She became unhappy and, I should imagine, pretty bored.

Chuck, in his usual fashion, took not the slightest notice of her and she began to feel that he must dislike her. The occasional bunch of flowers might have helped; or even a call to ask after her well-being, but not a bit of it; he was totally preoccupied with the task in hand. He had his wife with him so without compromising his principles too much, they could have had her out to dinner once or twice. They asked me out often enough. She could easily have been invited to join us.

Her well-being, as leading actress in the film, should have had some attention. She was not, after all, experienced in starring roles in films and was, most probably, more than a touch apprehensive. I put this to him, telling him that I had heard that was how she felt. His face became set and obstinate. "She has no reason to think I dislike her," was all he said.

That was that. The subject was closed. I am sure that this state of affairs could hardly fail to have had an adverse effect on their combined chemistry, never his strongest point at the best of times, when they came at long last to working their scenes together.

I remembered Sofia's remarks from *El Cid*. I believe that she had suffered from a similar state of things as Hildegard, but she was in a very much stronger position.

The film when it came out received, for the most part, lukewarm reviews with praise for Enobarbus, a fine performance as usual by Eric Porter, and I think Chuck collected some good marks for a brave attempt.

Many years later, Chuck and I found ourselves simultaneously on different assignments in Rome: I don't remember what they were. We met a few times for dinner. His film finished before mine and he invited me to the end-of-film unit dinner, which took place in a very hot restaurant in Rome. It was some time in the summer: the year also escapes me. The private room was packed with the entire film unit and it was sweltering.

He was seated at a very long table, some way away from me and I was sitting next to Lydia. After a perusal of the menu, she said, "Oh, they've got oysters!" I said that she was surely not thinking of eating oysters in that heat, but she was. She had half a dozen of them.

Half an hour or so later, Chuck was on his feet making a farewell speech when Lydia clutched my hand and said, "God, I feel so sick!" She had changed colour. "I'm going to throw up," she muttered. I got her up somehow and we found our way to an alleyway with dustbins, where she did indeed throw up, while I held her head and supported her against the wall.

"You're a soldier," she gasped, between spasms.

I got her to their car, put her in and went to get Chuck who, oblivious of her plight, was chatting to someone. He came out at once. I got into the car with them and we set off for wherever it was they were staying. As we were driving along the Tiber, an unhappy Lydia had to tell Chuck a couple of times on route to get the driver to stop while she fed the fish in the river.

I rang next day to ask how she was and, as she appeared to have recovered, we arranged to meet for a quiet dinner somewhere. They neither of them ever referred to it at all.

I believe that was the last time I saw them, although we corresponded from time to time. Then it dwindled to exchanging Christmas cards and finally faded out in the way things can when one does not meet for many years.

I was greatly saddened to hear of his long illness, some time ago, and even more saddened by his subsequent death.

Whenever Chuck had came to London in later years, I was living in Suffolk and I was either too idle or unwilling to go more than was strictly necessary up to town. I sometimes wish, in retrospect, that I had gone to see him in *A Man for All Seasons*, as I later heard he was very good in it. At the time, I could not envisage anyone in the role after seeing Scofield.

I should have made the effort, if only for old time's sake. I know he would have appreciated it.

An instance of his kindness and concern occurred one Sunday when Belita and I went to a bullfight in Castellon, during the filming of *El Cid*. It was a particularly hot and sunny day and the ring was packed even though the matadors were not well-known. There was the usual sense of slight dread, mingled with excitement.

Two of the six bulls were dispatched with no very great show of skill and, in the third, the matador, at the *moment of truth*, lunged at a vague area over the shoulder, leaving the bull still very much alive. It was trotting unhappily round the ring, clattering the banderillas and mooing pathetically, the sword still sticking upright from its back. The crowd had begun to boo.

One of the cuadrilla managed to get close enough to yank the sword out and return it to the matador who made four more attempts, each one with the same sickening result. By this time the bull was tottering and the crowd was booing its head off. The matador, green in the face, turned to them, shoulders shrugged, mouth open and arms wide apart, as if to say, "What now?" The president ordered on the butchery department, four men with knives, who finally dispatched the unhappy animal.

While this was happening and in spite of continual booing, unbelievably, the matador, started a *tour of triumph*, round the ring.

We were seated in about the third row of the *Sol y Sombra*, immediately behind a row of army officers. As the matador strutted past us, with arms raised in triumph, (I don't know how I came to do it), quite involuntarily, I hurled my cushion at his head. It was obviously my year to be throwing things. Four policemen converged on me and I was removed through the *entrada* to the promenade under the stands, my passport demanded and details taken.

It appears that the previous year a matador had been killed, not by the bull, but by a lemonade bottle, which had hit him behind the ear and a law had been passed, forbidding the throwing of any object whatsoever into the ring. I had clearly contravened this law and the police were looking unfriendly when

Heston, who had seen what had happened from the other side of the ring, made his way through the crowd, with the Spanish unit manager, to come to my rescue. They explained that I was English, and therefore not quite right in the head, that I was sorry and a very agreeable person really.

So, instead of arresting me, they said I could go back to my seat on the undertaking that I throw nothing else. I expressed my thanks to Chuck and made my way back to the ring.

As I reached the *Entrada*, I heard the sound of applause. "Sod's law," I thought. "I've missed something spectacular!" But that, it turned out, had nothing to do with it. They were applauding my re-entry. I clearly had popular support.

As I re-seated myself on the hard concrete tier, minus the offending cushion, the army officers in the row in front, turned and actually congratulated me on my action, saying that I had been quite right, it had been a dreadful performance and that I was "a true Spaniard", inviting us for a drink after the last bull.

We had seen enough for one day. I thanked them but, pleading urgent business elsewhere, hustled Belita, who had been much amused at my plight, out of the ring and back to our hotel.

So much for provincial bull-fights. But I was very grateful to Chuck.

19

The Fall of the Roman Empire

As I have already alluded to my great surprise at finding myself the only actor from *El Cid*, apart from Sofia Loren, to be cast in this film (or indeed any other) after my last disastrous encounter with Anthony Mann, I will not again labour the point.

Liz and I arrived in Madrid for all the necessary preambles, costume fittings and the like, and we had hardly entered our apartment when the phone rang.

A clipped and familiar voice said, "It's Alec ... Alec Guinness. Can you come to supper tonight?" I demurred and said we had hardly walked through the door when he rang. However, as he seemed strangely insistent, I became curious to know why.

At all events, he sent his car to pick us up later that evening, arriving at his palatial apartment shortly after. He and Merula opened the door to us and I saw Tony Quayle in the background. We all stood in the hall for no understandable reason, making awkward conversation for an unconscionably long time when, quite out of the blue, Alec turned and snapped sharply at poor Merula, "Are we going to stand here all night? When are you going to ask them in?"

Alec seemed shy of saying why he had so urgently wanted to see me and the first part of the evening was decidedly sticky. Quayle did his best with the chat until half way through dinner when, a certain amount of wine having gone down, Alec abruptly changed the subject. "Anthony Mann says you threw a rock in his eye. That's surely not true is it?"

"So *that* is what it was all about," I thought. I had to admit, alas, that it was perfectly true. They looked staggered.

Alec then told me that at their very first meeting to discuss the forthcoming production Mann had asked him if he knew a guy called Douglas Wilmer and that when Alec had said he did, Mann had astonished him, by saying I had thrown a rock in his eye. Tony Quayle said he had had the same question put to him. To both of them he had said, "The guy's crazy, y'know".

Alec then asked me what on earth had induced me to do such a thing. I thought it no bad thing for them to have some idea what Mann was like, which was, I believe, what Alec really wanted to know. So I gave them a brief run-down on our director's conduct on *El Cid*, culminating in the very regrettable event in question. I said I was sorry if I disappointed Alec, in any way, but after such a build-up of annoyance, suffered by me and the other British actors, almost throughout the film, something had suddenly snapped. I said that I thought it was unlikely that Mann would try it on with Alec but, since he had brought it up, it was no bad idea for them to be forewarned.

A formidable cast had been assembled, even for comparatively minor roles: Sofia Loren, James Mason, Omar Sharif, Stephen Boyd, Christopher Plummer and Mel Ferrer, to say nothing of Alec Guinness and Tony Quayle. Their fees alone, plus all the other costs, must have amounted to several millions of dollars. Such actors do not perform for peanuts, especially as the roles could have offered no particular inducement in themselves.

When the film was finished, it was, I believe, judged critically as "thoughtful and intelligent" but, in spite of Bob Krasker's brilliant camera work, it was a severe box-office flop and poor Sam Bronston was declared bankrupt. It finished his film career completely, after which, I later heard, he still went daily to his office, to sit behind his desk and simply stare at the wall.

I remember him as a pleasant and surprisingly unassuming little man, never much in evidence. Once I was standing among a bunch of actors and extras, watching a scene being filmed of the preparations for Sofia and Stephen Boyd to be burnt at the stake as Christians, when a quiet voice greeted me. It was Sam. He asked me how I was and then, with an amused smile, he added, "You have not thrown anything yet?"

So it appeared that, even though it had reached the ears of the great Movie-Mogul himself, Tony Mann's dire predictions for my future had been unfounded.

The scene we were watching had been brought forward in the shooting schedule and the costumes for the extras who were to be burnt as fellow Christians with Sofia and Stephen Boyd were not yet ready. When Mann was informed of this, he yelled, "C'mahn! C'mahn! Dress 'em up in *anything* - dress 'em up as *Christians*, for Chrissakes - you know, like *Judas* or somebuddy!"

He was very much of a *broad brush* director, relying on, though without taking much apparent interest, the great set and costume design team, Colosanti and Moore, combined with a wonderful cameraman, Robert Krasker, to work out the finer points. It may have had something to do with having made so many Westerns.

There was a scene in the script, where Eric Porter and I were described as driving a chariot apiece at full tilt down a narrow and winding mountain road for a longish way over what turned out, when we got there, to be thickly-packed ice.

There was also a sheer unprotected drop on one side to the valley below.

We were shooting high in the Guaderrama Mountains which, in deep winter, were not exactly the Malvern Hills. When I first came across this in the script, I naively assumed that some form of chariot training would be arranged beforehand. As the weeks went on, I mentioned this repeatedly to the Spanish assistant-director, always to be told, "Perhaps tomorrow".

Well, needless to say, the notorious Spanish tomorrow, *mañana*, never dawned until one day at lunch in the marquee, Tony Mann's voice bawled, "Wilner" - he never troubled himself to get our names right - " How's yer chariot-driving?"

"I don't know," I replied, "I've never tried it."

"Well, now's yer chance to find out," he said.

The dreaded scene had been brought forward and I thought I detected a malicious gleam in his eye. Was this, I wondered, how he was to exact revenge for the *rock* I had thrown at him?

Eric and I were put into a car and driven what seemed a long way up the icy mountain road. It was then that I noticed, with some misgivings, the fearsome drop and unprotected edge on one side. When we reached the high-up starting point, there were two chariots, one for Eric, which was hitched directly on to the camera car and one for me, hitched to two horses. Eric had no horses to bother about, but had to appear as if he had by simulated driving and holding the reins in an appropriate manner. A piece of cake, in other words.

I, on the other hand, was to drive close behind him, slightly to one side, I and my pair of horses being in full view for the duration of the *take*. We were told to look as if we were enjoying it.

Yakima Knut, the famous Hollywood stuntman and horse trainer was up there, rubbing his chin and not looking too happy about it. He knew, of course, that I had never attempted the chariot before. He said, "Just keep it away from the edge, that's all".

I said that surely the horses would see that they kept well away from the edge. He looked dubiously at me and remarked that one horse might do that but not necessarily a pair.

"Horses are stoopid animals," he said, "and when there are two of them, each one relies on the other. It's a bum deal, so just *keep 'em away from the edge*".

The director arrived and told me to keep close behind Eric and the camera car, and to love every moment of the drive. It was to be YIPPEE time! Hmmm.

I climbed into my chariot and Eric into the comparative safety of his. The camera-car moved off, with Eric attached. I giddy-upped or whatever got the horses going and we were off and gathering speed. I noticed the iron wheels slithering on the hard ice. I did my best to look happy as I noticed Tony's beady eyes on me just behind the camera. He was looking a tiny bit tense. He knew that the camera-car was unlikely to go over the edge ... but horses? Well?

After what seemed longer than was comfortable and a slither or two, by God's grace we at last reached the bottom intact. Feeling rather more than relieved, I dismounted from the chariot and walked over to Tony on the camera-car. Knowing his propensity for re-takes of anything either unpleasant or dangerous, I asked him if he wanted to go again. He eyed me sourly.

"No," he said, "I don't think we should push your luck *too* far."

Yakima, the head stuntman, came over and said, "You did great". Tony made no comment at all. In the final *cut* of the film, this hair-raising sequence was nowhere to be seen. Cut out. So perhaps my inward terror was more apparent than I had thought. Or perhaps the sequence was never intended to be in.

On the subject of horses, my introduction to Christopher Plummer, who was to play Commodus, the son and heir to the Emperor (Alec Guinness), was at a riding school somewhere in Buckinghamshire, well before filming started. When I arrived for my first practice, I saw him on a very quiet nag, on a leading rein ambling round and round at one end of the indoor riding school. He was looking most unhappy. He was being encouraged by the riding-master and it looked as if the latter would have his work cut out. Chris later told me that he had never been on a horse in his life and that he did not take to the idea one bit. He hated horses, in fact.

As a patrician and future Emperor of Rome, he would be required to appear perfectly *at home* in the saddle and this, at the time, looked far from likely. However, Chris had courage and great determination, and his teachers had patience so eventually he was able to cut a considerably more than presentable figure on a horse.

There was something very likeable about him, in spite of his unmistakable awareness of his own importance and, when in vino, his occasional lapses from generally acceptable behaviour. He was a most impressive actor of great flamboyance and *dash* and had an inner sensitivity. He was musical and a talented pianist and, in the right frame of mind, he was lively and fun to be with. This was fortunate for me as he appeared to like me and, from what I remember of the film itself, as Eric and I were playing his *side kicks*, much of my work in the film was in his immediate vicinity. To be liked is, of course, always endearing.

He was a dedicated actor who was undaunted by the myriad of difficulties inherent in any action movie, as in the instance of overcoming his fear of horses. There was much to like and admire about him.

I had been allowed to choose my own mount for the film from a selection of handsome Hispano-Arabs. There was one that caught my eye at once: a coal-black stallion, called Infante (meaning prince). He looked pretty fiery, with plenty of *go* and I asked the horse-master if he thought I could manage him. He said that, once we became used to each other, he thought I could. Liz, who was still in Madrid, took one look at the animal, which was impatiently stamping and pawing the ground, and tried to dissuade me but I felt sure Infante was the one for me and I decided to have him.

He turned out to be wonderful horse and I used to take him out for long rides in the surrounding country to get him used to me and, of course, vice versa.

At the end of the film, I had the opportunity to buy him and bring him back to England but, upon enquiry, all the livery stables I approached refused to countenance housing a stallion, as they said it would cause havoc with their mares. I told them that he was only interested in donkeys, which from my experience of him was the truth. Unfortunately I was not believed, so very sadly I had to leave him in Spain.

As a great deal of riding was involved in this film, much of it over difficult terrain, it was necessary for the best of us to keep up with our practice. This was done under the watchful eye of the Master of Horse, a former Austrian Imperial cavalryman, known as Friedrich Lederbur or, to give him his full style, Count Friedrich von Lederbur-Wicheln. He was a spectacular specimen of aristocratic manhood: six foot four in height with the face of a craggy Louis Mountbatten, piercing light blue eyes and a thick shock of gray hair. He also had delightful manners.

As we were filming in the Guaderrama Mountains in the depth of winter, much of the riding had to be done in thick snow and ice. One of Friedrich's tasks was to instruct and keep a watchful eye on us during practice. I got on very well with him and often enjoyed riding with him in the surrounding mountains, despite the severe wintry weather. I was trotting alongside him over what turned out to be a long sheet of ice, under the snow, when I foolishly decided to give Infante, who was eager to go, his head.

I broke into a gallop. Friedrich yelled, "Darklas! Darklas! Don't gallop your horse!" followed a moment later by, "Darklas - don't run after your horse!"

Infante had slithered and I had come off, luckily getting away with a few bruises.

Later on in Madrid, when Friedrich's English wife came out to see him, I had them both to dinner. She was formerly Iris Tree, the daughter of Sir Herbert Beerbohm Tree, the celebrated actor/manager. She was once a well-known wit, poet/painter, eccentric and so-called adventuress. She had modelled for Augustus John, Vanessa Bell, Duncan Grant and all the other Bloomsbury painters and she knew everyone.

She was formidable, but vastly entertaining and Friedrich visibly cowered under her frequently scornful glance. I once took them on a shopping spree in my car when she commanded me to stop. She sent Friedrich into the shop and when he returned empty-handed, she snapped, "Friedrich can do NOTHING! NOTHING! NOTHING!" Poor Friedrich. Not surprisingly, I heard later, they were divorced and I feel sure that they were better value apart.

I saw him only once after the film was finished. That was at the première in London. He was immaculate in his bottle-green, silver-buttoned, Austrian dress-suit. After that, he went back to Austria and I lost track of him.

Sofia also had to do a certain amount of riding in the film which presented no problem for her as she was an excellent horsewoman and very much enjoyed it. She, Friedrich and I frequently went off into the snowy mountains, riding just for the pleasure of it. She was amusing, occasionally wickedly so and, needless to say, not the slightest bit grand. I liked her very much.

Marooned, as we all were, in the hotel in Segovia, otherwise empty for the winter, she decided one day to send to Italy for a suitcase-full of pasta, the quality of which, she declared, had no equal anywhere in Spain. The following Sunday, having arranged to take over the entire kitchens of the hotel, she rolled up her sleeves and cooked pasta and made all the sauces for the lot of us. She had also sent for a couple of cases of a very good Chianti to wash it all down. It was a delicious change from the *sameyness* of the hotel menu and all the more appreciated because of the trouble she had taken for us. I cannot see many women in her situation, bothering to do such a thing.

Sofia was a trouper and a comrade. But I noticed that she was careful not to get too close to any particular one of us.

I have often been asked what she was like. I can only say that she was fun to be with but, from what I could see from working with her on two consecutive films, her undoubted glamour and allure were reserved strictly for her screen persona. Off-stage, as it were, she seemed almost to make a point of shedding it all and appearing as un-sexy as she possibly could by wearing little or no make-up, jeans and a shapeless cardigan. One completely forgot the film star, as she metamorphosed simply into being one of us.

One evening, to celebrate something or other, we had a party with a disco and I do not believe she danced with any man. She certainly danced, but either on her own or with her stand-in or the continuity *girl*, a lady of uncertain years. How she managed this, heaven alone knows. I cannot believe that no-one asked her. I did not because dancing is most definitely not one of my talents. But I can remember Tony Mann's face, as he watched her with total bewilderment. I heard him say to someone, "Well, I dunno about Sofia, I guess now I've seen about everything". What exactly he meant, I had no idea.

She was not in the least unsociable. One Sunday morning, towards lunchtime,

I came into the hotel lounge and there was Sofia, as usual in jeans, her long hair down, lying on a sofa with her feet up. With her was a particularly tedious American woman journalist, grilling her, notebook in hand, and the equally tedious film publicist, hovering nearby. I got myself a drink from the bar and sat on the other side of the room. Sofia was looking understandably bored. She happened to catch my eye and almost imperceptibly flicked her own upwards.

After a bit, in a short lull in their conversation, I went over to her and told her that I had found a remote place, about half an hour away in the mountains where they cooked the most wonderful baby lamb. All very primitive: no plates even. It was plonked down before one on a plain wooden board, at a deal table, with a large jug of delicious cold rosé. Would she like me to drive her there? Her face lit up. Yes, she would love it.

Then I noticed a moment's hesitation and she turned to the journalist woman, from whose clutches I was intending a rescue, and asked her if she would like to come too. And then to the dreaded publicity man and, to my dismay, invited him as well as one or two others. I said my car would not take that lot. "That's OK," she said, "we'll go in mine." She had no intention of being seen to go off alone with any man was the message I understood. So I said I would tell her chauffeur how to find the place and follow on in my car. I gave the chauffeur directions, saw them all pile into Sofia's limo and then I went back to the hotel for my lunch. She never referred to my failure to appear, but I am sure that she knew the score.

One of her favourite activities was poker. She and three others usually played in the evenings before dinner. It was always the same school. One day, soon after the incident of the baby lamb, one of the poker players, with a name not unknown in this world, approached me confidentially and asked me if I had heard, at any time, that he was having an affair with Sofia?

I stared at him blankly and said no, I had not. Well, if I *did* hear, he went on, he could assure me that such a rumour was quite untrue and would I please say so? I told him I thought such a possibility most unlikely and I really wondered why he favoured me with such unwelcome confidence. I later discovered that he had similarly approached two or three other people with the same nonsense, each of them, in the "greatest confidence, you understand".

Heaven alone knows what he was up to. I can only imagine that he was hoping to *start* such a rumour.

If so, it backfired badly as, needless to say, it came to the ears of Miss Loren and that was the end of the poker school. She totally ignored the man from then onwards and seemed, while still perfectly friendly with the rest of us, even more circumspect than before. Perhaps the spirit of Carlo Ponti was breathing down her neck; she most certainly went very carefully to avoid any whiff of scandal, determined, like Caesar's wife, to remain "beyond reproach". I was surprised when, later on, she left Ponti for someone else. It seemed so very unlikely.

Much of my leisure time was spent with Eric Porter, exploring Segovia on foot and listening to events in his life. This was our location base, for filming most of the *mountain in winter* sequences, such as the funeral and cremation of the Emperor Marcus Aurelius, not forgetting the aforementioned *coming down the mountain chariot sequence.*

Eric was an amusing companion, highly intelligent and excellent company. Despite being generally cast in coldly patrician roles, such as Soames, in the *Forsyte Saga* and Karenin in *Anna Karenina*, and a towering King Lear at the National, his general manner in reality was both cockney and extremely *camp.*

He came from a humble background. His father had been a London bus driver and Eric told me, with a wry smile, that, on his retirement, as a reward for a lifetime's service, he had been presented with a cheap watch. It was odd to remember that in my first London assignment Eric had been in the company, playing small parts, such as page to Dunois in *St. Joan* and had actually understudied me as Tybalt. I remember that he played all his bits and pieces extremely well and since when he had progressed, predictably, from strength to strength. His early death was a great loss to the English stage.

We both got on very well with Alec Guinness, who was not quartered with us in the hotel in Segovia but was living, in fittingly lofty eminence, in a lovely old former priory on the edge of the town.

I found a large 17th century wine jug in an antique shop nearby, allegedly from the priory, when it was still in religious use. I still have it and it bears the word *Prior*, indicating a prodigious intake of wine, holding, as it does, nearly a gallon.

But to revert to Alec: I had met him from time to time in London, usually at the Blatchley's house. He and I were joint godfathers to their son (Merula

Guinness being Chattie Blatchley's sister). I had always mistaken his reserve for a cold and unfriendly nature but in this I was mistaken. I got to know him much better in Spain and I found the more one got to know him, the kinder and easier he seemed to become. But there was always that shield of initial reserve. I believe that he was extremely shy, not taking too easily to those he did not know very well.

In Madrid, I once cooked dinner for Alec, Eric and Mildred McCargar, our charming American production secretary, and we drank long, deep and far into the night, the evening becoming more and more hilarious.

At one point Alec was on all fours, his bent head nearly touching the floor, giving an impression of a Japanese waiter, tentatively presenting an outrageous bill: almost impossible to describe, but there was very much laughter.

The phone rang next morning and it was Alec. After thanks, he was brief and, apologising for his "appalling behaviour", he assured me it would not happen again. I said I was very sorry to hear that. He had retreated behind his shield of formal reserve. But this was early days. He became very much easier later on and, as he had a great *penchant* for the grander restaurants of Madrid (and elsewhere, as I later discovered), he often took Eric and me out on the town to dinner, unobtrusively paying the enormous bills for which he would accept no return.

A striking instance of his extraordinary kindness was when I had a fortnight free in Segovia and decided to fly home. This meant an overnight stop in Madrid. As I had given up my apartment there, he arranged for his chauffeur to drive me over the icy mountains, to his palatial abode, having laid on preparation, including a splendid evening meal. He also rang from Segovia later on, to ask if I had all I needed. Had they lit a fire for me and provided plenty of wine? They had.

On a table, beside an open copy of the script of the film, there was a large old-fashioned, double-spool tape-recorder, with the tape set, ready to go. I pressed the start button, to hear Alec's voice, speaking just one of his lines from the film - over and over again - each time, with the tiniest variations, which gave me a remarkable insight into his method of working.

It only later occurred to me that this could have been an unwarrantable intrusion into his privacy and I should not have done it. Fortunately it was not but it could easily have been and I regretted it. I record it here, at risk of showing myself in a poor light, because I believe it to be of some interest.

For reasons financial, it was preferred to get Alec's part of the film, which was all in any case in the first half, finished as soon as possible. So, he was released before most of the rest of us and the sad day came for him to say goodbye. I well recall him coming out on to the location, to do so. For some unfathomable reason, one actor, Stephen Boyd, starring opposite Sofia Loren, had always shown an antipathy towards him so that, when Alec approached him, to say that he hoped one day to have the pleasure of working with him again, Boyd was uncivil enough to make clear that this was not a hope shared by him.

I can see poor Alec now, standing in the winter sunshine, with his black trilby hat, long dark overcoat, and holding his blackthorn stick, looking pale and shattered by the man's unwarranted behaviour.

Soon after Alec had gone, I had a card from him, from Beynac in the Dordogne, thanking me for a recommendation to a hotel there, with a brief description of the drive from Spain and a P.S. "But, where is the waterfall?" It seems that, in a fit of aberration, I had told him that the hotel, which was on the bank of the river, had a waterfall nearby. On reflection, I do not think it did.

A short time after, while we were still on location, some three or four of us were detailed to stand by at lunch-time in the marquee where we ate, to sit at a separate round table with Sam Bronston, who was bringing two Spanish notables whose identity was as yet un-revealed, to visit the filming. The *notables* arrived, their identity revealed and we had a very enjoyable lunch with two very charming people.

Half way through lunch one of the British actors, George Murcell, and his wife, Elvie Hale, strolled into the marquee, late for lunch. Seeing two vacant chairs at our table, they sat themselves down, uninvited, and cheerfully joined the conversation, which somehow touched on the subject of bull-fighting. Elvie, who could be described, most kindly, as forthright and, perhaps, less kindly, as distinctly abrasive, voiced her opinion that no-one but a sadist could possibly like bull-fighting. Whereupon the Spaniard gently replied that his grandfather was one of the kindest of men and he was a great aficionado of the corrida. To this Elvie scornfully barked, "Oh? And what was *he*? A Picador?" There was a distinct frisson round the table.

"No," came the quiet reply, "he was the King of Spain."

A short silence followed. The couple, as the reader has most certainly guessed, were Prince Don Juan Carlos and his charming wife, Princess Sofia, the present King and Queen of Spain.

20

Cleopatra 1961 and Marco Polo

Some time in 1961 my agent rang to say I had been offered a part in the forthcoming film of *Cleopatra*, with Elizabeth Taylor, Rex Harrison and Richard Burton. The role was of no interest whatever. It was Decius Brutus, one of the conspirators and assassins of Caesar who appeared in quite a few of the Roman sequences.

However, the fee was good with a very generous daily expenses allowance. Also I loved Rome, where it was to be shot and where I was promised a lengthy stay, so I accepted the offer.

In Rome, I found myself an apartment in an old palace at the top of the Via Veneto, overlooking the Pincian Gate, with a fine view of the umbrella pines in the Borghese Gardens. I was able to hire from my landlady, an amiable German lady married to an Italian marchese, an old Alfa Romeo *banger*, in which I drove about Rome. I was in seventh heaven and the film seemed almost incidental, compared with the pleasure of living in what was then my favourite city.

The demands were few: mainly that I should stay where I was and where I was more than happy to be. I was called for filming a few times where I met up with quite a few of my chums and where, for the first time, I met Richard Burton.

During my first few days on the set, in the many and endless waits, I talked with him, as he seemed disposed to be friendly. We had a few old friends in common, principally David William, who had directed him in the O.U.D.S. (the Oxford University Dramatic Society), and who had bestowed on him the epithet, the *Peasant Prince*, which had apparently pleased him immensely.

During these lulls, which occur on every film set, we used to chat as we seemed to have plenty to talk about. He soon got into the habit of seeking me out whenever he knew I was on the set. I liked him very much and found him interesting, extremely well-read and highly intelligent. He had a most engaging manner, with a particular brand of humour which seemed to accord well with my own, and a wry and quirky slant on life in general.

His very Welsh-ness, when he talked of his early and impoverished life in the Rhonda Valley, I found particularly intriguing. He was entirely without pretension or any apparent self-consciousness. But when I told him of my dollop of Welsh blood on my mother's side, he snorted with amused derision, telling me that Pembrokeshire was not Wales: it was *Little England*. I believe he considered nothing unconnected with coal mines could really qualify as truly Welsh. Whenever he was with Sybil, his very sweet and lovely wife, the pair of them became very Welsh indeed. He was clearly very proud of it.

He was talking one evening about how his family were all miners and she ventured to say that her father was also one. He jumped on that at once. "Your Dad was *never a miner* - he was *above ground, the mine manager*," turning to me, he jerked a thumb humorously in her direction, adding, "So you see, I married the boss's daughter".

They always called each other *Beaut*, presumably a pet name for Beauty, which seemed to reflect a deep affection for each other. They had been allotted a large and very grand house on the Appian Way, a few kilometres outside the city walls, where I often went for a drink or two. Quite often they would ask me to stay to supper with them. It was always very easy and relaxed, with just the two of them. We would talk and drink and laugh a very great deal.

He was a great romancer and loved to relate anecdotes, many I suspect apocryphal, telling me once, in his cups, that he was not really Welsh at all. He was really a Polish Jew. I took this, at the time, to be a drunken flight of fancy but subsequently discovered that, on his maternal side, surprisingly enough, he did have some Jewish blood although how on earth a mining family, living in the Rhonda Valley, managed to acquire such a commodity, defies speculation. I am sure it was not through coal.

I soon began to be aware that Richard had a considerable capacity for the hard stuff, both before and after supper, which Sybil appeared not to notice. I never once saw her make the smallest attempt to restrain him and I was certainly incapable, myself, of keeping up with him. I had also the slight problem of driving home. But, of course, in those bad old days, no-one seemed too bothered by the perils of *drink and drive*. On more than one such occasion, he would regale us with hilarious accounts of his doings of the day with his leading lady who, so rumour had it, was beginning to take a rather more than purely professional interest in him. This, it seemed, was a subject merely for mirth and the anecdotes were always shared with Sybil.

He once, on a more serious note, said of the lady, "She's a bloke, you know. She's not a woman at all."

Miss T. certainly bore this out, by her behaviour and salty choice of language on the set. This I heard myself, when she would call out to an assistant-director, addressing him as, "Hey, Shithead!" in not the most dulcet tones when she required something. She was always surrounded by her court of admiring hangers-on and I had very little to do with her in the film, as my department was almost entirely Roman and my role, such as it was, hardly crossed with hers at all.

Richard, on the other hand, had a great deal to do with her in the film, and in spite of her growing infatuation with him, he gave every appearance of regarding her entirely as a figure of fun. There were still plenty of jokey anecdotes at her expense.

One night I heard him relate, with glee, that Elizabeth had said, "You've got a pretty funny sort of wife, to have dyed her hair white". Sybil had very pretty hair, which had gone white at a very early age and which she had, very wisely, refrained from colouring.

On another occasion, when he was in the vein to talk about Miss Taylor, he told me that, some years back, when she was married to Mike Todd, he had been a guest at one of their dinner parties. At the end of dinner Todd apparently told her to go and fetch his latest present to her from the safe, to show it to the assembled guests. This she did and returned wearing the most enormous string of pearls which, once all the oohs and ahs had subsided, he told her to take back to the safe. As she left the room, he looked round his guests with a sad smile and said, "Well, that should keep her with me a while longer".

I thought that Rich related this to indicate a certain doubt on the lady's post-mortem protests, regarding how Todd had been the only man in her life. Odd that, later on, he should have showered her with jewels in much the same way. Perhaps both men enjoyed decorating a trophy wife.

I was at dinner one evening at their house when Rich's secretary came in and diffidently told him that Miss Taylor was on the phone and wished to speak to him. He brushed it aside, saying, "Tell her I'm in the middle of dinner, with friends". The man left and returned almost at once, smiling awkwardly, "She said tell Mr. Burton to get his ass over to the telephone ... *or else*".

Rich got up with a sigh, kissed Sybil on the cheek and went out of the room. I felt distinctly embarrassed and she gave me a resigned smile. He came back, looking grim, but said nothing of what had transpired. After dinner, he seemed to be drinking more than usual. I left early.

I had noticed, once or twice, that when he had really drunk a great deal, he seemed almost incapable of differentiation between the sexes. He could become embarrassingly tactile, putting his arm round one. Nothing gross, of course. Perhaps it was something to do with being Welsh and a boyo. I am not sure. Or perhaps it was simply to prevent him falling flat on his face. I was not mad on it, anyway.

He seemed to have deep feelings of guilt about having come by so much of this world's goods, so easily. He told me this himself.

So, he was overly-generous to the members of his extended family, with mink coats for his sisters-in-law and, later on, diamonds as big as eggs for Miss T. I do not know what he gave his brothers, but I certainly saw the ladies in their minks. I believe he drank, partly, for relief from these feelings. He also worshipped Dylan Thomas, following his pattern and identifying with him. I recall him early in the morning on the set before shooting had begun, holding a large balloon glass, filled with something I do not believe was cold tea.

Liz, that is to say, my wife, came out to join me once or twice. She got on extremely well with the Burtons and on one occasion we were with them both in a drinking club, called Bricktops, which was run by a large and ebullient black woman, with whom Rich seemed to be great chums. Why *we* were there, I cannot think, unless we were all on our way to dinner somewhere and Rich felt the need for a quick one or three beforehand.

He was already pretty far gone, I remember. He was sitting, staring glassily and silently at Liz and startled us by saying quite distinctly, "I want to fuck you". This was in front of Sybil. How the evening went afterwards, I do not recall, but I most certainly remember *that*.

Another strange thing was his habit of listening, apparently entranced, to his own voice on an LP of *Camelot*. Much later I was to experience, identically, the same thing with Richard Harris, who always played the same theme while he was in the make-up chair. There must have been something uncannily enduring about the role of Arthur, for it to have had such a lasting effect on both of them. Apart from heavy drinking, they had very little else in common that I can remember.

During that time in Rome, Howard Sackler, that great recorder of fine actors in the classics, came from America to make a recording of *Coriolanus*. He wanted Richard for the title role and to draw on the treasury of largely-idle British actors on the *Cleopatra* film, who would be at his disposal, for the other parts. As he had to work round the requirements of the film itself, the recording took a few days. On the second or third morning Rich turned up, looking really rough, obviously having been on a blinder the night before. It so happened that that morning I had had a letter from Liz, who had gone back to London (my Liz, of course), telling me of the death of a friend, Malcolm Baker Smith, a BBC radio producer. As Rich used to do a certain amount of radio work, I asked if he knew him and I said he had just died.

"What did he die of?" asked Rich.

I looked him full in the eye. "Drink," I said. He looked at me, long and hard, knowing quite well why I had told him. Then a wolfish grin came over his face and he said in his best Welsh accent, "Well, I'll be the next one, won't I?"

Like John Keats, he sometimes seemed "half in love with easeful death" himself. When I heard it had finally caught up with him, I was surprised his constitution had held up so long. I was also greatly saddened, knowing what a damned waste of such potential greatness it all was.

As to my own affairs, I had already appeared in several crucial shots in the film but had not as yet started any of my lines as the conspiratorial scenes, in which my stuff mainly occurred, were not scheduled until very much later on. During one of my latent periods, when I was not needed on the set, Julian, my agent, rang me to tell me that he had had an enquiry from a French film company, wanting me for a substantial role in a film called *Marco Polo*, with Alain Delon in the title role, and they would like me to play his father.

Julian had told them that, though I was committed to 20th Century Fox, for an indefinite period that, nevertheless, I had substantial gaps in the schedule and perhaps something could be arranged. The French company would require me for an initial period of two weeks preliminary shooting in Belgrade. The rest would have to wait until I was free of *Cleopatra*. Accordingly, I took my courage in both hands and went to see our director, Joe Mankiewicz, telling him of this offer and gingerly asking if I could be spared for two weeks. I even suggested that, as my lines could just as well be spoken by the other conspirators as by me, that perhaps they could be shared out among them.

I felt awkward about this as, after all, I did not want to appear disparaging of the screen-play which he, himself, had written. However, he was extremely kind and understanding about it and said he would have to consult the production office, but he would see what he could do. Production OK'd it, but stipulated that my release was to be strictly for two weeks and not a day more. This was because later shots, in which I occurred, had to marry up with ones already *in the can*. In a word, *continuity*.

In view of all that he had to contend with and bearing in mind the usual rigid conditions imposed on those under contract to film companies, this flexible attitude taken by Mankiewicz was astonishingly kind.

So I bade Rome a fond *au revoir* and, full of gratitude, I flew to Belgrade and the bleak mid-winter, having promised to return in time to say, "Goodnight, madam" to Cleopatra, my one line left in the entire film. I had shed all the rest, to be doled out piecemeal to my fellow conspirators, as I had suggested. I was actually a bit sad about this, but I really could not have it both ways.

In Belgrade, I was driven directly to the studio, which after Cine-Citta seemed a very ramshackle sort of affair. There I was kitted up with costumes and so forth and pitchforked straight on to the set. There I met Raoul Levy, the much-accredited director, whose chief claim to fame was to have *discovered* Brigitte Bardot. This was his venture and he was, in fact, the producer. He seemed amiable and fairly laid back, and introduced me to the director, whose name escapes me. I also met Alain Delon, who greeted me with surprising deference. I later noticed his bumptious manner to almost everyone else. I felt instinctively wary of him. There was also Bernard Blier, a distinguished French veteran film actor, who was to play my brother, and a sprinkling of Italian actors of some repute but of whom I remember little or nothing.

Most noticeable was a great feeling of camaraderie among producer, director, actors and technicians, not often found on the stages of the British film industry. The day always started with friendly smiles and handshaking all round: almost a *family* atmosphere and a most heart-warming start to the day.

Blier was a strange man. He seemed amicable enough, but was much given to anecdotage regarding his sexual conquests, his recollections being overly prefaced with the term, "J'ai baise," which, in French common parlance, carries a much stronger meaning than a literal translation would seem to suggest. Perhaps this had something to do with being plump, bald and middle-aged.

In the studio stage an entire boat had been built on rockers to simulate the movement of the sea. It had a gallery platform, running round it about three feet off the floor, to accommodate the various technicians. During a coffee-break, later on, I was chatting to Raoul Levy, who was sitting just under the prow of the boat, when I was astounded to see Delon, standing above us on the gallery, holding a cup of hot coffee which with much mirth he steadily poured on to Levy's head. This behaviour, I later discovered, was in perfect keeping with his general demeanour. For some reason that I was unable to fathom, he continued his politeness to me but I found myself unable to take to him and avoided him as far as possible.

As Levy had me for a bare 14 days, I was obviously kept pretty hard at it and for very long hours, Sundays included. The curious thing is that I can recall next to nothing of the film itself, or how the dialogue worked. It seems unlikely, but I think we all used our own respective languages, with the idea of dubbing it all into French in the final cut. Blier, I know, had hardly a word of English. I may have done mine in French, not, as it later transpired, that it mattered a damn.

A couple of days before my time was up, we had a cable from Fox's production office in Rome, demanding my return without fail, by the date, previously agreed. On the following day, I was shown a telegram from Rome, to the effect that I *might* be required on that day. I therefore relaxed somewhat and got on with the shooting. This was followed by an irate call from Rome, requiring immediate confirmation of my intention to return, as stipulated. When I spoke of the second cable and how it appeared to undermine the urgency of the first, they told me that no such second cable had ever been sent ... and certainly not by *them*.

Obviously an attempt had been made to delay my departure, with a cable, purporting to have been sent by Fox, but actually sent by this company's office in Rome. The telephone wires between Belgrade and Rome were fairly humming by this time and Fox production stated categorically that unless I was ready for shooting in Rome on the day previously agreed, they would sue the French company for substantial damages.

I felt distinctly embarrassed by all this commotion simply to enable me to wish Miss Taylor goodnight, but Fox was within its rights and I suppose it was a matter of principle. So, on the last day in Belgrade, I was kept hard at it, until two o'clock in the morning, when I was bundled into a car to the airport where a Dakota aircraft was ticking over, ready for take-off. This had been chartered for one passenger only to Rome, namely me.

In the rush, however, it appeared that they had forgotten to hire any heating for the plane, which was freezing cold. The air-hostess covered me in a cocoon of several blankets. "You are my baby for tonight," she crooned, thrusting a bottle of plum brandy at me, to ease the situation. I eventually managed to sleep for an hour or so, thankful to have left Belgrade, landing just after dawn at Fiumicino Airport in Rome. There I was again bundled into a waiting car and raced to Cine-Citta where, feeling far from my best, I collapsed into a make-up chair, closed my eyes and let them get on with it.

Hardly had I done so, when a familiar voice, from a nearby chair said, "Well, what about Master Richard?" It was Rex.

"What about him?" I asked.

"Didn't you know? He's gone off with her."

"Gone off? Gone off with whom?"

"Elizabeth, of course," he said.

I gaped stupidly at him. "You're surely not serious, are you? He *can't* have done. He thought she was a joke."

"Well, she's no joke now," he said.

At the end of the day's shooting, I immediately rang Sybil, who confirmed what Rex had told me. She asked me to meet her for lunch. My next couple of days were free, so I arranged to meet her at the Taverna Flavia. We met and were shown to our table which I saw, to my dismay, was immediately under an enormous portrait of Miss Taylor, as Cleopatra. I hoped Sybil would not notice but of course she did. It was almost as if Miss Taylor was listening to our every word and we could not change our table as, by this time, the place was full.

Sybil recounted to me how he had been drinking more and more, until he finally blurted out that he was having an affair with Taylor and wanted to live with her. It is difficult to believe that in the space of two weeks such an abrupt change could have taken place in his attitude to the lady. All that mockery of her must have been a cover-up for something he had secretly started long before, all of which left rather a bad taste in the mouth.

I did my best to comfort Sybil. I reminded her, as if she needed reminding, "You know Rich well enough. He's done this a few times before and he'll probably do it again. But I'm sure he'll come back. He always has."

She said she was not so sure. This time she thought it was serious.

I asked her if there was anything she thought I could do ... though, for the life of me, I could not think what. She asked me to try to get him to meet me somewhere for a meal, somewhere where we could talk. I said I would try, but privately I did not have much hope.

Somehow, I managed to catch him and he agreed, reluctantly, to meet me for lunch on our next free day, the following Sunday. He named a place called The Welsh Pub, where he said they had steak and kidney pudding. His manner was quite different - evasive.

On the Sunday I got there early but clearly not early enough. He must have been there some time as he was already pretty far gone. He was glassy-eyed and holding on to the bar, safe behind his alcohol barrier. Any coherent conversation was out of the question. I did not even try.

I had only one more conversation with him, when he told me how Ifor, his much older brother, had beaten him up when he heard about it all. And that, sadly, was that.

Richard Burton had once had the capacity for becoming our greatest living actor, surpassing even the great Olivier. He had splendid looks, a magical voice and, both on and off-stage, an irresistible charisma. Added to this, he had a fine intellect and could have pursued a distinguished academic career, had he so wished. I know that, with part of himself, he did so wish.

It was terrible to see it all thrown away.

I tried once or twice to contact him, when he and Taylor were staying at the Dorchester, but he had adopted the Hollywood pattern and surrounded himself with an impenetrable wall of minions. My messages were never returned. As things were, I think he was probably right.

As to *Marco Polo*, that was the end of that too. Levy had been getting money in spasms, shooting whenever he had it. When he got more, he would shoot more film. It was very much hand-to-mouth. Eventually he ran out of money and also the providers thereof, and the film was never finished. Equity pursued Levy for well over a year, to induce him to pay his contractual fees, as I imagine did others in the same boat as myself.

One day Julian rang me to tell me the poor man had shot himself. I felt pretty dreadful about it.

This is an episode in the many sagas of *Cleopatra*, which has nothing to do with either Burton or Taylor. It concerns the day of the great ceremonial when Caesar, played by Rex Harrison, is brought in a triumphal procession with animals, camels, elephants and heaven knows what else to meet Cleopatra. All of this involved a great deal of organisation and kerfuffle. Everything in the procession had to be lined up; Caesar was to be borne aloft in a palanquin, the animals in order of march and the multitude of extras, forming the crowd of spectators, instructed when to roar and what to do.

When the procession arrived *on its marks*, Caesar was to leave his litter, walk up a long flight of steps to the throne, turn and begin his speech. As the shot was one of such ambitious length and complexity, the director decided to shoot it without rehearsal, hoping to get it in one. When everything was at last in order, he called, "Action," the cameras rolled and we were in business. The whole shooting-match set off, animals, senators and soldiers and the rest of it at a measured pace. Caesar was deposited at the foot of the stairs, up he went, the cameras following him, he arrived at the throne and opened his mouth to speak. Not a word came out. Poor old Rex had understandably *dried* stone dead.

"OK, cut," called Mankiewicz. "That was a rehearsal, we'll go again."

The floor was swept after the animals and the whole laborious process set up again, which must have taken a good two hours. I could see Rex, silently mouthing his lines.

"OK, shooting this time" and again "Action".

Off went the whole caboodle again, Rex went up the stairs and turned and *dried* stone dead again. I really felt for him. It was enough to unnerve an ox. "Sorry," he said and looked it. A third attempt was made with predictably the same result.

"OK," said the director. "It's a *wrap*. We'll go again tomorrow."

About an hour or so later, I saw Rex in the bar, understandably fortifying himself after his ghastly experience, with a stiffener. Rachel Roberts, his lovely wife was with him, holding his hand. They were surrounded by sympathetic chums, including me, when quite suddenly Michael Hordern lurched up to Rex and claimed his attention. He had clearly been fortifying himself as well.

"Rex, d'you remember that play you directed me in some years ago? Can't remember the name."

"Hell-o, dear boy!" said Rex. "Yes, of course I do."

"Have you any idea what it was like, being me?"

"Er- no," said Rex, with a puzzled smile.

"Well, you made my life a bloody misery. D'you know that?"

"Come, come," said Rex with a nervous laugh, "I can't have done."

"Oh yes, you did. You ruined my life for months and months. And d'you know, when I was watching you today, being carried along, with all those bloody animals and when you got to the top of the stairs and then made a bloody arse of yourself in front of all those people, d'you know what I felt? I was bloody DELIGHTED!"

Wham! Rex had slapped him across the face. Michael staggered back, his hand to his cheek and then, looking round at the embarrassed assembly, "There!" he said. "D'you SEE?"

I think he felt he had made his point.

21

Curious Coincidences

I have had for many years a great friend called Peter Bentley whom I first met when I was with Liz, staying in a very pleasant lakeside hotel in Montreux in 1947. He was with his mother, a delightfully amusing lady with a most entertaining turn of phrase and a fund of fascinating stories and racy anecdotes of a bygone era.

They were both converts to the Roman Catholic religion, which I remember considering, at that time, a pretty preposterous thing to be. *Brideshead Revisited* had not at that time appeared, not at least on my horizon. I was an agnostic, which suited my book quite well. We talked about it a few times and I well recall my increasing incredulity and saying to Peter, "But you can't possibly believe" this, that or the other thing, and his quiet affirmation that he most certainly did.

It later transpired that he wanted, above all things, to enter the priesthood and had indeed already tried his vocation at the London Oratory but, for some reason which we did not go into, had had to give up.

I remember a strange happening at that time in Switzerland. It was in early Spring and the vast fields of narcissi were all in full bloom and Peter and his mother had made an expedition into the country to see this dazzling carpet of flowers, apparently stretching for miles. They had walked into the fields, quite at random, and sat down to rest for a few moments. When they returned to the hotel, Ma Bentley, or *Marb* as we came to call her, was in a state of some distress as she had taken off her glasses when she sat down in the middle of miles of narcissi and had left them there.

Peter said he would pray to St. Anthony of Padua, the patron saint of lost property but *Marb* said there was not a hope as they would never find the spot again in such a vast area. However, Peter, hoping with the faith that moves mountains, insisted on driving there the next day and having a search. They set off into the fields, looking about them to no good effect and certainly not the slightest idea where exactly they had been the day before. There were no trees or other landmarks to guide them. At last *Marb* said she would have a little rest, before giving up and returning to the hotel, so they sat down again.

She put her hand down for support and, with a gasp of astonishment, she said, "Peter, look!" and there, right by her hand, were the missing spectacles.

Some few years later, after Peter had in fact been ordained priest in the Oratorian order, he came to spend a few days with Liz and me in Campden Street. By this time, Liz and I had also converted to Rome. I was going through a pretty barren patch, with trashy and uninteresting scripts, and I had a moan about this to Peter, who suggested that we should all make a Novena to Our Lady to send me something worth doing. I felt that this was a bit like asking the BVM to do my agent's work for him and I really felt it was not quite on. Peter said, "Well, why not?" So we did.

Peter went back to the Oratory and, after the nine days of the Novena had elapsed, he rang me to ask if there had been any result. I laughed and told him of course not. I had hardly finished speaking to him when the phone rang and my agent told me that Rudolph Cartier of BBC TV wanted to see me about a part in his next production.

It so happened that I was reading the life of Charles de Foucauld, a French nobleman and a reformed rake, who, after his conversion, became the founder of a religious order to work among the poor in French North Africa and who was murdered by a Senussi raiding party in his desert hermitage in 1916 and was later beatified. At all events, I went to see Cartier, whom I had never met, and he started talking about the character he had in mind for me.

I was astonished and, interrupting him, I said, "It sounds very like Charles de Foucauld".

He looked surprised in his turn and asked, "What do you know of Charles de Foucauld?"

I told him I knew quite a lot as I was reading his biography, a book entitled *Desert Calling*. Rudy stared at me and said, "It *is* Charles de Foucauld" and he offered me the part on the spot.

It all turned out very well and was one of my rather better TV efforts: at least, so the press led me to believe.

Two quite interesting coincidences.

22

Sherlock Holmes And The BBC

In 1963 the BBC created a series entitled *Great Detectives*. This included many fictional sleuths of note and was intended to serve as a collection of pilots, or try outs, for possible future series. Unsurprisingly, it was to include one of the Sherlock Holmes stories and to do a dramatisation of one of Conan Doyle's personal favourites, *The Speckled Band*.

I was approached to play Holmes and Nigel Stock was offered Watson. It was to be directed by the excellent Robin Midgley.

In due course it was put on and judged, with only one of the other pilots, to be good enough to warrant a series. I had only once before been in a *serial*, as distinct from a *series*: there was a great difference, as I was to learn fairly forcefully later on. I had played Charles II in *Pepys's Diary*, a serial with Peter Sallis, for the BBC and had very much enjoyed the experience. When I was asked to do Holmes, assuming that I was on the same ground, I was perfectly happy to accept. This, however, was subject to an undertaking, promised by the overall producer of the series, of certain provisos. The first was that, as I was not a quick study of lines, I should receive each script no less than three weeks ahead and secondly that there should be no more than three directors in all, in order to ensure maximum continuity of style and that one of them should be the original director, Robin Midgley.

These conditions were all agreed by the production office. I very soon discovered, however, that they were far from being as good as their word.

The scripts invariably arrived late and were often of such unacceptable quality that I was obliged to rewrite them, burning the midnight oil, sometimes until two or three in the morning. They had been produced by six different writers with no inter-reference and, so far as could be seen, no supervision from the production office or the series script editor.

As to the second proviso, we ended up with no less than eight different directors, not one of them Midgley. Furthermore, half of them were on their first directorial assignment, having just emerged from a course at the BBC school of training.

In short, we were to be used as a teething-ring for novices. We were given four who knew their job. Mercifully, one of them, Shaun Sutton, borrowed I believe from Children's Television, directed two of the episodes which was a great relief. Of the rest, one was a middle-European with apparently not a clue about the mores of Victorian England. He could not understand, as an instance, the predicament of the *fallen woman* in *Illustrious Client*. "Couldn't she have got a job in a shop?" he asked. "Not without a *character*," I had to explain. I do not think he *got it*, even then.

In near desperation at one point I ran into Douglas Allen, the head of what was, at that time at least, the more prestigious Department of Serials, and I told him something of our plight. He was very sympathetic. I had just seen Clellan Jones's brilliant job of Henry James's *Portrait of a Lady*, which was, of course, a serial. I complimented Allen on it and asked him if we could not have this excellent director for at least one of our future episodes.

He looked at me, open mouthed and aghast. "You can't have him: he's *Serials*, you're *Series*." He did not say *only Series*, but I think that is what he meant.

It was as if *British Home Stores* had asked *Harrods* for the loan of their Sales Manager in Christmas Week.   .

The bulk of the burden and responsibility of delivering the stuff *on the night*, so to speak, was to rest on my shoulders. Stock, while privately totally in agreement with me, had rather less to say on the matter. He had, also, considerably less to say in the actual scripts themselves. Holmes has to be dead accurate and razor-sharp at all times. One slip and he has lost credibility and is no longer in character.

The upshot of all this was that it invariably fell to my unhappy lot to insist on consistency of style and to the necessary corrections in the writing.

The direct result of this was that I became gradually more and more the exasperated villain of the scenario. The stress began to take its toll and I became, I fear, pretty short-tempered, particularly with the production office, to whom the series appeared to be just another no-account pot-boiler, where practically anything would do.

Somehow we managed to get it all together and it is remembered by those old enough to do so as a piece of work which bore, at least, some quality. Both Nigel and I came out of it with a certain amount of credit.

My stock with the BBC drama department, however, was, perhaps understandably, at zero. At risk of self justification, perhaps, I will allow myself to cite one or two instances.

I was given a script entitled, *The Red-Headed League*. It contained no less than 14 characters completely extraneous to Doyle with names like *Harry the Horse* and stemming, apparently, from an over-addiction to Damon Runyon. The script opened in a "Mews Flat; [sic] with *Merryweather* the banker in bed with his mistress". The script writer called for "saucy pictures" on the walls and had a comic policeman climbing in and out of the window.

Instead of portraying John Clay, the villain, as so interestingly described in the original, as the bastard son of a Royal Duke, he was portrayed as a run-of-the-mill roughneck of no particular interest. All reference to his lineage was simply disregarded, presumably as being of no consequence. I rang the production office at once and asked if they had looked at it. They said they had "been a little worried about that one". That had not stopped them just sending it on to me without any previous comment. Possibly it had been hoped I would not notice.

When I told them I had not the smallest intention of appearing in such drivel, panic-stricken, they said, "But we start rehearsing next week".

"Not with me, you won't. It's found a suitable home: in the waste-paper basket." I added, "You can tell the script editor to get off his arse, have a good look at Doyle and just copy out the excellent dialogue, as written". Thus far into the series, I had done his job for him. And that, of course, is all he had to do. There was no time to exchange courtesies. The result was fine.

At risk of labouring the point, there was, among many others, one particularly gross piece of mismanagement. When we came to do *The Devil's Foot*, I was handed a script which was to fill a 50-minute slot but which contained exactly 20 minutes playing time. This slight discrepancy had clearly been through the Production Office, escaping their notice.

On this occasion, Stock and I had to buckle-to and produce a workable script. The unhappy scriptwriter, a man of some considerable reputation, owing to years of overwork, had suffered a mental breakdown, followed almost at once by his tragic suicide.

I believe it is not generally realised just how voracious a medium TV can be and this is particularly the case with scriptwriters whose work, unlike those writing for the theatre, is swallowed up in an hour or so and then, if the writers are in demand, as this one most certainly was, it is immediately on to the next assignment.

I was thankful when I reached the end of it all but when the BBC discovered it was regarded as a critical success, they got in touch with me in Hong Kong, where I was filming as Nayland Smith, a poor man's version of Holmes in some twaddle, called *Fu Manchu*. They asked me if I would do a second series, adding, almost as an afterthought, that, for reasons of economy, the rehearsal period for each episode would have to be cut down to 10 days.

I said, "It cannot be done, or at any rate, not by me". I had been momentarily hesitant about it, but a 10-day turn-around quite definitely put the tin lid on it. I hesitated not a second longer. The prospect had not been an inviting one in any case, but *10* days! What a nightmare!

Needless too say, this did not go down too well with the Beeb.

In the first place, they had been screwed down by Adrian Conan Doyle for a pretty hefty whack for the TV rights and he had insisted on them buying 52 stories or no deal. We had used up 13 of them and I am quite sure that the Beeb was confident that I would be perfectly happy to do the lot, in which case they could hope to sell it as a package to the USA and points east for quite a tidy figure. Instead of attempting to come to some arrangement whereby I might be tempted to take up the cudgels again, they stuck to their 10-day schedule with an aunt-like drawing aside of skirts and started doing the rounds to see if anyone else would be foolish enough to take it on.

I believe Eric Porter and John Neville were approached among others who refused the bait. Finally, they hit on that fine actor, Peter Cushing, who, in my opinion and later also in his own, as he himself told me, unwisely agreed to do it.

What the result of all this was like I leave to the judgement of those old enough to have seen it. Certainly the production values were in the firing line, although our particular producer cannot be held to account for that. As soon as our series was over, he left the BBC and took his talents to the Antipodes where I heard he prospered exceedingly.

I was in a Hammer Horror with Peter some time later and the subject of the series quite naturally came up. He said it had been the worst nightmare of his entire life, that he had hardly had time to breathe, let alone learn his lines and that when he watched some of the episodes, he did not think, "There's Peter Cushing as Sherlock Holmes," he thought only, "There's Peter Cushing trying to remember his lines".

He added, "I'd rather sweep Paddington Station for a living, than go through it again". It had clearly been another saga of incompetence. The BBC once again had shot itself in the foot and thrown away a splendid opportunity of making what should have been a fine classic series.

At the possible risk of exhausting the reader's patience, I have gone into the foregoing exposé at some length, as it is, I believe, not often that someone in the far-from-unusual predicament in which we found ourselves to be able, without risk of reprisal, to blow the gaffe on the dysfunctions of that particular department of the BBC. Now, happily beyond the reach of possible come-back, I am particularly well-placed to do so!

Whenever the end result appears to be smooth and lovely, it was very often because those in the firing line, so to speak, in this case Nigel and myself, who were left to pull the chestnuts out of the fire, actually did so. Things may well be different now, of course. One hopes so.

It may well be the case that the reader has had his fill on the subject of Sherlock Holmes; then he will certainly be forgiven if he skips the remainder of the chapter.

I persevere with it only because if there is any episode in what may derisively be called my *career* which is at all likely to have made any mark, this may be possibly it. I can hardly claim too much personal credit for this as the very nature of the subject of Sherlock Holmes is, apparently, of such universal interest as to be well documented and the *raison d'être* and focal point of numerous learned societies and publications.

The series was made well over 40 years ago and I have long ceased to be surprised by fan mail, which admittedly arrives no longer in torrents, but certainly still in a surprisingly steady trickle. I am also invited to appear at various public functions for this and no other reason, either to speak or read or simply to put in an appearance.

This situation is brought about largely because it appears that all the long term Sherlocks, other than myself, are long since gone to their Baker Street in the sky. It may be tempting Providence to say so, but sometimes I believe it has much to do with my determination to do no more of them, that I attribute my present extreme longevity. My sole lapse from this determination was an unfortunate one, undertaken solely for the basest pecuniary reasons.

I refer of course to the film *Sherlock Holmes' Smarter Brother*. But, as one of my critic's once pointed out, even actors have to eat.

I am also not infrequently questioned about my attitude and approach to the character itself, how I arrived at it and so forth. I once gave an after-dinner speech to the *Sherlock Holmes Society of London* on the subject. Asked if I was an avid fan before the series, I replied truthfully that I was not, without adding however that, after the series, I was even less so. But I had most certainly enjoyed first reading the stories, which I had done many years before and was indeed familiar with most of them.

I have for the last 10 years or so been an elected Honorary Member of the above-mentioned Society and enjoyed going, fairly regularly, to the Annual Dinner at the House of Commons. But I do not, however, dress up in Victorian gear and go with them on their European pilgrimages to the Reichenbach Falls. I have also been made a Baker Street Irregular, an American society, much aspired to by all avid Sherlockians of the USA, election to which is strictly by invitation only. Also, there are a number of other societies, such as *The Boston Bull Terriers*, who have likewise done me the honour.

A frequent question I have had to answer is if I was at all surprised to be offered the role. I have replied quite truthfully that I was not too amazed. I was considered, at that time, an experienced and, possibly even, over-exposed TV actor and was therefore reasonably well-known. My suitabilities for the role, such as they were, could well be assessed beforehand. I could appear to have, when required, an incisive persona and an appearance that seemed to suit most people's idea of the part.

I had, as the press were quick to notice, rather more than a passing resemblance to the original *Strand Magazine* illustrations by Sidney Paget. Quite how they were able to make this assessment, I am not quite sure, as most of Paget's drawings of Holmes bear not over-much resemblance to each other and certainly *none* that I can recall resemble him as described in the text.

When asked if I had been familiar with other impersonations and, if so, had they had any bearing on my own construction of the character, the answer was "Yes" to the first and, superficially speaking, "No" to the second. Upon reflection, of course, they must have had some effect, subconsciously if in no other way. There were obviously some aspects, for instance, that one would reject and others, sometimes consciously, sometimes not, that would have been assimilated. But had I modelled my performance on another?

The answer is most decidedly no.

To be truthful, I had never seen a character construction, which totally fitted the bill. They all missed out on what I considered, in my doubtless ineffable arrogance, some aspect or other; so that, for me, at any rate, they failed to add up to what I felt as a credibly satisfying whole. When I was invited to play the part and re-read the stories again, this conviction became even stronger. I made up my mind to do my level best to make good these deficiencies which I had quite clearly defined in my own mind. Whether or not I eventually succeeded in this bold venture, I have to leave to the judgement of others who saw it at the time or subsequently on the video tapes later published, at the continued insistence of the S.H. Society, by a reluctant BBC.

There is one small testimonial that perhaps is worthy of mention. It is something like a play-bill flyer. It is framed and hangs on the wall of the loo. It has two portraits of me as Sherlock from the series and bears the legend in large letters:

"The only man who ever got it right"
A Celebration of Douglas Wilmer
as Sherlock Holmes

The Cremona Fiddlers of Williamsburg
Marshall-Wyeth School of Law
Williamsburg, Virginia
Sunday, 4 October, 1998

So, at least in one small exotic corner of the world, I had scored in my intentions, enabling me, in my occasional fits of despondency, to repair to the loo for total reassurance that not for nothing was I born.

In case it should be of some interest, as to how I approached the actual construction of the character, I can only say that it was in much the same way as

I do so with any role. I first read and re-read the relevant story several times and, having switched on my imagination, I allow it to soak, so to speak. This would be a gradual process out of which would emerge the general shape of the character. I would then, during the process of rehearsal, gradually elaborate the detail, always on the watch to preserve the truth of how the character would react to the situation in hand. In other words, I would proceed much as would a painter or sculptor, by trial and error, self-critical addition and subtraction with the further dimension, in the case of acting, of the critical requirements of the director.

Any artist or actor can create only within the limits of his imaginative and physical capacity and creative powers. Sometimes, one sees a performance where the actor seems out of his depth and appears out of touch with what Glen Byam Shaw was wont to call the *truth* of the character.

This can be for a number of reasons. The actor has failed to find the truth of the central core of the role; he may be miscast or it is possible that he has not devoted enough thought to the job. Or it may be because he is attempting something beyond his artistic comprehension. He could also have been misled by the director: a case of the blind leading the blind. Or more simply, that he has missed his vocation and would be better employed selling groceries.

For a summary of the character as I saw, and continue to see, it, I can only reiterate a version of what I came up with on the occasion of the *Sherlock Holmes Society* Dinner, with apologies to those for whom it may be *déjà vu*.

From the experience of seeing previous Sherlocks, it would seem that, in many cases, they had either chosen to ignore, or failed to notice, certain salient traits in his nature. There has been a tendency to portray him almost as a Victorian paternalistic hero of derring-do, ever chivalrous, over-serious and, consequently, somewhat cardboard. Possibly owing to my own sardonic nature, the way in which I saw him, whilst certainly containing most of these elements, had also, I felt, a decidedly *black* side to his character which, possibly, it had been formerly found too difficult or unsympathetic to incorporate.

For whatever reason, I decided that I would paint him *warts and all*. He was a towering and commanding figure, often forbidding and silent. Such men cast great shadows. They can be intimidating and inspire fear.

He was totally devoid of the spurious values of the establishment, with no great regard for rank or material prestige. Witness his open contempt for the King of Bohemia and the Noble Bachelor, also the possible offer of honours.

He was certainly capable of chivalry to women, for whom, generally speaking, however, he seems to have had scant regard. He was also capable of complete callousness, as shown by his treatment of Milverton's housemaid (he wooed her in disguise to obtain vital information about her employer's house and his habits). It is true that these peculiarities are almost always relieved by humour, but it is not always humour of a noticeably kindly nature. It is more usually quirkily sardonic.

There is also his almost total and habitual lack of any consideration for the comfort of his faithful and long-suffering friend, whose capacity for toleration almost defies belief. Who else but Watson would put up with such a companion who, in a moment of *ennui,* would lie back in his armchair, a smoking pistol in hand, decorating the wall with an enormous VR, picked out in bullet holes.

There was also his disagreeable habit of performing chemical experiments, resulting in Watson being driven out of the room by the appalling stench. There was his frequent adoption of lofty airs and arrogant and superior attitudes, punctuated by periods of surly silence and his playing of melancholy airs on the violin, whenever the mood took him. Also his total disregard of Watson's medical sensibilities, by jabbing himself with cocaine whenever a black mood descended on him.

He has every qualification for the description, "A stable-companion from Hell" but he must have provided a great deal of adrenalin-charged excitement to make up for that and much else besides. There was, of course, very much on the credit side to admire but, as that is self-evident and has been amply demonstrated by most other interpreters of the role, there is no need for me to go into it here. I have concerned myself in drawing attention to what I feel are the important aspects that are most frequently ignored and which I did my best to incorporate.

Such was the climate of the times that there was to be no mention in any of the scripts of anything so utterly depraved as a cocaine habit. I was therefore unable to include it, much as I believe it should have been there.

Tempora mutantur. [The times are changed]

It may be argued that the portrayal of Holmes by the late Jeremy Brett did, in fact, contain many of the elements to which I have referred. This is perfectly true but his performances, if I may be forgiven for pointing it out, were given considerably long after mine.

Perhaps then, it is in order at this point to relate that Jeremy came to dinner one evening at my house in London, not long after my series was shown, and that he was kind enough to express his admiration for my portrayal of Holmes. This could, of course, have been merely actor's *flannel*, but he had no particular reason to refer to it at all. I had certainly not brought up the subject.

He was a much younger man then and it was 20 years later, almost to the year, that he was to give his own long and memorable interpretation.

As matters stood, there were many complaints when my series was shown, that I had made the man too arrogant and unsympathetic. Well, I had tried to portray, not a sugar-coated version of Holmes, but a true all-round one, as I saw him and continue to do. I believe that I was faithful to Doyle's intention and there are those who would agree with me.

This is not an apologia and if, in spite of the lighter touches and humour that I was able to introduce into it, my performance was ultimately unlikeable, then I must freely admit defeat and that I failed in the role.

I would like very briefly, however, to refer to the stories as written by Doyle.

They are narrated, with two exceptions, entirely by Watson and it is only on his say-so that we can be reassured that his idolised companion has any redeeming features. He is at pains to tell us of how his "clear, hard eyes were dimmed for a moment and the firm lips were shaking. For the one and only time, I caught a glimpse of a great heart as well as of a great brain." Note, if you please, *the one and only time*. Elsewhere Watson describes him as an automaton and a calculating machine. He would appear to have had not a friend in the world, save Watson.

It is perhaps stating the obvious that such observations can have no explicit place in any dramatised version, but can find expression only in narrative form and as is clearly indicated in the original text. In a dramatic context, therefore, Holmes is thereby deprived of any *softening* qualities and we are left, unless we are very careful, solely with the cold, hard calculating machine. Small wonder most actors go for the Establishment Hero of, in my view, popular misconception.

I have dealt at some greater length on the foregoing than was my original intention, for which I hope to be forgiven. I have done so as it was a major event in my theatrical life and therefore of some importance to me, if to no-one else. These are, after all, my memoirs and they record six gruelling months, spent not entirely agreeably, in the production of a series purporting to deal with probably the most world-famous fictional character in literary history.

My own efforts in that direction seem to have been appreciated more in retrospection than they were at the time, as fashion and trends apparently now favour the anti-hero rather more than they did. Sherlock Holmes is now seen, largely due to the efforts of Jeremy Brett and, before that, to perhaps a lesser extent myself, as no longer the straight-batting Establishment paragon previously so frequently depicted.

Doyle did not like him and I believe, at close quarters, not many would. Brett certainly did not and said so quite plainly. In the light of his words of sooth, I am able to feel, even if only to myself, largely vindicated and I can only hope that the foregoing has been of some interest.

At all events, I have at least got it - or most of it - off my chest after all these years.

As to the *Sherlock Holmes Society*, I owe a great debt to Tony Howlett, one of the original Founders and a most distinguished President. For many years, he laboured to induce the BBC to put out our 1964/5 series again, writing them countless letters. For reasons best known to themselves, the Beeb had been most secretive as to the whereabouts of the tapes and indeed to their continued existence. It was generally believed that they had been *wiped* for re-use or otherwise lost: a belief that the Beeb was happy to nurture.

I had become reconciled to this state of affairs, when, without warning two of them, both in excellent condition, surfaced at the National Film Theatre. It transpired that the Beeb had them all in their archives, virtually intact except for *The Bruce-Partington Plans*, which had a chunk missing. So, thanks to Tony Howlett's persistence, they at last decided to release two episodes: *The Speckled Band* and *The Illustrious Client*, under the banner of *BBC World-wide Productions Ltd*. They told me that should sales be in excess of 5000 copies, they would consider spending time and money, brushing up the remainder, with a view to their publication.

I asked specifically if the format envisaged would be that which could be used in the USA, and I was assured that, of course, it would be. Consequently, I felt every confidence that, in spite of being one of the last of the series to have been made in black and white, this target could be reached, with the enormous possibilities of the American market. My optimism was, however, short-lived.

Just prior to publication, the head-lady of *BBC World-Wide Productions Ltd.* telephoned me in some embarrassment to tell me that, "Owing to a dreadful oversight," the two videos had been made in a format unusable in the USA. She was full of apologies.

The remainder of the series still remains in the BBC Archives, unheralded, unsung and certainly unpublished. The target had nearly been reached, but without the American market, alas, not quite.

They had shot themselves in the foot, yet again.

It had been my intention to leave it at that, but I had subsequently been approached by Sir Christopher Frayling, the Chairman of the *Arts Council* and Rector of the *Royal College of Art*, who is writing a book on the culture of oriental evil in art and literature. He wished to ask me some questions, regarding my performance in two films, dealing with *Fu Manchu*, and based on the novels of Sax Rohmer. As they, along with such dross as *Jason and the Argonauts* and *Vampire Lovers* were hardly high on my list of mentionables, I was proposing to ignore them completely and, as I was not happy with the result, I had jettisoned them from my mind as so much rubbish. When I told Sir Christopher this, he said that would be a pity as, in his opinion, what I had told him was worth recording. Furthermore, like so much preposterous twaddle, the films had now achieved some sort of *cult* status.

I hope he is right. He suggested that I write it as an appendage to Sherlock Holmes. My role was actually one of the longest in the film. It was the Commissioner Nayland Smith, the implacable enemy of Fu Manchu, the latter played with great conviction by Christopher Lee.

My role was a function, rather than a character, which could best be described, I suppose, as a filleted Sherlock but conceived, written and certainly acted, without the spark of life. His companion, Dr. Petrie, played by Howard Marion-Crawford, is a pale crib of Dr. Watson, while Fu Manchu is an oriental representation of Professor Moriarty, the most evil man in the Holmesian world. In short, my role did the donkey work, leaving Fu Manchu to skim off the cream.

Nigel Green, a talented ex-student of mine whom I had taught at RADA, had played the role of Nayland Smith, in the very first of the films, reputed to be the best of the bunch, and had wisely declined to do any more, handing over the baton, as it were, to me. I was mug enough to take it.

One of the films was made in Hong Kong and later on in Dublin. I cannot remember much about the other, except that it was supposed by some to be the better of the two. The actual *Brides of Fu Manchu* in the title, consisted of an international gaggle of Beauty Queens, imported from the Lord knows where, who had nothing very much to do, except look decorative and yelp with terror occasionally. There was a formidable lady, appointed as a sort of police woman chaperone just to keep them in order. This unfortunate woman nearly went mad as hardly any of them had ever seen London before and frequently some went missing just when their services were required, having been picked up on the previous night by men of evil intent.

On the Hong Kong film, on our first evening in Kowloon, the Chinese actress, Tsai Chin, took me to a *proper Chinese restaurant*, some distance from the smarter area where our hotel was situated. I remember an enormous warehouse-sized eatery with hundreds of Chinese, all chomping and slurping, amid the deafening noise of chatter. We had what Tsai recommended, which was, to my untutored palate, bland and uninteresting. However, I felt obliged, out of politeness, to simulate the full enjoyment of a gastronomic experience.

Privately, I thought I had often done better in Soho.

On the way back to the hotel in a taxi, she was suddenly seized with violent stomach cramps and felt very unwell, just managing to make it in time. Ironically, I got away with it myself. I do not quite know how.

We started filming the next day in an appallingly grubby studio run by two Chinese brothers, fortunately most of it on the *lot* and therefore outside in the open air. I seem to remember a communal dressing-room, with wash bowls and pee buckets, also Christopher carrying his loose change around in a sock. During one of the set-ups, I saw him reading a paperback and asked if he was enjoying it. "It's hardly for me to say," he replied. "I wrote it myself."

His name was not that on the cover. Perhaps he was using a *nom de plume?*

With considerable justification, of course, he always managed to give the impression that he held himself in the highest esteem and there was never very much humour about. But then, if one spends one's life as the *nasty* in films, steeped in horror and gloom, perhaps that is understandable. I have always believed him to be a very good actor and much under-used in quality drama. But had he done more of the latter and much less of the Hammer style of work, he would probably have been much less well-known.

When I first knew him, as a young man, before he ever went into the business of acting, his great ambition was to sing in opera. He indeed had a very fine singing voice. What a loss that there was never a musical *Dracula*.

His handling of the role of Fu Manchu was masterly, when it could have been utterly ludicrous. Tsai Chin was also impressive, as his equally villainous daughter. Indeed they were the only roles in the film of the smallest interest. I could certainly not bring Nayland Smith to life and I am not often defeated. When I saw the films on video, the impression I had of my performances was of a suit of clothes walking about.

In one of the two films, I believe it was the Hong Kong one, I was supposed to be a Chinese homicidal maniac whose face had been surgically changed to mine. Accordingly, I was obliged to appear at one point in the film, with my visage improbably seamed with cuts and surgical stitches, and not looking quite at my best. A *stills* photo, presumably to aid continuity, had been taken. Many years later, someone sent me a copy of a horror magazine, called *Monsters*, in which this particular photo appropriately appeared. It was captioned, much to my relief, "Who Is It?"

By a curious, not say suspicious, circumstance on the night of the very last shot of the film, the enormous Temple of the Heaven-sized Palace of Fu Manchu was mysteriously burnt to the ground.

Was it insured, I wonder?

23

Rediffusion and Joe Orton 1962/67

I was cast by Rediffusion in a number of TV plays, one of which was made memorable by a chain of sequential events. This was a slight affair called *The Tortoise and the Hare*, which was virtually a three-hander: a man, his wife and his mistress.

The wife was to be played by the lovely actress, Sian Phillips, wife of Peter O'Toole, and I was to be the man. It was directed by a volatile Russian lady called Tania Lieven, the one-time wife of the Hollywood actor, Albert Lieven. She was also the more recently former wife of Miles Malleson, an extraordinary-looking man, with neither chin nor eyebrows but a very obvious wig and who enjoyed a success with the ladies which was as enviable as it was inexplicable.

The divorce having been recent had clearly left its mark on Miss Lieven, which showed all too soon as rehearsals got under way. For no discernible reason, she seemed to take a strong dislike to Sian and showed it very clearly. She began by picking on her, early on in rehearsal, while Sian was beginning to feel her way into her role. I can only imagine that it was Sian's unusual good looks that irked her, reminding her, perhaps, in some way of Malleson's peccadillos.

Matters reached such a pass that poor Sian felt unable to walk into the rehearsal room but would wait in the street outside until I, or the other actress, appeared to escort her in.

This was getting us nowhere so I tried to reason with Tania as her mishandling of Sian was clearly going to end in disaster. Towards the end of rehearsals, she said we would "run through again and this time, Sian, let me see a *performance*. You have shown me *nothing*, as yet."

How the woman could be so stupid or what really prompted her, I was never able to discover. My own patience, never my strongest suit, gave way and I tore into Tania, tearing her off a considerable strip, telling her that Sian was a fine actress and that any shortcomings were entirely the director's fault and I told her to leave her alone.

That was probably not the wisest thing to have done. It certainly set the cat among the proverbials. Tania went to Peter Willes, the head of drama and told him that I had been abominably rude and undermined her authority in front of the whole cast. Willes, a remote figure with something of a reputation for waspishness, without speaking to me on the matter, banned me forthwith from any future Rediffusion productions.

This embargo remained in force for some years until one of their directors wanted me for a leading role in a two-part blockbuster called *When the Kissing had to Stop*.

It so happened that this coincided with Peter Willes being on leave and thereby unable to exercise his veto. By the time he returned, we were in the final stages of rehearsal, so his displeasure was tempered somewhat, especially as he could see that I was having one of my better moments with the difficult leading role. In the hope of a *succès d'estime*, he sensibly left things alone; not that he had very much choice in the matter, at that stage. Uncharacteristically, he took to drifting in to watch rehearsals in progress. Occasionally he would venture some half-humorous remark. "You do know what an evil fellow you are, don't you?" All very playful.

I was never quite sure if he was referring to the role I was playing or if he was impugning my personal character. I was certainly not about to enquire.

From a markedly hostile position, he became gradually more friendly, culminating in an invitation to Liz and me to a formal dinner party in an Italian restaurant, somewhere near Marble Arch. Perhaps it was his birthday, but it was all very grand - black tie, no less - there were several guests, most of whom seemed to be titled.

There was one odd fellow who turned up attired in denim. His name was Joe Orton.

At that time he was unknown to me as he had not yet become a figure in the theatrical firmament. Far from being in any way self-conscious of any difference, either in class or attire, he seemed quite at ease with himself. He had an amusing turn of phrase. He had natural, easy manners and there was something very likeable about him. He sat next to Liz, with whom he got on very well. He said he wrote plays, which Peter was going to promote. I remember him well and have completely forgotten Peter's grandees.

Apparently, Joe and Liz had exchanged 'phone numbers because a few days later he rang up to ask if he and his friend could come to tea. It seemed an unlikely time to have chosen, but to tea, he and his friend both came.

His friend was introduced as Kenneth Halliwell and I was immediately struck by the complete disparity between them. He was an odd-looking man, solemn and unsmiling, with a plump, heavily-featured face, surmounted by a bouffant wig, perched on the top of his head, like an egg-cosy.

The two of them sat, side-by-side, on the sofa, Joe lolling comfortably back, while Halliwell, in marked contrast, perched on the edge, as if poised for imminent departure. Apart from their obvious sexual orientation, they seemed an unlikely pair to be friends. But this, of course, was a very superficial observation. I had, after all, met Joe only once before and his companion not at all. The few remarks that Halliwell made were always to do with the importance of his own contribution to Orton's work.

Joe, on the other hand, chatted amusingly about their six months in prison, for "defacing library books". I forget most of the obscenities that they were supposed to have perpetrated, but I remember him describing a book on Sybil Thorndike, containing an earnest-looking photo of her, apparently intently regarding an enormous sexual organ attached to a Greek torso. They had also pasted a grotesquely tattooed naked man on a book of Betjeman's poems. There were others that he described, with obvious remembered delight.

I am sure that he had heard it all before, probably *ad nauseum*, but Halliwell sat glumly aloof during this hilarious litany of misdeeds. I noticed that Joe made no reference or complaint, as to the severity of their sentence. It was the funny side of it all that was paramount in his recollections. They came again a couple of times; I think it was for drinks in the evening. We did not ask anyone else because we selfishly enjoyed Joe so much, but also because there was Halliwell's uncomfortable presence to contend with.

The last time I saw them, they were together in the men's shop in Harrods. I asked how *Loot* was doing and said I very much wanted to see it. Joe said that I had better get on with it, as it was about to come off. He told me that they were getting kitted out in Harrods for a visit to Morocco. Presumably it was in preparation for this, that Joe had pomaded his hair into little hedgehog spikes all over his head: rather like little black Topsy in American comedy films.

I wished them a happy holiday. The next I heard of them was reading the sensational account of their deaths (Halliwell having murdered Orton) soon after.

As a result of this tragic occurrence, *Loot* went on for an extended run.

24

Budapest 1963

It is strange how some episodes in one's life linger on in the memory, almost more by nature of their circumstances than by the actual incidents therein.

In the autumn of 1963 I spent several weeks on a film in Communist Budapest. During the course of my stay, I was quartered in shabby grandeur in a one-time palatial hotel on Margaret Island, in the middle of the far-from-blue River Danube. Two of my co-exiles in the hotel were George Sanders, the quasi villain of the film, and his wife, the former widow of Ronald Colman, Benita Hume. As a rule, I dined with them.

I remember very little about them, except their somewhat improbable preoccupation with a sausage factory that he had recently purchased.

What the film was entitled or what on earth it was about almost completely eluded my memory, until, raking through some ancient papers, I came across a letter from Julian Belfrage, my agent, complaining angrily to the film people that I was not receiving the correct daily expenses. It was headed with the unlikely title *Millie Goes To Budapest* and bore Julian's counter-remark in ink, "What a shower!" as his uncomplimentary opinion of my employers.

My curiosity being aroused and in order to convince myself that the events I describe were not an entire figment of my imagination, I decided to surf the net in an attempt to track down the film.

After some difficulty and cross-checking, I eventually found a brief account of its content. The title had been wisely changed to *The Golden Head* and it was said to be an Anglo/Hungarian co-production, the first of its kind. It was further described as a *cherishable*, being, in all probability, the "worst film ever made" and unsurprisingly scarcely ever to be seen outside Hungary itself.

Having contributed, in some degree to this treasure, I was intrigued enough to dive further, to discover that one of the Hungarian actresses, a dancer, was said to have displayed a noticeable amount of underarm hair, which may be acceptable in Eastern Europe, but rather less so to Western eyes: especially in Wide Screen.

George Sanders was described as adopting a series of ludicrous disguises and I was referred to as "the ever-reliable Douglas Wilmer," which, I suppose, could have been worse.

One of the more enduring memories I retain was of an unrepaired and revolution-ravaged city, of unusually beautiful-looking women, poorly and shabbily dressed, of seething discontent and forlorn resignation; and everywhere I went, a deep hatred of Communism and all that it stood for. As in East Berlin, the Soviets had forbidden repairs of any sort, as a constant reminder to the Hungarians that defiance does not pay. The city's scars from the *Rising* were everywhere and, as it was forbidden to film anywhere which would show them on screen, this narrowed the field more than somewhat in attempting to film in the city itself.

The Russian presence was *felt*, rather than actually seen: manifest through the endless vetoes and regulations passed on through the regime. This was reinforced by the knowledge that large numbers of Soviet troops were immured in barracks, surrounding the city. They were kept out of sight, but no-one was unaware of their presence. Every so often a convoy of enormous military canvas-covered lorries would drive through the city. I can remember seeing the canvas backing momentarily drawn aside, allowing a glimpse of fur-capped Tartar faces and rifles with fixed bayonets.

It was forbidden for social groups of more than four to gather together but, behind closed doors, this injunction was more honoured in the breach than the observance. Finding myself with little affinity with many of my fellow-countrymen in the film, I began to spend more and more of my leisure time in the more congenial company of Hungarians and I was present at many such illegal gatherings. There was always much lively discussion on a multitude of interesting topics, artistic and political, and a most noticeable detestation of the regime. This was always washed down with copious quantities of cheap Hungarian wine which, like most items available under the Soviet yoke, was of a very poor quality. The plum brandy, which usually followed, was generally much better.

At one such soirée, there were two doctors, a married couple, who had both been imprisoned for their part in the *Rising*. To my embarrassment, the wife was bitter in her condemnation of the West for failing in its promise to come to their aid, to which I feebly replied that had we done so, none of us here might be alive to discuss it.

I remember her crushing rejoinder. "Would that matter so much?"

We had a number of lively young English-speaking students attached to the unit as interpreters and some of them asked if I would give a talk to the English Class at the Karl Marx University of Economics. I dislike speaking in public but, feeling that it would be churlish to refuse, I asked them what they would like me to talk about. "Anything British, but whatever you like."

The day came and I presented myself at the University. I was led to the class where I spoke on the British Royal Family, making it as racy as possible. It seemed to go down very well and they certainly laughed a lot, particularly at the more scandalous revelations.

There was one young man, I noticed, with cropped hair, who laughed not at all but glowered through all my possibly feeble jokes, slouching off at the end of my talk. I asked who he was.

"Oh, he is the Government spy. We have one or two in every class. They report on our political correctness. It depends on their report, whether or not we receive our degree."

Almost everywhere I went, I was aware of this heavy blanket of oppression, an intense interest in the West and a longing to escape, which was strictly forbidden but not, as I shall later describe, entirely impossible.

There is one particular incident, which I will certainly never forget, involving a day on location. Filming was due to take place on the banks of the Danube a few miles outside the city. We were told that it was unlikely to be the next day, as scheduled, on account of Soviet army manoeuvres taking place, it was rumoured, nearby. I was looking forward to a lazy morning. However, I was woken before dawn and told to be ready as soon as possible. Having shaved and abluted and downed a hot coffee, I stumbled, still half asleep, down to the unit car. As I was getting in, one of the assistant-directors thrust a bundle of papers into my raincoat pocket. When I asked what they were, he said that they were my "papers for the day".

As we drove off, I idly thought I would give them a look. They appeared to be ID documents but, as I had no Hungarian, I asked the driver to look at them and tell me what they were. They described me as a Hungarian set-designer, with a photograph of a man, not remotely resembling me. He even had a heavy moustache. And what about the damned Russian army, I asked myself?

My fears were suddenly realised when we found ourselves crawling behind a slow-moving convoy of tanks, which we were completely unable to pass. I remembered the recent case of the American butterfly hunter, arrested as a spy in Romania and the endless negotiations to obtain his eventual release. But worse was to come.

I wound down the window and saw that we were slowly approaching a check-point, with soldiers armed with machine guns and one of them holding a red flag. Hastily closing the window, I thrust the papers at the driver, deciding to simulate sleep. We were stopped, of course, and words were exchanged between the red flag man and the driver, who handed the papers to him. Slouched in my corner, I could not see the man's face, only his hands opening the papers. It was an eternity before he said something and without bothering to look at me, handed them back to the driver and walked away.

Relief was quickly followed by fury, that I had been exposed to such an ordeal and when I got back to the unit office, I bounded out of the car and yelled, "Don't you bloody well dare to put me in such a situation ever again!" I believe that they thought me unreasonable.

Even bad things come to an end and I had been back in London a month or so when there came a ring at the door. It was one of our Hungarian interpreters, accompanied by his daughter. I noticed that they had each a very large suitcase, which I thought looked ominous. He told me that he had managed to worm his way out of Hungary on a "brief holiday visa" in order to attend a fictitious religious meeting in London and they had no intention of returning. He had been able to wangle this by virtue of his calling as he was a Hungarian Presbyterian pastor! His name was Konkoly and he would appreciate my help.

This was a bit of a facer as Liz and I were about to go on holiday to Italy. So I telephoned the Pastor of the London Presbyterian Church and apprised him of Pastor Konkoly's plight. After much questioning, he grudgingly suggested that I had better bring them to his manse in Pont Street. So, later the same day, I did.

The Pastor of Pont Street did not appear to be overjoyed at meeting his

AND SO TO LUNCH....

DAGGERS flash; blood spreads over a white toga . . . and Julius Caesar dies once more in Rome. This time, for the film "Cleopatra."

Clearly, a good morning's murdering, because the director orders "Break for lunch" almost before there is time to change a toga.

So—lower picture—there's Caesar (Rex Harrison) sitting contentedly in the studio restaurant beside actor Douglas Wilmer. But look back to the top picture—to the assassin on the left behind Caesar. It was Douglas Wilmer. No hard feelings about that murder. . . .

Exclusive Sketchpics by Monty Fresco and Robert Penn.

Cleopatra, the film shot in Cine Citta, Rome. It was cast with almost every well-known British actor, idly hanging about in Rome, waiting to be called to the studio. It suited me as I loved exploring the city. I had also made friends with Richard Burton, seeing a lot of him and his delightful wife, until his notorious affair, after which he made himself scarce. Rex was an amusing raconteur and I felt most uncomfortable about plunging a knife into his back. He was very forgiving about it, as the photo indicates

As Niger, a character in *The Fall of the Roman Empire*. I was very surprised to be in this after the dreadful incident in Anthony Mann's previous film, *El Cid*, when he told me he would see to it that I would never, ever work again. Luckily, Alec Guinness was playing Marcus Aurelius, so I was not without friends. Sofia Loren was delightful and we got on very well. I also had the amusing company of my old friend, Eric Porter

Above left: My wife Liz, enjoying a drink in my dressing room in the Savoy Theatre, London, after the first night of *According to the Evidence*. It was not well received by the critics, one remarking that he could not imagine why actors of our quality could be doing such stuff, adding philosophically that he supposed even actors had to eat

Above: In the film *Patton*, as Gen. Sir Freddie de Guigand, Chief of General Staff to Montgomery in the N. African campaign. On the right is that fine actor, Peter Barkworth. This was a most successful film, in which George C. Scott as Patton scored a great personal success

Right: As Fairfax in *Cromwell*, looking depressed. When Cromwell's council were required to sign King Charles's death-warrant, Fairfax was the sole member who refused. This did not please Cromwell. Richard Harris did the same for me: possibly the reason for the despondency

Left: The Coronation of King Charles II in Westminster Abbey, from the BBC serial *Pepys' Diary*. When I chose this, rather than a glum play by Ibsen, the director asked why. I said that when I thought of playing Charles II, I smiled; when I thought of playing the Ibsen, I did not

As Fairfax in *Cromwell*, who was, in the film, demoted from his actual historical role as Commander in Chief down to merely General in command of the cavalry. For the purposes of the film the CIC had of course to be Cromwell. I am seen here enjoying a gallop, during a charge in one of the battles. I believe it was either Naseby or Marston Moor, which, as everyone knows, are both situated in northern Spain, where all the battle sequences were shot!

Playing the Sultan in *Sinbad's Golden Voyage*. I was hidden behind a golden mask for most of the film when I was merely the Grand Vizier, and where I was guide, philosopher and friend to Sinbad in his adventures. My face had been hideously burned by the wicked magician, to be finally healed in a magic fountain and revealed at the very end, as shown here in all it's manly beauty. It will be readily understood that, for my face to be hidden behind a mask, during most of the film, was a decided plus. I have not included it in my memoirs. Ray Harryhausen's monsters, however, were a *tour de force* and were the real stars of the film

With Amy Dalby in *A Public Duck*, one of two plays in the *Love Story* series which I did for ITV. I played a lonely old man, who feeds the ducks in a public park and has a disagreement with an old lady over feeding a particular duck. Both of them feel they have prior claims on its affections. Needless to say, they become friends and she invites him to tea. As the title of the series indicates, they fall for each other, always meeting at the same park bench, by the duck pond. The story ends with the old lady alone on the bench looking anxious and very sad, and wondering where he is. He has of course died. A rather mournful little tale, but beautifully written. I enjoyed doing it with Amy

For my second appearance in the *Love Story* series, I played opposite the lovely Wendy Hiller. It was entitled *Never Too Late* and was a charming tale of the widow of a famous conductor, who meets and befriends a lonely old retired General in a hotel in Harrogate. She is there for the Music Festival and he to indulge his passion for touring old battlefields of the English Civil Wars

As Sir Roger Burroughs, the shy octogenarian General in *Never Too Late*. Burroughs was attending a regimental dinner to celebrate his 80th birthday. At Wendy's character's decided determination, they form an unlikely friendship, eventually falling in love and marrying. It was beautifully written and the improbability was most cleverly handled, becoming entirely plausible. The programme was a great success and playing with Wendy was one of the most enjoyable experiences in my career

With Eric Porter during a relaxing break in the filming of Charlton Heston's directorial début of Shakespeare's *Antony and Cleopatra*, in an unposed photo by Lydia Heston. As well as directing the film, Chuck also played Antony, an ambition he had long cherished, and Eric played Enobarbus, with his usual success. The whole venture was shot in Almeria, in Andalusia. Unfortunately, it was a season of high winds and much of the dialogue in the open air had to be post-synchronised because of that. However, I greatly enjoyed working again with Heston, who was, as ever, his usual generous self

Thorley Walters as Dr. Watson and myself as Sherlock Holmes in disguise in *The Adventure of Sherlock Holmes' Smarter Brother* in which Gene Wilder was director and star turn. Marty Feldman, the cross-eyed comic, always arrived at the studios driving an ancient, but immaculate Rolls-Royce. I was obliged in the script, which of course had nothing to do with Doyle, to appear in a variety of disguises. It was a bizarre experience

Gene Wilder putting a point of direction to me. I am here completely unrecognisable (at least I very much hope so!) in disguise as a street musician. I cannot remember how we faked the violin-playing. We must have done so because, talented as Thorley certainly was, he had to play the harp, which I am pretty sure was not one of his accomplishments. If you find this sort of thing amusing, then you would find the whole film hilarious. I have to confess that I did not do so. I have always found the combination of Mel Brooks and Wilder extremely funny but, on this occasion, Brooks was not with us

Glenda Jackson played Sarah Bernhardt in *The Incredible Sarah*. I was Montigny, her employer. My old friend Daniel Massey was also in what I thought was a dreadful film. Glenda faced it bravely and, with such sheer acting skill, got away with it. I, on the other hand, nearly got the sack for my outspokenness to the veteran American director

As Jim Fanning in *Octopussy* with Roger Moore as James Bond. In Sotheby's Auction Rooms we are watching the villain bidding for the mysterious Fabergé egg before, to my horror, Bond enters the bidding, which is already in millions. To my astonishment, I got more fan mail from all over Europe and the UK than I have ever had in my life for anything including Sherlock Holmes, which itself was pretty prodigious but confined to the UK. Roger was fun to work with and light-hearted

co-religionists, but evidently his Christian principles carried the day and he said he would see what he could do to find them somewhere to stay. This, it transpired, proved less than easy, as Pastor Konkoly placed difficulties in accepting any of the options going. The Pastor of Pont Street rang me up, obviously having had more than enough and holding me responsible. He said, with some asperity, "Pastor Konkoly is a deeficult mon to hailp".

I forget how it was all resolved but I heard that the persistence of Pastor Konkoly resulted, somehow, in their passage to America. Not very much later, I heard from him that he had acquired a well-to-do parish and was driving a very large car.

As to the film that brought this about, I have never seen it and am acquainted with no-one who has. It sounds a *lulu*.

25

Cromwell 1969

Following hard upon *Patton* came the film, *Cromwell*, for which the battles of Edge Hill and Naseby were to be shot in Spain. I was delighted to hear that Alec Guinness was to be in it, playing King Charles. I was to play Thomas Fairfax, who had been suitably demoted for the film, from Commander-in Chief of the Parliamentary army to Cromwell's lieutenant. After all the *star* role in the film *was* Cromwell and it was to be played by Richard Harris.

I found it a less than happy assignment as Harris was to throw rather more than his weight about, throughout the film, with objections to anything that might show Cromwell in a less than favourable light. He carried this to such paranoid lengths that he identified himself with his own idea of the character, regarding anyone opposing him in the plot of the film almost as an actual personal enemy. Very nearly out-methoding *Method*.

His performance started well enough, having established that Cromwell was in fact a lovely lad from Limerick. As the character developed in the script, becoming a good deal less pleasant, this interpretation became more difficult to sustain.

As Fairfax, I had to support him, but only up to a certain point. That point was reached with the Death Warrant of the King, which Fairfax refused in council, to sign, maintaining that to do so, would be regicide. In the script, as in history, he then rises and leaves the Chamber. At this Harris, at rehearsal the day before actual shooting and perhaps not having read the script beforehand, rose in his might and flatly refused to countenance such a proceeding.

"I'm not having him fuckin' walking out on *me* - turning this into a fuckin' kangaroo court."

Ken Hughes, the director, mildly pointed out that that was what historically happened and that, having refused to sign the Warrant, Fairfax could hardly be left to sit there and sulk.

"Look," said Harris, "what's the fuckin' picture *called*? Eh? What's it called? *Who gives a fuck about Fairfax?*"

Nothing had been settled and the scene was to be shot the next day. I went home with some jitters, having learned the lines as per script and being strongly allergic to last minute changes thereto. So far nearly all of Harris's whims had been law, backed by threats to walk off the set. However, on this occasion I was favoured by fate. Harris arrived next morning in his sunniest mood. He told me that he had enjoyed a most agreeable evening at home, with his *stand-in* and two of our lady *extras*. He seemed to have forgotten his objections to the *kangaroo court* and the scene was shot, as scripted.

I was sitting, waiting for the scene to be lit when he appeared and flung himself into the chair next to me. After an account of the evening's pleasures, he went into thought and then said, "You know, Doggie, I'm thinking of giving a couple of Richard Harris Scholarships, to LAMDA (London Academy of Music and Dramatic Art)".

I expressed some surprise at this, as they had booted him out as "unlikely to earn his living on the stage".

"Yes, I know, but I think I'll do it, all the same."

I remember thinking that perhaps he should give the candidates a talk on, 'How to succeed, without trying, in spite of *being extremely* trying'.

His stand-in, a large fellow with cauliflower ears, then appeared, bearing a large cardboard box which he placed on the floor. In it was a pint tankard of beer. Then, noticing me, "D'ya fancy a pint, Doggie?" Harris asked. As it was still about nine in the morning, I declined, with thanks. He then noticed Robert Morley, who was sitting a few feet away, with his back to us, chatting to Charles Gray and called out, "Would you like a pint, Bob?" Morley took no notice, so Harris repeated the offer, but louder. Bob slowly turned his head and eyed Harris with something like disbelief.

"What?" he said.

"I asked, would you like a pint?"

Bob stared at him. "It's all over," he said. "When the star of the film offers you a pint of beer at nine o'clock in the morning, it's time for us all to pack up and go into the grocery business."

At this crushing rejoinder, Harris said, "Bob, you've got me all embarrassed now. Is there anything else you'd like?"

Bob waved a dismissive gesture. "Oh no, no, I don't suppose there's any Champ...." and broke off. "No, no, of course there isn't."

Poor Harris looked completely confused and then sent for a couple of bottles of Dom Perignon, which Robert also waved aside.

I felt almost sorry for him: at least, momentarily.

On location in Spain, we all had to ride frequently. Depending on the weather or Harris's changeable moods, we were all obliged every day to go to the battlefield site, get into make-up and part-costume, ready to go at a moment's notice. Those of us not directly in use were supposed to practice their riding. As the horses were in use in all of the battle scenes, either that or engaged with the second unit elsewhere, there was not very much opportunity, in practical terms, for riding practice at all. We were all called, nevertheless, involving us, for most of the time, spending day after day in our caravans, hanging about in costume and make-up without a horse in sight.

Alec was a particular sufferer from this daily production muddle but, as he was slow to complain, they just let him get on with it. Finally, after some weeks of this inconsiderate treatment, he wrote to his agent in London, sending a copy from his diary, which read, "called for costume, make-up, and riding practice: no horses, so not used". This occurred day after day.

The agent complained to Irving Allan, the panjandrum of the whole film, whose tyres screeched down to the unit office, bearing the great man to vent his wrath on *production*.

I was with Alec in his caravan, listening to some Haydn quartets, when there came a knock at the door to reveal a chastened-looking production manager. Uneasily he enquired if everything was all right, "because, if there is anything you need, you only have to tell us".

Alec acknowledged this, with a "thank you". The man turned to go and then, as if an afterthought had just struck him, he said, "Oh, and, er, Alec, if you have any cause for complaint, don't tell your agent, just tell me".

Alec looked him over and, pursing his lips, he said quietly, "And what good do you suppose that would do?"

During some of our interminable waits, Bob Morley came into my caravan for a chat. He was always an amusing raconteur. In a brief moment in between anecdotes, I told him how well I remembered his most touching portrayal of Louis XVI, in an otherwise forgettable film called *Marie Antoinette*. He looked at me thoughtfully and said, "I believe that was the last time I ever gave a performance".

He was denigrating himself, of course, because although Morley was invariably Morley, he always turned it to good account and gave distinguished performances: in such roles as Undershaft in the film of *Major Barbara*, as Prinny (Prince of Wales) in *The First Gentleman* and his own very successful play *Edward My Son*, not to forget his Oscar Wilde, for which he was a natural. He told me that he had disliked his army-officer father and gave me to understand that this resulted in his own views being decidedly *Left*.

If so, he was a classic example of the Champagne Socialist, as he was not only very fond of that wine, but also of good living in general.

As soon as we were back in England, Alec was able to resume his consummate portrayal of Charles, to which he had given his customary concentration of thought and detailed analysis, resulting in a performance which, as always, epitomised *the art that concealed art*. Harris took to watching him, frowning with grudging admiration. He once turned to me and said, "By God, you've got to hand it to him. I think that you can really learn from watching him."

This, of course, was unlikely as Harris's way of going about things was the total antithesis of Alec's. He would throw himself into the make-up chair, having first put on a disc of himself, singing in *Camelot*, and perusing the script for the day, memorise it almost at once, with his truly remarkable photographic memory and that, so far as one could see, would be that. I believe that he relied on his natural boundless self-confidence and what, for some at least, was his animal magnetism to carry him through. He never showed much sign of giving his work a great deal of thought beforehand.

I had seen a thoughtful performance by him a long time ago, in a TV play by Joseph O'Connor, called *The Iron Harp*, in which he played a blind Irish poet. It was the first I had ever heard of him and I was much impressed. So much so, that when I first met him in *Cromwell*, I congratulated him on it. To my surprise, my compliment was ignored and he launched into a long tirade against O'Connor, liberally seasoned with four-letter words.

As the filming went on, he took more and more to watching Alec working. This, it transpired, was no longer in admiration, but in order to look out for anything that might show Cromwell in an unduly unfavourable light. As Alec's character developed in sympathy so, of course, Cromwell's declined. He made frequent protests, ensuing in arguments with the director, occasionally with some success. In one instance, after the *rushes (Rushes: a re-run of the previous day's filming)* next day, I asked Alec how it had been resolved.

He looked at me quizzically for a moment. "It turned out to be *out of focus,*" he said. It was never re-shot.

I cannot imagine how Alec retained his patience throughout the film. I was made of less sturdy spirit, being considerably depressed by it all. One morning, in the make-up chair, he noticed this and said, "Come on, let's go somewhere dizzily smart for dinner. Where would you like to go?"

I suggested Prunier's in St. James, adding, "Provided we don't say anything, or talk at all about this bloody film," to which he agreed.

Remembering his punctuality, I arrived at the restaurant early. He did not appear to be there. I then noticed, in a tucked-away corner, a wide-open copy of *The Times.*

It was Alec, in hiding.

We had a couple of huge Dover soles and I asked for some nutmeg on my spinach. Alec waved it away. "Nutmeg on spinach?" he said. I gave him a taste of mine. He caught the waiter's eye and asked for some to be grated on his.

I had a letter from him, the Christmas before he died. In it, he recalled this and said, "I've had nutmeg on spinach for the rest of my life".

At last the final day of filming arrived and we all gathered together for a drink in the studio bar. Richard Harris had presents for all of us and he gave me a very handsome cigar box in red leather. I thanked him and I said, "I will keep this always on my coffee-table and every time I look at it, I will think of you".

It is there to this day and contains nothing but his card, "For Douglas, with many, many thanks, Richard".

I appreciated the thought, but what he was thanking me for, I don't know: certainly not my golden opinions.

26

Dame Wendy Hiller 1972

In the 1970s, *ITV Playhouse* put out a series entitled *Love Story*. They enjoyed varying success: some had charm, others were so-so, and some were distinctly mawkish.

I was sent the script of one which caught my very definite interest. It was called *Never Too Late* and concerned a late-blossoming love story between a shy octogenarian General, Sir Roger Burroughs, to be played by me, and the widow of a renowned conductor.

The old man, who had lived alone, was entirely preoccupied with historic battles, which he would re-enact with match boxes on table tops before actually walking round the old battlefields on foot. In this case he was preparing to do so on the following day round Marston Moor, a few miles from Harrogate, the site of the Parliamentarian rout of the Royalist army in the English Civil War.

The part of the woman was also not quite young, but she had to be still attractive, charming and certainly pretty forceful.

They meet for the first time in the hotel lounge in Harrogate after dinner where she is staying for the Music Festival. She notices the old boy, sitting alone with ordnance maps and manoeuvring his matchboxes into battle formation on the coffee table. She is intrigued and curious to know what he is doing. He soon becomes aware of her interest, which he finds embarrassing and intrusive. She eventually feels impelled to ask him what he is doing. He gruffly tells her that it is the preamble to walking the battlefield the next day. She is not put off so easily and continues her interest and, much to his surprise, he finds himself explaining how the action was fought, the course of Prince Rupert's cavalry charge and where Fairfax's right wing was routed before Cromwell's Ironsides finally won the day.

To his consternation she not only expresses much interest, but also asks if she might perhaps accompany him on his expedition the next day. She brushes aside his prevarications as to the roughness of the terrain and he agrees, somewhat reluctantly, to her request. She tells him the next day that her husband always used to conduct at the Music Festival and invites him to accompany her to a concert in the evening.

To his astonishment, they do both the battlefield and the concert. To cut a long story short, the association warms up until, after a decent interval, she actually proposes marriage to him and takes him on as her second husband.

The play was charmingly written and the gradual ripening of their relationship entirely convincing and had much humour. She gradually cures him of many of what, in her not entirely humble opinion, were his less attractive ways. I forget the exact ins and outs of the plot, except that he finally expires quite peacefully in her loving arms, having enjoyed a short but blissfully happy marriage.

Naturally I rather wondered who was going to play this forceful lady and was surprised and delighted to hear that Wendy Hiller had agreed to do it. I had long admired her from her youthful beginnings, both in the theatre and in such films as *Major Barbara* and *Pygmalion*, to which Bernard Shaw had given his consent only on condition that she played both leading roles. She came, armed not only with a formidably distinguished career, but also with an equally formidable reputation for being difficult to manage and accustomed to having her own way.

Well, we would have to see. Very soon we did.

When she arrived at the first rehearsal, I was most agreeably surprised at her youthful and attractive appearance. She must have been pushing 60, but she still retained the bloom of youth in her cheeks, moving gracefully and with a lovely speaking voice. She showed very few signs at all of her age. She was still most decidedly a proposition. Well, so far so good.

She lost no time, however, in demonstrating her reputation for forcefulness. After we had done the first read-through, she outlined for me her views on my role, including my appearance and the sort of clothes she considered I should be wearing. I heard her out, thanked her for her helpful advice and then, with equal emphasis, I told her that I had already given the matter considerable thought and that I had made up my mind how to proceed and that that, subject to the director's approval, was what I intended to do.

She eyed me with a moment's consideration and then decided to leave it at that ... at least for the moment.

I am happy to say that from that moment, we got on famously. She was able to channel her not inconsiderable forcefulness into that of the character she was playing and that seemed to keep her perfectly happy. We ended up really very fond of each other and she confessed to me after the filming of my demise in her arms, that she had found it most upsetting. We had been good friends and I loved working with her and people, the press included, were very kind about the finished result.

It remains one of the most delightful television episodes that I can recall.

27

Daniel Massey

I first met Dan in 1966, when we did *Major Barbara* for ITV. He played Cosens while I did Andrew Undershaft, which was undoubtedly the most rewarding role in the entire play.

The title role was taken by that splendid actress, Eileen Atkins, who unluckily had less success with it than she should have done. She was excellent in rehearsals but, somehow, lost the edge in the actual performance.

As Cosens, Dan gave of his most charming and carefree best with a performance which seemed to be almost a reflection of his own personality, containing, as it did, an element of worldly wisdom curiously combined with his own particular brand of high-spirited innocence. I took to him at once and we became very good friends. Later on, I was to see that he had very different moods. There were long black depressions and apparently unreasonable irritability. However, there were no signs of these during *Barbara*.

He informed me that, when he had told one or two people who was going to play Undershaft, they had told him to make sure he had a goodly stock of Valium as, with me, he would most certainly have need of it. Who these people were I never knew. He very kindly added that in his experience, at any rate, my reputation for being difficult was entirely undeserved.

In this, of course, he was being over generous. I was often very difficult indeed and, in certain quarters, I had earned this ill opinion. A classic case in point was the BBC series of *Sherlock Holmes*, which, although successful, earned me no laurels for refusing to put up with crass incompetence. When things went wrong, I could not rest until I had done my best to put them right and this, in turn, could give rise to cross words and crossed swords. With competent direction and a halfway decent script, I could be as nice as pie. With *Major Barbara*, we had a sound director in John Frankau and really not too bad an author in George Bernard Shaw. Consequently, all went well.

But having touched on one of my hobby-horses, I digress.

I return to Daniel. He had not had a happy childhood or an easy adolescence, his parents being separated or divorced. His father, Raymond Massey, was domiciled in America while his mother, Adrienne Allan, in whose care he and presumably his sister were nominally left, was not exactly a model of maternal affection. They were brought up by nannies while she swanned about, he told me, as a fashionable lady about town. His parents, having thoughtfully provided him with Noel Coward as a godfather which stood him in good stead, later packed him off to boarding school at Eton.

This appeared to have given him a pathological dislike of his mother, about whom he never wished to speak. This, in turn, almost certainly gave rise to his many later psychological difficulties. During the time I knew him, he was always in the hands of a succession of psychotherapists, to whom he must have been a veritable goldmine. As siblings, he and Anna also appeared to have a somewhat dysfunctional relationship, keeping themselves well apart from each other and being reconciled only when Dan was literally on his death-bed.

Like so many of us, they both had unsuccessful marriages: he to Adrienne Corri and she to Jeremy Brett.

Dan could never hear Adrienne mentioned without seething with anger. Over the not ungenerous-sounding financial arrangements of their divorce, he told me that she would lose no opportunity to defame him, both socially and in the press, with accusations of how short of money he had left her.

I recall that, when she played the part of my wife, in *The Revenge of the Pink Panther*, she opened the boot of her car, which contained two mink coats, and how she pondered, with finger on chin, as to which one she would wear for the filming. At the time it struck me as somewhat at variance with her much advertised poverty. But perhaps they were *hired* for the occasion. Who knows? She was a very beautiful woman, but garrulous and wildly theatrical. Dan must have found her exhausting.

Adrienne is not a particularly common name. It was curious that both she and his mother bore the same name and both, in their very different ways, were *grandes dames* of the theatre. The psychos must have had a field-day with that.

When I first knew Dan, he and Lydia Bedford (the Duke of Bedford's former wife) were very much an item. She was considerably older than he was, so that, on the face of it, the arrangement seemed that of mother and son. However, there was more to it than that. She clearly doted on him and did her best to fulfil his every whim. What she could have hoped for from such serious misalliance, I cannot imagine. I think she blinkered that and simply lived from one day to the next. He was certainly emotionally dependent on her, but I know he worried about any long-term future, as he once said to me, with some anguish.

"Oh God, Doug. What *am* I to do? I can't *marry* Lyddy!"

For her part, I believe she allowed herself to hope, although she must have known that such hopes were unrealistic and that one day she would have to let him go. She was very stage-struck and even wrote fan letters to me after some of my performances, probably because I was a friend of Dan's. She also lent me her flat in London when I was stuck for somewhere to stay and she stayed with us once or twice in Suffolk, where she had never been before.

She certainly looked after Dan at a time when he greatly needed emotional support. Young in spirit, she had converted Woburn Abbey into the first great house to be a major tourist attraction and was a lively and most amusing companion. She had a wonderful fund of anecdotes of her many years at Woburn. She was the third of four sisters, all of whom, on the face of it, had made brilliant marriages and all of which had come unstuck. I met her skittish sister, Denise Ebury, on quite a few occasions. She had been married to Lord Ebury and, despite being no longer quite young, still enjoyed risqué stories and playing kneesy-kneesy with me, under the table: somewhat, I must confess, to my embarrassment.

There were two other sisters whom I never met. One had been married to Aly Khan, before he ran off with Rita Hayworth, and the fourth, Primrose, had married Earl Cadogan. All four sisters were very close.

Dan's quandary was perfectly understandable but in the end, of course, it had to finish. They did, however, manage to remain close friends, even after he married the lovely Penelope Wilton, whom I think he met when they were together in *Bloomsbury*, a play about Lytton Strachey and the *Bloomsburies*, as the group of artists and writers was called. Dan was brilliant as Strachey, giving a wonderfully camp and entertaining performance.

He had to lose a lot of weight for this, as Strachey had been skeletally thin, and I can see him now, slumped in an old-fashioned deck chair in our garden in Suffolk, just before he started rehearsals, his finger tips together, knees pointing upwards and a Panama hat tilted over his eyes. "I'm practising being Strachey," he said. He loved coming down to Suffolk and going for extravagantly fishy meals at Pinney's, in Orford. Sometimes we would buy huge Dover soles on the beach at Aldeburgh, which I rather fancied myself as a dab hand at grilling.

Not long after his marriage to Penelope, he started his dark moods again when he would sit, silent and morose, refusing even to listen to his beloved music. He would confine himself to the house, gloomily contemplating the world from an upstairs window. At such times, any communication with him was impossible. I tried a few times to be met with a blank wall of depression, with the occasional burst of irritation. I think most of these moods were triggered by gaps in his professional work. He cannot have been like that when he was either rehearsing or actually playing. He really did live for his work and I believe he regarded such gaps as a form of rejection. I recall his unreasonable fury with our excellent mutual agent, Julian Belfrage, when his daily telephone calls produced nothing in the immediate offing.

I found it surprising that a man of Dan's professional experience should be so often taken off-guard by such eventualities, inevitable in the lives of all actors, no matter how successful. He told me that, after his brilliant filmic portrayal of his godfather, Noel Coward, in *Star*, for which he received an Oscar nomination, he had had a very long period out of work. He was convinced that this was because he had so successfully portrayed a homosexual. I was equally convinced it was not and that it was purely the luck of the draw. However, he was used to being in demand so that was that.

In spite of producing a lovely daughter, Alice, these *black dog* moods of his returned and poor Penelope found him more and more uncommunicative, and felt increasingly that he was drawing away from her. She put up with it for a very long time but she was, after all, an attractive woman and she was working in the theatre. Inevitably, she fell for someone else, who paid her some attention: in this case, Ian Holm. She divorced Dan and re-married.

Dan told me that, quite naturally, she had found living with him impossible and had found someone, to use his own words, "who would give her a good time", whatever he meant by that.

During his marriage, however, he gave several performances of distinction, among them his Othello, which I went up to see at the Nottingham Playhouse. Although he was, I felt, cast against type, he gave a fine portrayal, conveying a tremendous dignity and a true nobility of mind. However, I remember he was not happy with it and felt that Iago, played by Timothy West, was in some way undermining his performance. I said that was the nature of the play but he remained, I am sure, unconvinced. I wonder how he would have coped with Olivier's Iago?

There was a considerable period of time when I knew that he did not want to be bothered with me so I left him alone. When we re-met, we resumed our friendship as if it were yesterday and no such gap in time had occurred.

He had got together with Penelope's equally lovely sister, Lindy, and he appeared to be very happy with her. She was not in the theatre itself but none-the-less seemed very much of it. Whenever I saw them together, they seemed to be happy, although Dan still had a tendency to his old down-moods. They came up to stay with us every so often and we would all repair to our old haunts like Pinney's in Orford. Both Anne (my third wife) and I loved it whenever they came and would look forward to it very much.

Lindy and Dan had a few years together before Dan was struck down with Hodgkin's Disease, which had not been diagnosed, in spite of all the investigations of our wonderful Harley Street, until it was far too late to save him. He fought like a lion and bore heavy doses of chemotherapy with incredible bravery. Whenever we visited him in hospital, he remained cheerfully optimistic. In March 1998, he died. I read at his Memorial service at St. Paul's, Covent Garden, which was attended by most of the elite of the profession he had loved so well.

I fear that all the foregoing has paid inadequate tribute to his debonair charm, both on and off the stage. He had a delightful singing voice and it was a most poignant moment, almost unbearably so, when it was heard, resonating round the church, singing, "I've got a little lock-up in the Portobello Road," from *Make Me an Offer*.

His distinguished career needs no focus from me. It has spoken for itself. I have done my best to record the man I knew as my friend with only enough background detail necessary to make it comprehensible.

His last public appearance was as Furtwaengler in the play *Taking Sides*, in which he gave a performance of towering dignity. His deep love and understanding of music gave his portrayal a passionately quickening vein of truth. He was quite simply magnificent. He undertook this, despite two previous onslaughts of chemotherapy which had not only deprived him of his fine crop of hair, but which, I am sure, had far deeper repercussions than he cared to reveal. On his last visit with Lindy to Suffolk, in the middle of our usual bouts of mirth, I remember his sudden and sombre look when he quietly said, "There's no doubt, Doug - I've been winged". This was in marked contrast to his more recent outward attitude of optimism.

On a less sombre note: when I went to see this last performance, we went for supper after the play to Fortnum's where he, despite the actor's usual preoccupation with his appearance, strolled in as bald as an egg with total nonchalance and without the smallest sign of self-consciousness. This was in 1997 and long before shaven heads were a commonplace. An amazing friend.

He was fortunate indeed to have dear Lindy for the last few years of his life. Her unremitting care and love during his last long illness must have done much to alleviate his final sufferings. So thank God for her and God rest his sweet soul.

28

Hamlet, Nottingham And London 1970/71

In 1970 the Nottingham Playhouse invited Anthony Page, the young associate director of the Royal Court Theatre in London, to direct a production of *Hamlet*. With a transfer to London in mind, Alan Bates was invited to play the part and I was offered the role of Claudius, the King.

As I believed that Bates would be an interesting Hamlet and as I had long admired him as an actor, I was reasonably excited at the prospect. I asked who was to play the Queen and was told it was to be Isabel Dean, who seemed an excellent choice as she was slightly younger than me and a very attractive woman. She was also an actress of considerable experience and distinction. Furthermore, I knew her quite well and had always got on with her: all qualities of enormous importance to the successful realisation of Claudius and Gertrude. So far so good.

At his request, I went to see Page for a chat about the role and the forthcoming production and I was looking forward to hearing his views. However, he seemed to be more anxious to hear mine, venturing none of his own at all which I found rather surprising. Nor did he give me any idea as to the direction in which he proposed to take the play. I assumed that perhaps he had not yet made any decisions in detail or that he preferred, for the moment at least, to keep his cards close to his chest.

A week or so later, he rang me to say that Isabel Dean had pulled out as she had decided to take another offer. When I expressed disappointment at this, he hastened to reassure me, saying, "Don't worry, it's much better. We've got Celia Johnson!"

I was staggered and dismayed at the news. Celia Johnson was indeed a lovely actress and I had long admired her, but at no stage in her very long career would she ever have been right for Gertrude. She was, I believe, over 60 and looked, if anything, rather more.

How was I going to play Claudius, one of whose main motives for murder was the irresistible sexual allure of the Queen? In the *prayer for repentance* scene, Claudius makes clear reference to this, as does Hamlet in the closet scene with his mother, raging against the sexual nature of her ties to Claudius.

The casting of Celia Johnson in such a role made something of a nonsense of this, as in no possibility could her sexuality be considered as a credible motive for murder and I said so. Page appeared to be moved not one jot by this and all he said was, "Celia will be splendid".

Quite clearly I had either to rethink the role and find some other credible way of playing it, or withdraw altogether which, in all honesty in retrospect, I should have done. Wrongly, I decided on the former course, which was to concentrate on the only motives left to me, "my crown, mine own ambition," and to forget "my Queen", treating her merely as a gullible means to achieve those ends. This, I felt was hardly fair to Miss Johnson, Gertrude or Shakespeare, to say nothing of short-changing the audience and myself. However, I thought I would try to make the best of such difficulties as, having played the part as a schoolboy, I very much wished to repeat it. Rehearsals got under way and I began to re-fashion Claudius into a man who would conceivably marry a much older and not over-nubile Queen.

A further difficulty was that that the play was to be performed in its absolute entirety, taking over four hours, despite pleas from the Nottingham authorities that most of the audience would disappear before the end of the play.

We were shown the costume designs which, for the most part, were acceptably conventional. These were to be worn against what must have been the most unsuitable set for *Hamlet* ever to have been devised. It was an enormous tin box of uniform and shiny aluminium, resembling, in some aspects, a modernistic airport and, in others, the interior of a refrigerator. It was furnished with a variety of metal boxes in the same material, which served as thrones, beds and chairs. It had fidgety sliding panels. It seemed mindless and meaningless, and my heart sank.

At the dress rehearsal, it was lit entirely from the front, in a bright white light, making no concessions to atmosphere and presenting a most disconcertingly reflected glare to the auditorium. What was in the director's mind, only he knew. As may be perhaps surmised, he and I, by this time, had had certain disagreements and I regret to say that, in some considerable degree of exasperation, I once told him that I had been familiar with this play before he was born.

Alan, on the other hand, took everything he said, almost as *writ on tablets of stone*, following dutifully his director's every requirement without any apparent question. I found this extraordinary as I had formed the opinion that he was otherwise a man of some considerable intelligence. The results were not encouraging as his performance, from a promising first reading of his role, gradually dwindled into something very much less.

At the dress rehearsal, Alan told me, in desperation, that when he started out he had felt like a prince but now he felt like a Lowestoft trawlerman. A curious choice of words, but that is what he said. Possibly it was because of the lumbering top boots he was required to wear.

Happily Celia, with whom I got on very well and of whom I became very fond, almost always took my side in the disagreements with Page. We worked very well together as a team of two and did pretty much as our own mutual view dictated. She knew she was too old for the part and said that she should never have undertaken it. I lied and said that was nonsense, but I know she was not deceived. Either consciously or unconsciously, she was aware of my predicament and fell in with the course that I was taking. Without any discussion or planning, we worked together in perfect harmony, relying on our instinct and, certainly in her case, her not inconsiderable sense of theatre.

Page had been right (but perhaps not in the way, meant at the time), when he told me, "Celia will be splendid". I think we pulled it off, if not as Shakespeare intended, at least in the only way open to us in the circumstances. The press notices indicated that we had done so, being largely laudatory for Celia and me, although one or two complained, quite predictably, that we were "short on sensuality"! I am *sure* we were!

I have been reading a crop of these old press notices, which bear me out in much of what I have said. Poor Alan came off badly with hardly a word of unqualified praise that I could see in any of them. There were complaints of inaudibility and many references to his eccentric phrasing and meaningless pauses, often in the middle of sentences, reducing the text to total incomprehensibility.

Then, of course, we had had the very difficult set to contend with which did attract some considerable criticism, not to say ridicule.

Towards the end of the period of rehearsals, Page, perhaps having some understandable misgivings, summoned his friend John Dexter from the Royal Court Theatre to the dress rehearsal, at the end of which Dexter, I believe, strongly advised the stringent need for cuts.

Whereupon, instead of having presented us, from the first, with a well-considered and sensitively-cut version of the play, there was little time to do other than lop off the entire first scene on the battlements (probably one of the most atmospheric beginnings to any play, ever written) with other internal amputations, to the detriment of our confidence on the opening night. How we got through it as well as we did was a minor miracle.

In contrast to his past and subsequent distinguished record, I find it difficult to understand Anthony Page's handling of this particular production. I can only assume that he was trying to do something original with it but what that might have been God only knows. I also found his casting of Celia as the Queen, much as I had come to love her, equally strange. Some time later on I met Isobel Dean somewhere and teasingly chided her for backing out. She looked at me in some astonishment and said that she had been given no choice in the matter. She believed she had simply been replaced with a more illustrious name.

On Alan's fame in films, the production transferred, undeservedly, to the Cambridge Theatre in London, where it enjoyed a respectable run. Anthony Page continued with a most distinguished career, both on television and in the theatre.

29

Suffolk And East Anglia

I am sometimes asked what brought me to Suffolk to spend the rest of my days and the answer is Sherlock Holmes. It was a direct result of the series in the mid-'60s.

In the beginning I certainly enjoyed my moment of fame but my pleasure was to be short-lived, soured by the loss of any privacy I might have previously had. I took to wearing horn-rimmed spectacles and a hat pulled down to my eyes.

I used to visit my brother-in-law, who had a house in Norfolk where I greatly took to the wide-open skies and seclusion, and where people seemed content to mind their own business. I may have become paranoid but London had become difficult. Liz and I scoured Norfolk for a rural retreat but without success. So, passing through Suffolk on our numerous house-hunting forays, we decided to settle for there, eventually finding a semi-derelict cottage on the edge of Dallinghoo Wood. It had a bit of land with it and, blissfully, total seclusion.

As soon as we could, we took to weekending there whenever possible. I loved it, basking in our acre of garden, which we filled with old-fashioned roses. We planted a willow behind the cottage and generally made ourselves at home. We acquired some decent sticks of furniture in the antique shops of Woodbridge and Framlingham for practically next to nothing, as one so easily could in those days. Liz did not have quite the same feeling as I did about it as she bore the brunt of packing up provender for the week-end with which she, understandably, soon became weary. Neither did she have quite the same motivation to get out of London as I did.

Sometimes, later on, when I had times off between acting, I would drive down on my own and stay as long as I could.

Gradually and cautiously we made friends in the area and eventually, when my *fame* had simmered down, we were able to develop a pleasant social life in our rural retreat. I started to take pleasure in playing the country gent. I even had a gun in a nearby shoot. I was an erratic shot, but I greatly enjoyed bringing home game for the deep freeze, which I *ripened* first in the little adjoining barn where we kept the car.

However, I still had to earn my bread and cheese and continue my acting career though I certainly did not do so with the same zest as before.

Unfortunately, this ran concurrently, and with rather more enthusiasm, with my amatory career and eventually my poor wife felt she had had enough. To our mutual grief, she divorced me.

I left the London house and bought one in trendy Fulham, an area I was never able to take to. I set up home there with one single bed and bedding, one bedside chair and really not much else until I was gradually able to furnish it, which took me about a year. I wore my discomfort as a well-deserved hair-shirt and, despite all the lawyers' efforts to stir up maximum strife, we remained extremely fond of each other until the recent sad end of her life.

She had somehow managed to obtain an annulment on the grounds of my inability to produce children. I had to attend some sort of tribunal of priests from Westminster who presented for my signature a document, certifying my *impotence*. As it was my very potency, in the first place, that had caused all our problems, I asked them how I could possibly sign such a document?

"Well, as you can never be a father, that constitutes *canonical* impotence," I was told. A fine distinction.

"That means," said I, "that, in the eyes of the church, I am ineligible for marriage, under any circumstances whatsoever. Ergo, either I live in sin in the future or like a monk for the rest of my life, which, on present showing, seems rather unlikely."

The spokesman said yes, that was indeed the case. He was sorry. Not half as sorry as I was.

However, I had brought it all on myself. As a divorced person, I would not have been eligible for re-marriage in any case and neither would Liz. But in the case of annulment, however, she at least would be able to re-marry, whereas I, the *impotent* Lothario, could not. Fair enough, I thought, and signed the paper, wondering how she had managed it. She later told me that on a visit to Lourdes she had made friends with a Catholic psychiatrist, who, in his specialist capacity, had served on the second Vatican Council. He had taken up the cudgels on her behalf and it was under his expert guidance that it had all come to fruition. Good for her, I thought.

When I next saw her, I said with a wry smile, "So, darling, we've *never been married*". She looked straight at me and said, "Well, you and I know better, don't we?"

About a year later, she told me that a mutual friend, who had been widowed, had asked her to marry him and had offered to buy me out of my retained half-ownership of the house. I said that if she wanted to marry him, then I would obviously not stand in her way. I had made over half the house to her already under the divorce settlement. However, in the event of her pre-deceasing me, the whole house would have reverted to me. As soon as it was all put to rights, she married him and I am sure he was good and kind, and a much better husband for her than I had managed to be.

While he was still at Lloyd's in the City, I used to go up to London occasionally and take her out to lunch, which he did not seem to mind. One day she told me that this would have to stop, as he was not really too keen on me seeing her alone, not even in public. I was sad about it, but I quite understood.

I had my own life to get on with, which I did with some unwisdom, by marrying again. Her name was Barbara and I had met her in Nottingham, when I was in *Hamlet*. It was ridiculous and I should have known better. She was 22, but looked appreciably older, and I was 50. She was also extremely good-looking, which could have had something to do with it.

When the play finished in Nottingham, I went back to London but we spoke most days on the telephone. She was most anxious to join me there. I was very dubious as to the wisdom of this, bearing in mind the enormous age difference between us, so I demurred, giving her my reasons, to which she remained totally deaf. Then, one day she turned up at the house in Fulham with a suitcase, announcing that she would sit there until I agreed to let her stay.

Weakly, I finally agreed to this, but only for a short term. Well, the *short term* became longer and longer until, after a considerable amount of pressure, mainly from her parents, I married her. It was at Caxton Hall, with a wedding breakfast in the evening at the Garrick Club attended by a dozen or so of our friends.

Barbara took to my rural retreat in a big way and, being of a social turn of mind, started making friends there. I happened to bump into David Ball, the lighting assistant and lover to Angus McBean, the great theatre photographer. Both were professional acquaintances from way back in 1948 at Stratford-on-Avon and intermittently ever since then. They were living in Fleming's Hall, a most picturesque and moated medieval manor house in Bedingfield, near Debenham. They had given up photography and were running a highly successful and decidedly up-market antique shop in Debenham itself. There was a third member in the business, Norman Kelvin, who looked after the management of the shop, while David waltzed about to find the stock and, every so often, took journeys off to stay with Robert Carrier in Marrakesh.

Angus was a most colourful character, usually attired in a tailor-made boiler-suit over an extravagantly flowery blouse with a flamboyant bow tie or *pussy* bow to set off the whole bizarre ensemble. His conversation entirely matched his appearance, with an oddly child-like manner, which was most endearing. He was also highly intelligent and a genius, not only in photography into which he had introduced his own particular brand of dreamlike surrealism, but in many other branches of design, from hand-blocked period wallpapers to very fine and wonderfully imaginative pictures, executed in fine resins, often incorporating odds and ends of bric-a-brac: impossible to describe.

I own one of them, a six foot high work, called *Rubbish Owl*, in resins, incorporating discarded spare parts from a car scrapheap. It has two cogwheels for eyes and arrests the attention of anyone entering the room.

He had photographed everybody who was anybody in the theatrical profession of his and my generation, from the Oliviers to Marlene Dietrich. In fact, it was his photograph of Audrey Hepburn, at that time completely unknown, that first put her on the map. He was missing his life in the theatre so he got David to invite us to lunch.

As the two *boys*, David and Norman, were I suspect both suckers for glamour, they appeared greatly taken by Barbara's obvious pulchritude and amused by her high camp manner. We were gradually introduced into the inner circle of the elite gays of Suffolk, meeting Frederick Ashton, the great choreographer of the Royal Ballet; Freddie Fox, the Queen's hat maker; Robert Carrier, the cookery writer; Angus Wilson, the author and Anne Hoellering, who owned the Curzon Cinema in London, and many others.

Anne, who had a lovely house in Norfolk, appeared to be greatly smitten with David, who was outrageously amusing and rather like Michelangelo's head of *David*. She was often entertaining the *boys*, who would drive Angus over for lunch and much of the rest of the day. These occasions almost always included us. Anne had taken a great fancy to Barbara, who certainly had a way with her.

There was something almost *Bloomsbury* about those lovely long days in the Hoellerings' garden. It was very remote from the real world, as I know it today. There would be half a dozen of us, on rugs on the lawn, chatting, drinking or having a nap, while Angus snoozed in a deck-chair under an enormous willow, a large straw hat over his eyes, with his venerable white beard on his chest. Anne always made quite a ritual of the food and wines that she produced on these occasions. Nothing short of the very best would do, often travelling up to London, raiding Fortnum's and recherché Italian delis, for *bonnes bouches*, to put before her beloved *boys*. She was something of an expert over such vital matters.

When I eventually married Barbara, Anne insisted on buying her a long dress by a top Italian designer for the occasion. I suppose it was in the nature of a wedding present, but it was extremely generous of her and was certainly much appreciated by the wearer.

Those idyllic days, alas, eventually had to end.

Anne had taken David on a trip to Italy where they stayed *en prince,* I would imagine, wherever they went. It seems that in the Duomo in Florence they had some sort of disagreement over something or other and David stalked off in a rage and that was that. I believe they never spoke to each other again. She continued to ask us over for the week-end, from time to time, again for the most lavish meals, but it was never quite the same, of course, without the *boys*.

We sometimes had them all over to the cottage: Wood House, as it was grandly designated on the ordnance map. Barbara would dollop out cassoulet, or something simple, like chilli con carne. I remember once when Bob Carrier came. There was rather a good cassoulet on the go and he told me that his very favourite meal was baked beans on toast. The *boys* had persuaded him that Suffolk would be a great place to open a gourmet restaurant and that it would go very well. I believe the wish was father to the thought and they suggested

Hintlesham Hall, which was on the market at the time. It was a very beautiful Georgian house, set in extensive grounds and approached by a long drive. So he bought the place and spent a very great deal on doing it up in great style, and eventually opened with a fanfare of trumpets.

I fear that it turned out to be a disappointment for him. The *Right People*, on the whole, stayed away and it was visited mainly by the *merchant princes* of Ipswich, which was not quite, I think, what he had in mind.

Barbara and I went to dinner there and it was certainly very impressive. But the attendance was sparse and mainly as described. I have noticed that the *County* are, generally speaking, reluctant to spend on such luxuries as dining out. Bob's friends, on the other hand, did extremely well out of it as he often gave lunch or dinner parties in his own private wing of the house, in a large and splendidly-appointed private kitchen.

One Easter he gave a lunch party at a long dining table, laid out with silver and decorated; I cannot remember how or with what, but I know that the effect was perfect if slightly over the top. In every place-setting there was a real wren's nest with tiny *eggs* and a little trinket for the women and something small and appropriate for the men. Where he found the nests I cannot imagine, but the whole effect was quite delightful.

I was amazed at the ease with which he cooked and played host, producing a most elaborate and epicurean banquet. He had a couple of waiters, of course, but they simply served at table.

Another time we were asked over for a special occasion: a photo session with the New York equivalent of the magazine *House and Garden*. Bob was to cook lunch and the preparation of each course was to be photographed. It was to be entitled *Robert Carrier cooks lunch for friends*. The *boys* were there, of course, and some other friends, whom we had never met, and it took for ever. Shot after shot of the same subject. Bob had to flambé something or other: so, on with the cognac and whoosh! Several *takes* on that too: flames not high enough or too high. In the meantime, Bob's guests were becoming ravenous. However, when it eventually arrived, hot from the maestro's hand, it was of course pretty splendid.

After a very late lunch indeed, we all trailed out for photographs of the kitchen garden where I noticed, to my astonishment, a large bed of full-grown red pimentos. I was with David Ball, who bent down to look at them. He beckoned me over to look more closely. They were all Sellotaped on to the plants! Bob had been determined to make a splash.

He drove himself pretty hard. When he told me that he had been approached about running a cookery magazine, I looked at him aghast and said he would kill himself. He had Hintlesham to run, with a cookery school attached; he was also still running *Carrier's* restaurant in London. How did he think he could take on the added responsibility of producing a magazine as well?

I recall his reply, with a thoughtful look in his eye. "Well you know, I need to be stretched or I get very lazy." In the event, he did undertake the magazine but for a short time only. It had clearly been one *stretch* too many, even for him.

During the few years after the *Sherlock Holmes* series, I found that I had become seriously disenchanted in the exercise of my profession. A sequence of disappointments had contributed to this. There was the Alan Bates *Hamlet* which had certainly been a great disappointment. Although Celia Johnson and I personally came out of it very well, the production itself had not been a happy experience. I had looked forward to it greatly and I should have enjoyed it, but the circumstances I have described elsewhere made it impossible. No-one does well out of a flop whatever praise may have been lavished on an individual performance.

A script of a play arrived in 1967 for my perusal, called *According to the Evidence*. It was a transcript of a novel by Henry Cecil, otherwise Judge Henry Leon, and it was a type of *whodunnit*. The play needed a lot of rewriting to make it work. It was to go on tour and then in London where we were to have the Savoy Theatre. I was asked to play the lead. I suppose the lure of star billing in the West End, coupled with Naunton Wayne, the charming Muriel Pavlow and my old dear friend Michael Gwynne were my reasons for doing it. Either that or extreme penury.

One critic said of it that he could not understand what actors of our quality were doing in such a piece, adding philosophically and quite correctly, "I suppose even actors have to eat".

Looking back, there was a production in 1956 at the Saville Theatre directed by John Clements of Congreve's *Way of the World* in which I played Fainall, the villain of the piece. It had a star cast with Clements himself, as Mirabell, and his wife, Kay Hammond, as Millament: they were both too middle-aged for the parts. We had the great comic actress, Margaret Rutherford, extremely funny and a delightful person, but totally miscast as Lady Wishfort. Margaretta Scott, Harry Corbett and other stalwarts completed the cast.

We were ridiculously over-dressed by Doris Zinkeisen, tottering about on four inch heels, with cart-wheel hats with upstanding ostrich feathers. Katie Hammond, who was a star and a charming person, had begun to speak so slowly that the rest of us were encouraged to gabble our lines as quickly as possible to get through the piece at all. During rehearsals, I mentioned one or two of my misgivings to John Clements, who patted me indulgently on the shoulder. "You worry too much, dear boy," he said.

I do not think, personally, that *he* had worried *enough*: not until he read the press notices.

In 1959 I had been in a double bill of two excellent pieces by Anouilh, *Traveller without Luggage* and *Madame de..* with a very strong starry cast headed, in the first instance by Denholm Elliot, and in the second by Elizabeth Sellars and me. However, the very eminent director made less of a success of it than was his wont. It should have been a sure-fire successful transfer to the West End. We were all convinced that it would be until, half way through rehearsals, when I knew it had not a chance. It sank without trace.

In 1974 there was David Hare's first West End venture: *Knuckle*, with Eddie Fox, which was a promising piece of writing. Again I came out of it reasonably well but it was very much an early play, full of promise certainly but not really good enough. Nevertheless it enjoyed a respectable run at the Comedy Theatre in London. Eddie had had a great success with his film *The Jackal*, which clearly extended the run of *Knuckle* more than somewhat. Hare has written many more brilliantly successful plays since.

In 1975, there was also a film called *Sherlock Holmes Smarter Brother*, with Gene Wilder in which I, mistakenly, reprised my old role of his nibs; this time I appeared in a variety of absurd disguises, including one in *drag*. This was supposed to be highly comical.

The combination of Wilder and Mel Brookes was often hilarious. Unfortunately on this occasion, Wilder had decided to go it alone.

Then there was a film in 1976, with Glenda Jackson, in which Dan Massey and I had biggish parts, called *The Incredible Sarah*, about Bernhardt, with an infantile American script in which the emphasis was definitely on the *Incredible*.

I suppose it had a showing. I certainly have no recollection of ever seeing it anywhere, though I gather it was nominated for two Oscars and Glenda was nominated for a Golden Globe.

When I was a young actor, I had made a decision that if I had not made a considerable name for myself by the age of 40, then I would feel in honour bound to pull out. Here I was, well into my 50s and, apart from *Holmes*, still only known to TV audiences although I was, of course, well-known in the theatre among my fellow actors. Anyway, it had all become too stressful and I was really no longer enjoying it.

Eddie Fox asked me to play Polonius in his forthcoming *Hamlet*, but I still had the lingering sour taste of the last production of the play in my mouth and I simply could not face it. I think Eddie thought I had turned it down because the part was not good enough, but Polonius is quite as good a role as Claudius and not nearly as difficult.

Various TV offers and bits and bobs in films such as *Patton* - together with the experience of supporting Richard Harris in *Cromwell* - all combined to form my decision to *cut and run*. It had all begun to be stressful so, in short, I felt I had had enough. Adding to my malaise, I felt my memory was not up to scratch. Therefore, I was obliged to consider how best to fill my life and to earn my bread and cheese. I had always had a great interest in wine and given it a fair amount of study.

Woodbridge was a charming town but, like so many country places in those days, not over supplied with up-market watering holes and the concept of a *wine bar* was not exactly current. So I wondered if I could open one and make a success of it. I put the idea to Barbara, who seemed enthusiastic. She could look after the catering side, with assistance, and I could run the wine department. A friend called John Jacob, who was the chairman of Radio Orwell, had his ear pretty close to the ground so I asked him what he thought of the idea. He thought it a good one and suggested a visit to Simon Loftus, of Adnam's Wines, in Southwold.

This I did, telling Loftus my ideas and asking his advice. His reply was most encouraging, asking, "How much do you need?" I was a touch nonplussed by that and told him it was his advice I needed, not finance. I added that if I accepted finance from Adnam's, I would be tied to their wines, would I not?

"Not at all," he said. "You could get them wherever you like." I asked him what they had to gain from financing me. He replied, "To promote wine interest in Suffolk".

I thanked him, but I thought I would be able to go it alone so he advised me to serve some sort of apprenticeship in a wine bar, if I could find one, or even a pub.

It so happened that there was a wine bar in Hadleigh, about 30 miles away from Woodbridge, so we went to see the owner and asked him if he would take us on, as un-salaried labour. This he consented to and it was arranged for us to start work there the following week. After a few weeks of our *apprenticeship*, we began our search for premises, finding some, far from ideally situated on the first floor over some shops in the main thoroughfare of Woodbridge. This we converted into our wine bar, aiming for an atmosphere that was primarily masculine but at the same time where women would be happy to be.

We decided on a Holmesian theme and it was to be called *Sherlock's*.

I drew up a wine list, comprising carefully tasted wines at the lower end of the scale, rising in price to fine wines and classed growth Bordeaux, of which I had a considerable number, imported from my former home in London and which could be dispensed only by the bottle. There was luckily an unused cellar under the premises, ideal for the storage of wines.

After a number of unavoidable setbacks in the alterations to the interior, the building of a bar and all the other necessary paraphernalia, we were set for an opening date. We had found various good ladies in the neighbourhood, who catered for weddings and so forth and who could make excellent quiches and other delectables. We intended, and indeed produced, a large and varied buffet and salads, cold roast sirloin of beef, delicious black Suffolk hams, Aldeburgh crabs and Lowestoft smoked mackerel. While, for something hot, we had various home-made soups and a chilli con carne: not very original by today's standards, perhaps, but it would more than do to kick off with.

At last came the opening night: almost as nerve-wracking as a first night in the theatre. The place was packed to the gunwales and it all went off amazingly well. So far so good. We were off to a flying start.

We had taken on extra staff, mostly local debs and a very capable manager, a Dutchman called Hugo, who eventually did most of the cooking. So it continued, both day and night.

We had our regulars, who came in almost every day: sometimes at lunchtime, as well as the evening session. Very soon it became like a club where everyone knew each other. It had an original atmosphere and, almost at once to our amazement, we found ourselves in Egon Ronay's guide.

Unfortunately we suffered one serious casualty: my marriage to Barbara. She had begun to cross swords with my manager, Hugo. For some time, she had been leaving more and more in his highly efficient hands, coming in later and later, at the same time becoming resentful and critical of his methods. In the end, matters came to a head when she said he would have to go, or she would. By this time he had been with us for two or three years and was well entrenched in the running of the place, which meant I could have a day off, completely free of my responsibilities: also that I could even go off and do the odd assignment in my old world of the theatre. However, she was adamant. She was incapable of performing all Hugo's duties. I pointed out that, without him, we would have to shut up shop, as well she knew of course. I tried to reason with her, but she was unmoved. I am sure she had grown bored with the routine, once the novelty had worn off, and she simply wanted out. Poor old Hugo was just an excuse. She left the bar entirely to Hugo and me, with our *Pixies*, as our young serving wenches were called, and became a complete lady of leisure, which suited her nature far better. In a way, I was surprised that she had stayed the course as long as she did. However, she did continue to visit the bar, when not otherwise amused, but only as a very good non-paying customer.

About that time Bob Carrier decided he needed a hostess at Hintlesham: someone who would greet his guests, or rather his clientèle, on arrival, take their coats and lead them to where they could sit in comfort and enjoy an aperitif. It would have to be someone personable, with an out-going social manner, who could make the punters feel like invited guests. Well, he did not have to look very far before offering the job to Barbara. She was, after all, at a loose end and prone to getting into mischief on trips to her sister in London so I was pleased when she accepted Bob's offer, which suited her style much better than her former bread and butter job with me.

She got on very well with Bob and his guests and, on the rare occasions when I visited Hintlesham, she appeared to be doing her stuff very well. I am sure he was well pleased with her. She stayed on at the cottage until we finally decided to part. I had in the meantime moved into a very convenient flat, which I had bought, immediately opposite the wine bar. She then shook the dust of Suffolk from her feet for ever and I am sure, with no regrets or afterthoughts whatsoever, happily took up residence in the flat I had to buy her in London, very near to her sister.

I slogged on with the wine bar for about another year, when I began to feel that I had had enough of it. It had been a four-year stint, Hugo had departed, having eloped with one of my more attractive customers, and the atmosphere seemed not as it once was.

I put it on the market and it was bought, to my amazement, by a dwarf and his girl friend, who ran it with reasonable success for many years longer than I had been able to stay the course. Having changed hands again, it is still open to this day, but no longer as a wine bar. It is now a much more ambitious affair, as a restaurant serving elaborate meals with Malay overtones.

30

Marrakesh

One Spring during this time, Barbara expressed a great desire to go to Marrakesh, mainly I came to believe, because Robert Carrier was in residence there at the time. The place itself had always had a lingering attraction for me. I liked the sound of it, nestling at the foot of the Atlas Mountains: spicy Arab food, a maze of souks and of course the fabulous Djemaa el Fna, the huge square at its centre, filled with fortune-tellers, snake-charmers, acrobats, story tellers and musicians. I also wanted to see the wonderful Koutoubia Mosque, the original model for the later Giralda in Seville. Mari, Barbara's amusingly naughty younger sister, was to come with us.

I had read of it as a city in the grip of delirious imagination - a feverish dream of honey-combed alleys, minarets, quivering in the moonlight, haunted by the restless carnival, which had lasted a thousand years without ceasing - and a lot more hyperbole, most of which, in realisation, turned out to exist largely in the delirious imagination of the Moroccan Tourist Board.

However, we arrived and settled in at our large and characterless hotel, which could have been anywhere, and made for the Djemaa el Fna, mentioned above. This turned out to be a monstrous bear-garden, teeming with the most aggressive and persistent touts I have ever encountered. We bore it for a short time and then attempted to make our escape down an adjacent alleyway, the touts still in hot pursuit. Finally we ended up in a bar, with the door firmly shut in their faces. We had a drink there and when we made to leave, three of them were still there and ready for the off. I eyed the most aggressive of them in a fury and told him to "Bugger off!" He gave me a villainous look and said, "You tell me to bugger off? I tell you to fuck off! All English are Jews!" They then left us alone.

Not the most auspicious introduction to Marrakesh we could have had. However, we managed to find a taxi to take us back to our hotel, where we remained until the evening.

We then went out and found a restaurant nearby which was almost empty, in which the seating arrangements consisted of recliners round the walls. We were shown to a set of these, next to a Moroccan gentleman in European dress. He was holding a long glass containing something amber and tinkling with ice. I was virtually next to him on my chaise-longue, with Barbara and Mari at right angles to me.

To our slight irritation, he seemed inclined for conversation. "Bonsoir, monsieur. Vous êtes ici avec votre harem?"

I explained, perhaps a little stiffly, that one of the ladies was my wife and the other her sister. "Ah, vous êtes en vacance." He then offered his assistance in any way possible, producing his card with a flourish. "Oh God, not another tout?" I thought. But no, he was a Captain in the Palace Guard in the Suite de Sa Majesté, which was clearly meant to infer that he was a personage of considerable influence. It would give him intense pleasure after our meal, he said, if we would honour him by taking a glass with him at the Mamounia: the local Claridges, made famous by Churchill's repeated residence there.

It was our first night, so why not? Perhaps somewhat unwisely, we accepted. He escorted us outside to a battered black Renault, reeking of petrol, in which he hurtled us through the considerable night traffic of Marrakesh, weaving in and out, first on one side of the road and then the other, keeping up a flow of chatter all the while. He said something about an obligation to call first at the Palace and asked me to request that the ladies do not descend from the *voiture*, once on the Royal premises.

We rattled through a pink stone gateway, past sentries with sub-machine guns, who leapt to attention. He then pulled up sharply outside a large caravan, which he invited me to enter, leaving the girls in the back of the car. This was his command-post, with an officer and a couple of men in uniform. There was much saluting and an interchange of throat clearing, after which he led me to a table with telephones. From here, he told me, I could telephone anywhere I liked in the world. "Telephonez Londres, New York, ou vous voulez - pas de problème."

As he clearly wished to demonstrate his power to dispense *largesse*, I felt it would be churlish to refuse. Also, by this time I was more than a touch tight. I wrote out Liz's number and handed it to him and in less than the rub of a lamp, I heard Liz's bemused and sleepy voice, enquiring anxiously if I was all right. "The

Palace at Marrakesh? A hotel? Not a hotel. Are you sure you're all right? I was asleep actually."

Oh Lord, I had forgotten the hour's difference and had woken her up. "Damn. Sorry."

"Allons-y," said Mustafa, taking my arm. Back to the girls in the malodorous Renault and another nightmare race to the Mamounia. The enormous bar, under massive chandeliers, was ablaze with light and empty. He ordered huge whiskies, clinking with ice, which we sipped by a bogus-looking Moorish fountain. Mustafa would not hear of me buying a round. He had obviously decided to like us and was babbling about a wonderful fish tagine, he could arrange for lunch tomorrow. I had rashly expressed a fondness for fish.

We thought he would most probably never be seen again, or would be too tight to remember next day, so we agreed to wait in our hotel around lunchtime. If he did not appear, we could always go in and have a late lunch there. Around one thirty, he rang. He was desolated, but he had been held up by the security arrangements at the royal golf-course. He would be with us in half an hour in the hotel bar.

On the dot of two, I found him, elbow on the bar, short and plump in a tight blue uniform, with the usual large Scotch on the rocks. He was full of apology and explained that, on the last appearance of Sa Majesté on the royal links, terrorists had lain in wait at the 18th hole with a machine gun and that Majesté had just escaped death, by diving into the royal bunker, as they opened fire. Such a thing must not be allowed to occur again. It would not be good: not for Sa Majesté and certainly not for Mustafa.

He downed his Scotch with a sigh and greeted the girls as they joined us, kissing their hands. After the usual enquiries as to well-being and the quality of last night's sleep, he clapped his hands and led us outside to the car. Then we, and for some reason never explained, also the barman, found ourselves crammed into the careening Renault, narrowly missing mopeds, taxis with live goats and other strange items of traffic.

Leaving the city, we hurtled and bumped along forlorn and pot-holed highways, finally pulling up outside a lone tumbledown building, some 20 kilometres from the town. It looked unpromising and I noticed that the girls seemed shaken and none too happy. Inside, there was a sad-looking bar with no alcohol visible. There were several sets of bare trestle tables with folding chairs and, in a recess, a small bar-billiards table. *Our* barman, whose English appeared to have been limited to the names and prices of drinks, shuffled uneasily in the background. I invited him in French to join us but he held up his hand, his head deprecatingly on one side, muttered something I failed to catch and followed Mustafa who had disappeared through the swing door.

There followed almost at once a most diabolical shouting match in the kitchen, with Mustafa's voice the loudest. It rose to a crescendo and suddenly stopped as he kicked open the swing door and strode into the bar, bearing four bottles, which he plonked down on the table before us. "Je regrette, mes amis, il n'y a pas de poisson. Je suis désolé." Then followed a long tirade about how his life was beset by imbeciles.

Barbara caught my eye. She looked desperate. "When's he going to pour the bloody wine?" she hissed. Mari looked pale and her eyes were shut.

Mustafa indicated a treat in store. He rattled on about tagines of this, that and other ingredients and their varying degrees of succulence: but still no wine, not in our glasses at least. Mustafa seemed to have forgotten about it; evidently it really took the hard stuff to concentrate his attention. I stole a look at my watch. It was 4.30pm. Barbara muttered that she was dying for a drink and did I think, perhaps …? I shook my head.

As if divining our thoughts, he broke off and the wine at last arrived in the glasses. It was white and it was warm, but it was certainly welcome. "Santé," he beamed. Barbara downed half her first glassful in one.

"Le roi," I enquired. Did Sa Majesté himself take a drink? He eyed me gravely and said "Sa Majesté… est très discret," at which point the door was kicked open by our friend, the barman, who, with a modest smile, sailed across to our table, bearing an enormous dish of kebabs. He was followed by a small boy, carrying a tray with bowls of steaming sauces, which gave off the odours of paradise. We fell to and they were every bit as good as they smelt. Mustafa knocked off half a dozen or so at great speed and, wiping his lips and fingers, watched us with the benevolent smile of a philanthropist.

"Ça vous plaît?" he enquired, picking his teeth with a quill. Matters then became really serious, with a monster tagine of young pigeons, nuts and unidentifiables, best not enquired into. We were finally defeated by the arrival of yet another confection, this time of young chickens and salted lemons, with couscous. By this time the bottles had been arriving hard upon each other and I saw and heard Mustafa through a rosy haze.

What a splendid fellow he was, to be sure.

Great heavens, he was already weaving his plans for dinner. "Perhaps a little fish?" he coaxed. By this time we were as wax in his hands. I looked at the girls, who were too exhausted to protest. But first, he said, we must have a little rest so we piled into the car, leaving our friend the barman behind, and rattled our way back into the mêlée of Marrakesh. For reasons which will remain forever obscure, we stopped somewhere in the town to pick up a totally silent Moroccan lady before driving up to a large hotel. We went up in the lift to one of the bedrooms where he seemed quite at home, ringing down for a bottle of Scotch. I sat on one of the two beds, between Mustafa and the silent lady, while the girls retired to the bathroom to repair the ravages of the day. I made an attempt at being polite to her, but was told by our host that, as she was Berber, she was unable to understand.

"Does she please you?" he enquired. Somewhat flummoxed and in the hope that he did not mean what I thought he might mean, I mumbled something to the effect that she seemed charming enough. "Then she is yours," he said with an expansive gesture. Taken aback, I reminded him that I had a wife in the bathroom. He looked genuinely surprised, "Mais Monsieur, vous êtes en vacance!" That settled, he shrugged and poured the Scotch.

When the girls came out, he disappeared for a moment, returning with a small pot of what appeared to be thick cream. He took some in a teaspoon and handed it to me. When I hesitated, he said it was a special honey called *majune*, which he strongly endorsed. I tasted it gingerly and found it indeed very pleasant. He then handed some to the girls and then took some himself. The Berber lady merely observed. It certainly had an effect. Almost at once, life assumed a rosier hue and our situation appeared irresistibly comic. A very special honey it was; and clearly well-laced with hash. We were laughing immoderately at whatever was said. I remember very little of the remains of the evening. We must have somehow extricated ourselves from the threatened fish dinner, probably pleading fatigue from an excess of delights already enjoyed.

Somehow he got us back to our hotel albeit in a state of near collapse and we promptly retired for the night. It was only our first day in Morocco and he had threatened to visit us on the morrow with a further parade of pleasures.

I was awakened next morning, by no means quite at my best, with a commanding knock at the door. With a sinking heart, I enquired who it was. Needless to say it was the gallant captain, come to fulfill his promise. Barbara sat up, looking as bleary as I probably did.

"Oh, no!" she wailed and, throwing herself back on the pillows, she yelled, "Tell him to FUCK OFF!"

To avoid an international incident, I shushed her as best I could. However, she really meant it. I cautiously opened the door a fraction and there he stood, beaming with goodwill and as fresh as paint. Summoning all my talents for diplomacy, I begged for a couple of hours' grace. His face fell momentarily, then brightened. Was there meantime any way in which he could serve us? I thought desperately, then remembering that, in making our escape from the touts, I had broken the strap of one of my sandals, so I snatched it up and asked him to have it repaired for me.

This was a faux pas. He went pale and stared at me in disbelief. Then, with a short bow and holding my battered sandal like a dead rat, between finger and thumb, he turned on his heel and left. We never saw him or the sandal again.

Although our brief, but intense acquaintance had ended on a somewhat ungraceful note and our recent volatile friend had been, in some ways, almost endearing, it had become abundantly clear that enough had become more than enough. We had five days left and it was time to move on.

As Robert Carrier was at home in his Marrakesh house and, as the girls were most anxious to see him again, I rang him. He sounded pleased to hear from us and invited us over for lunch the next day. Having made previous abortive attempts to explore the city, thwarted by the ubiquitous touts, I took the advice of the reception clerk and summoned a taxi to the hotel. With a quick dive into the cab, we slammed the door and were away, leaving the baffled touts standing. We went as far as we could *en voiture* and continued on foot, through a maze of insalubrious alleys, mercifully free from touts, being directed at last to an unpromising door of blackened wood, studded with iron, set in a whitewashed wall. After a few moments, our knock was answered and we stepped into a magical courtyard, straight out of the Arabian Nights.

A fountain bubbled in the centre of a pool, surrounded by exotica in pots, oranges and lemons and Robert was advancing to greet us, beaming with welcome. There were three or four men standing about with drinks in their hands, none of whom we knew. I noticed a tall man in white Arab dress, whose striking appearance was marred by a wall eye, adding a sinister note to his otherwise majestic demeanour. He was talking to Robert in French and after a light, but excellent lunch, he produced from his robes a small silver pot, which turned out to contain *majune*. This appeared to produce, among those who partook of it, a mild euphoria but without the hilarity of our recent experience.

I felt it wise to refrain, as did Bob, who had undertaken to take us on a tour of the souks. The girls did likewise, which hardly surprised me. He told me it was lawful for Moroccans to use hashish, but apparently not Europeans. With alcohol, it was the other way round. In private, people did as they liked. When his guests had gone, he took us on his promised tour of one or two of the souks, which need no description here but which we were able to enjoy in comparative comfort. The touts, who presumably knew him, kept well away.

I had wanted to visit the 12th century Koutoubia Mosque, with its magnificent towering minaret, but had to content myself with the exterior as entry is forbidden to infidels. That, with our adventures with Mustafa and our visit to Bob, were the only memorable features of our stay in Morocco.

I have never felt any great urge to return.

31

Here And Now

It is well over 30 years ago that I last trod the boards as an actor. This was in *Knuckle*, an early work of David Hare, in which I am told I gave one of my better performances in the *live theatre*. I took the role of Patrick Delafield, the father of Curly, who was played by Edward Fox. The play itself was very nearly very good, with flashes of the brilliant writing one has since learned to expect from the pen of Sir David, without, however, proving ultimately as successful as the sum of its parts.

In short, it was a near miss.

As I was fortunate enough, myself, to receive a good press, the experience was not in any way a sad or inglorious swan-song to a career, which had certainly had golden moments, but of which I begun to weary. I had, perhaps, grown out of it: or perhaps it would be nearer the truth to say that it had outgrown me.

Life in the theatre was altering. Times are bound to change, of course, but in my case the changes were no longer to my taste. Money was becoming increasingly a governing factor and with *money* one could also read *time*. Production costs were increasing at an alarming rate, which meant shorter rehearsal periods, with less time to study one's role, to say nothing of the bare essential of just learning the lines. This was particularly the case in the commercial theatre and even more so in TV and film, which had become the *bread and butter* of most actors. It was much less the case, of course, in the subsidised theatre, such as the National or the RSC.

In most cases a play would go out usually on tour in the provinces on trial, as it were. This was particularly necessary in the instance of a new play to enable time for any necessary adjustments to be made and which could only be judged before a live audience. These tours were becoming something of a bugbear, as the theatrical landlady had all but disappeared in the new economic climate. This meant staying in hotels which were either expensive or hideously uncomfortable, or sometimes both.

I well remember the words of my old friend, Dan Massey. "You know, Doug, you really wouldn't like it now. It's just not a *gent's* life any more."

Another factor was causing me increasing unease. I was never, in any case, what was called a *quick study*, needing a decent amount of time, not only for the bare mechanics of learning the lines, but also for the role to *soak*, as it were, and for its possibilities to develop. The curtailing of this was my ultimate reason for rejecting a second BBC series of *Sherlock Holmes*. I had found the first one taxing enough; I would have found matters much more difficult under the new system.

My last assignment on filming was when I was invited by Bryan Forbes to play the part of a *presenter* on a remake of *National Velvet*. This involved a very long speech, to be shot in the arena at Olympia, and it had to done within an unnervingly tight time schedule: between two horse shows. There would not have been much time for re-takes or to redress mistakes, either on my part, or, more forgivably, on the part of *camera*. I would really have to have my lines unshakably word-perfect.

My wine-bar was in full swing at that time but I had my admirably capable Dutch manager, Hugo, so I took time off to really sweat it out, leaving him and Barbara to get on with it, until I really felt rock-solid on the words. As luck would have it, I promptly went down with a severe bout of gastric flu, which left me feeling considerably below par when the day of shooting this sequence was upon me. Hugo insisted on taking the day off to drive me to London so that I would not have transport difficulties to face.

We arrived at Olympia where Hugo left me, hot-footing it back to the wine-bar. I was feeling ghastly and, despite all the work I had done, I found I could not remember a single line of the script. So, I was put in the hideous position of having to tell Bryan Forbes that I simply could not do it. Bless his sweet soul, Bryan, instead of going mad, took the news quite calmly and sympathetically, saying that, as he had written the whole screen-play, he was quite able to do it himself and I was not to feel bad about it, and such a thing could happen to anyone.

There are not many directors, I believe, who would do that.

I then had to break the glad tidings to my agent, who was putting me up for the night. He too expressed sympathy, but I believe I knew what he was thinking.

It was a humiliating experience and I felt dreadful about letting everyone down. Further coals of fire were heaped on my head when I had, almost the next day, a charming letter from Bryan, saying that he hoped I was feeling better and repeating his words of comfort and, what is more, enclosing an entirely unexpected cheque for half my fee.

I shall never forget the full horror of the situation and I know that it played a large part in my decision to leave the theatre, films and TV for ever.

Nor will I ever forget the understanding kindness of Bryan Forbes in the matter.

I had in any case been gradually doing less and less in my old life and living more and more in my country retreat, opening the wine-bar, which was going well, and having friends to stay: like Dan Massey and his girlfriend Lydia, which I greatly enjoyed. So, the parting was hardly a sudden wrench.

There were, some years earlier, visits from another close friend, who will have to remain for the time being, at least, nominally, *Nick*, for that is what, for the purposes of these memoirs, I will call him. Should he become recognisable to those who have known him, then so be it. He is an actor, not unsuccessful and indeed now very well-known.

He would turn up and stay with Barbara and me, often for several days at a time. He was tall, with the head of a satyr. Highly intelligent, he was a voracious reader, an amusing and gifted conversationalist with a beautiful speaking voice and an easy and appreciative guest. He was also a prodigious consumer of gin and tonic, affecting a strangely elusive life-style, which can only be described as *of no fixed abode*. He was apt to turn up with nothing but a tooth-brush in his top pocket, a *modus vivendi* which we regarded as an amiable eccentricity.

Whenever we threw a party, we would always try to get *Nick* to come down for the week-end, as he was usually quite at his scintillating best at such gatherings. Our friends found him amusing, interesting and excellent company. He was not short on charisma.

I became, in keeping with my new style of country life, a keen, if erratic, shot and *Nick* and I, with one of my guns apiece, trudged across the nearby fields in the hope of a pigeon or two. He was always game for anything. It so happened that, about a mile or two from the house, Peter Hall, who knew us both, was filming some sequences for *Akenfield*, the epic documentary of rural Suffolk, based on Ronald Blythe's book of that name. So we thought we would stroll over and surprise him, as indeed we did.

As soon as he spotted us, a couple of armed and dishevelled actors advancing towards him, he threw up his hands in mock-surrender, wearing his famous *mandarin* grin.

For about two years *Nick* remained in close touch, coming to stay quite often. On what turned out to be the last time he was to do so, he seemed his usual amusing self. He left as usual with hopes to see us again very soon. A couple of days later, I had a letter from him, written in a most uncharacteristically agitated vein. I made him a suitable and friendly reply, complying with a certain most urgent request. From that moment on, he disappeared, as if into thin air and we were dropped like a couple of hot potatoes.

After an initial enquiry or two, from which I was able to learn that he was still at his last address, and apparently perfectly all right, I made no further attempts to get in touch with him; I figured that when he was ready to do so, we would hear from him again, but only when he was good and ready. But, sadly, that was never the case. One has no right to be disappointed, of course, but that was how I decidedly felt. After all, we were fond of him and he had seemed to be so of us.

Many years later, however, when we were running our wine-bar, I heard that the long-running TV series, in which he was starring, was to be filming some sequences in Suffolk and that, furthermore, the unit, including *Nick*, would be staying for some days in a Woodbridge hotel. After the first day of filming, I strolled over to the hotel and sat myself down where I had a good view of the stairs. The hallway was empty and very soon down he jauntily came, on his way to the bar.

"Hallo *Nick*," I said.

He froze and stopped dead in his tracks, saw me and covered his face with both hands. I walked over to him and, taking his wrists, I pulled them gently away. I smiled at him and said, "You're a very silly fellow, *Nick*".

The poor devil looked desperately ashamed and then asked me what I was doing, so I told him about the wine-bar we were running, at which he cheered up and said he would come that very evening to see us.

That evening and every single evening for the remainder of their time in Woodbridge, he turned up, in his most roistering vein, roaring with laughter, spending like mad, drinking a great deal of gin and tonic, standing drinks all round and as jovial as you please with Barbara and me, as if he had stayed in touch all the intervening years.

He never once referred to the strange letter he had written me or to the request it contained. But, on the very last night of his visit, I noticed that he was holding a large book in his hand, which he pressed upon me, telling me how interesting I would find it. It was the life of Charles Stewart Parnell. The subject of Irish Nationalism was not one of my most absorbing interests but, of course, I appreciated the thought.

I have watched him once or twice on TV and, when I sometimes forget the mute button for the adverts, I detect his dulcet tones, but have seen neither hide nor hair of him otherwise since. I digress yet again but, really, why not?

I have very often been asked if I missed my former life in the theatre and I have always answered quite truthfully that I do not. This sometimes occasions surprise, or even in some cases, incredulity, as if I should have been left at a total loose end with absolutely nothing to do.

To return to the *new* life, which I had almost imperceptibly come to adopt: my second home and rural retreat from London became, after the very painful divorce from Liz, and over a period of time, my principal place of residence. There was a circle of new friends and, in any case, I had a number of interests to take up more time than I now had at my disposal. As I have related elsewhere, I ran a wine-bar for over four years, which took up much of my time and energies. There was bird-watching with the wonderful reserves of Minsmere and North Norfolk at my disposal. I had also developed a great interest in the ancient and historic churches, with which East Anglia happily abounds. There were my innumerable roses and a fairly extensive garden to be tended.

I had always retained a modest talent in painting with memories, perhaps, of *Holy Joe* my mentor in that gentle art, from my architectural time with Seeley and Paget, in Cloth Fair. Accordingly, I enrolled in classes, under the supervision of Ken Cuthbert, a painter of considerable repute, in order to learn how to make the best of it.

In the appropriate season of the year I had a *gun* in a nearby shoot; I had become a keen, if erratic, shot, which I kept up for a number of years, until one day, like many middle-aged men, I believe, I decided I would rather watch birds than kill them.

I built a new wing to the cottage, making it more of a comfortable house. I had also bought a new home in Fulham, an area which I cordially came to dislike, selling it a year or so later. About that time, I also formed a modest property development company, in conjunction with a choleric Baltic baron, buying and renovating houses and cottages in the area. The financial side I found boring and uncongenial so, at his suggestion, I left it to him. This I did for a time until I discovered that, whereas I was putting up my half share of the purchase price in each case from capital, my partner was secretly arranging mortgages on the property in question to furnish his half share, whereupon I terminated our hitherto agreeable arrangement forthwith.

It is, perhaps, stating the obvious when I say that any interest in my memoirs resides mainly in the number of persons of note whom I have had the good fortune to know, both during my theatre life and after. It is at the continued insistence of those who have been, over the years, exposed to my rambling conversational anecdotes, that I attempt to record them in some form of coherent order. This, as I believe I have said, may have been a possible attempt to stem any such further anecdotage. I can only hope not.

In the case of my good friend, Philip Porter, however, I feel perfect confidence as he has, perhaps rashly, but certainly repeatedly, undertaken to publish them.

It is entirely due to him, that, in the early 1990s, I was winkled out of my rural seclusion and into the *Sherlock Holmes Society of London*, an event from which much has stemmed. He remembered me from 1964, when, as a young and impressionable boy, he was allowed to sit up and watch my series of *Sherlock Holmes* on BBC TV. This had been his first encounter with the character and had started a life-long interest in all matters Holmesian. At the time of first contacting me, he was Chairman of the Society and he kindly invited me to lunch at Simpson's in the Strand. We had never actually met. There were two or three other members of the Society at lunch, close friends of Philip's: Peter Horrocks, Elaine Hamill and Tim Owen.

I was invited to the Society's Annual Dinner and then, at the end of the evening, Philip asked me to speak, as guest of honour, for the following year. I think it was 1994. Mellowed with wine and good cheer and heartened by the performance, just put on by the Bishop of Durham, whose speech had been one of the most cruelly boring ever to assault the human ear, I rashly agreed. I felt that whatever I did thereafter in the following year, it could hardly be worse.

I spoke in due course and was invited to become an Honorary Member, an honour I was delighted to accept. This was followed by Philip's invitation to make audio tapes of two of the stories for the Society's members. I chose *Speckled Band* and *The Devil's Foot*. Philip asked his good friend, Richard Lancelyn Green, one of the leading authorities in the world on Doyle, to co-produce, which he was delighted to do.

I had had a veritable avalanche of mail in 1964 and thereafter, at the time of the original TV series, and had kept back a few of the more interesting ones, in particular two from a boy of 11, written from his prep-school. In the second one of these, he asked if he could visit me at the theatre after one of my matinées, telling me that he also had received his Sherlockian baptism from my series and that he "longed to meet the living spirit of Sherlock Holmes". It was signed "Richard Green". It was long after I met him as an adult that I connected the events. He never referred to it himself. I could hardly have had, with Philip, a more auspicious co-producer.

The recordings in due course were made, under their watchful eyes, in between noises of aircraft and trains, in a rather amateur studio in Leominster. They were considered good enough for Richard to take them to Penguin, who happened to be his publisher. They were enthusiastic and commissioned the three of us to make three or four further recordings of selections of four short stories, to be followed, in time by *The Complete Adventures*, and then *The Sign of Four*.

The subsequent making of these were among the happiest and most harmonious moments of my entire professional career. We never had a single disagreement, that I can recall. I named us *The Triumvirate*.

We met at the studio in London on a regular basis, every few months, giving me time at home to do as much practice-recording as was needed between sessions. The edited scripts, by Richard and Philip, were always on time and totally faithful to their author.

I invariably stayed with two other very dear Sherlockian friends in Chiswick, Elaine and Jonathan McCafferty. After the day's recording was done, a somewhat weary but triumphant *Triumvirate* would walk back to their house, with three or four stops at our favourite pubs, on the way. This became an absolute ritual. On arrival, *chez* McCafferty, there would be further generous libations, followed by an invariably excellent dinner, prepared by the deft hand of Jonathan.

This, like all things good, eventually came to an end, alas, but our friendship remained firm and intact. This was particularly so in the case of Richard.

Being the only bachelor among us, he seemed to adopt Anne and me, almost as surrogate parents. He visited us here in Suffolk, sometimes with the McCaffertys, or with our mutual very good American friend, Marina Stajic, but more often alone, staying with us for two or three days at a time. He came with us on Sherlockian visits to New York on three occasions where he was as at home as in London. He and I got together a double act with which we toured in Boston, Washington, Philadelphia and New York. Our *performance* consisted of a brief and witty introduction by Richard of me in the person of Sherlock. This was followed by questions, carefully prepared, which I would answer before throwing it open to the house. It always seemed to go down very well.

Richard also came with us twice on Italian holidays, where he was a most delightful travelling companion and highly knowledgeable guide. He appeared to have close acquaintanceship with most of the art galleries in Europe and America, also their museums, opera houses and concert halls. He was also a connoisseur of tucked-away and hidden corners of London, and we had many an enjoyably informative prowl round the City, which he knew almost better than the back of his hand. He never thrust his knowledge upon one, but his almost encyclopaedic mine of information was always there, when required.

On two occasions he, Jonathan and Elaine McCafferty came on holiday with us to Malta, where we stayed at our brother-in-law's villa, swimming and doing the sights, collapsing by the pool at the end of the day with a bottle or three of wine and much hilarity. It was also not without other social delights. We were lavishly entertained by the elite of the island, who seemed delighted to know our friends.

Some years after, Richard became increasingly concerned about the letters and papers of Sir Arthur Conan Doyle, which, as one-time literary executor of Dame Jean Conan Doyle (Sir Arthur's daughter), he was convinced should go, on her death, to the British Library. The remaining few distant members of the family, however, had different ideas. They were to be put up for sale, by public auction. With increasing preoccupation, Richard, convinced of Dame Jean's wishes in the matter, tried every means at his disposal to block the sale. Richard himself already had in his possession probably the most extensive collection of Doyle material and Sherlockiana in existence, and it was his intention to write the definitive biography.

At the British Library, had they gone there, he would have had access to most of the necessary remaining documents. As it became increasingly clear that he was not to succeed in the matter, he became depressed and preoccupied. He was sleeping badly and we were shocked and worried by his changed appearance and demeanour when he next came to see us. He was most certainly not himself and left to go back to London, by an unusually early train.

Two days later, the telephone rang for me. It was his mother. She said she had some very bad news. She told me that Richard was dead.

I experienced considerable difficulty in coming to terms with this. He had become so much a part of our lives, that I probably took him for granted. Like a son, I suppose, I thought he would always be there: either there, or at the end of a phone. It was not easy to get back on track. Even writing about it, however briefly, and thereby, in a small way, re-living it, I find some difficulty in getting back on track with my writing.

We buried ourselves in Suffolk and I got on with my painting as the best therapy I could devise. It was a couple of years before I felt able to face the *Society* Annual Dinner. I think it slowed me up a bit.

However, I am still here and more or less vertical. I am probably happier than I deserve and can look back on my life with pleasure. I am fortunate in having friends young enough to last my lifetime. Although, of course, one can never be sure.

I am content to be where I am.

It was 45 years ago that I first made acquaintance with what has become my beloved county, just barely long enough to qualify, hereabouts, as being a *Man of Suffolk*.

Living as I do, I have been almost entirely divorced from my former life, both in the theatre and otherwise. I have not been to the theatre for many years, as I suffer a degree of deafness, which prevents me from following the plot. The same holds good (or bad) for the cinema, unless it is a foreign film with sub-titles. This is an unfortunate legacy of my years in the Royal Artillery and is known as *gunner-ear*, which, to preclude misunderstanding, is best not pronounced too quickly!

I have a good wife, Anne, who spoils me by attending to all the mundane details of my existence, such as finance and paper-work, at which she is brilliant. She is Maltese and flamboyantly Mediterranean, still very striking to behold, in spite of being married to me for 25 years.

I believe we love each other, in an exasperated sort of way. She nags me mercilessly, which I have no doubt I well deserve. I have to be kept up to the mark.

She has a lovely daughter, Katharine, who is like my own and she has two equally lovely and extremely clever children. Unfashionably enough, she also has a husband. We all get on extremely well, providing me with a ready-made family without the bother of having had to make one of my own.

We are not very well-off, but there always seems to be enough for a foreign holiday or two every year. We eat wisely and well, and there is always a decent bottle of wine. We have enough in common: our religion, good cooking, wine, bird-watching, travel and a few good friends. She is a very fine player of bridge, which exacting game she plays for the county and from which I keep very well away. There are not enough hours in the day to accommodate all my interests without that.

In law, Anne is my third wife but I am told that, in the eyes of the Church, she is my first. Liz had achieved an annulment, in what seemed to me an uncharacteristic piece of equivocation, on the grounds of my *canonical impotence*, after a civil divorce on the grounds of my *unbridled potency*. So *that* marriage apparently did not count.

My second wife and I were married in Caxton Hall, which, being a registry office, was therefore also invalid. My present wife had obtained an annulment over 30 years ago, marrying me in the very same church in Malta, 16 years later. The rules of canon law had, in the meantime, *moved the goalposts*, regarding my *impotence*, so now it appears, no longer a bar to matrimony. Ergo, Anne is my *first* lawfully-wedded wife. Hmmm!

One hopes the goalposts do not move back again and make me a *canonical bigamist*!

We go to Malta each year, which I have come to count almost as a home-from-home. It is full of interest for me, soaked in history and, architecturally speaking, one of the richest 17-mile long stretches of land in the world, abounding in magnificent churches and splendid palaces. Having reverted to my water-colour days with *Holy Joe*, at Cloth Fair, I have done a large collection of paintings of buildings, some of which are, alas, no longer still standing. I find my painting a wonderful way of relaxing and if I make a mess of my work, at least it is *my* mess and up to me to put it right, if I can.

I am, luckily, seldom bored and have learned to enjoy my moments of solitude. They are seldom over-protracted. I have enjoyed writing my memoirs.

Life is not bad, after all, and I can best sum up, in the words of Edith Piaf but, with one terrible reservation, which may or may not be guessed:

Je ne regrette rien!

Index